Dixie's Best-Kept

An Introductory History of the Confederate Navy

By

Mark K. Vogl

Wake Forest, NC
www.scuppernongpress.com

Dixie's Best Kept Secret
By Mark K. Vogl

© 2021 – Mark K. Vogl

First Printing: 2021
Second Printing: 2023

All Rights Reserved – No part of this book may be reproduced by any means without the express written consent of the copyright holder

Published by:
Rebel Mountain Enterprises
PO Box 825
Gilmer, Texas 75644
www.confederatewarcollege.com
e-mail johnyreb43@yahoo.com
Tel. 903-725-3175

The Scuppernong Press
PO Box 1724
Wake Forest, NC 27588
www.scuppernongpress.com

ISBN: 978-0-578-84996-6
Library of Congress Control Number: 2021901653

Front Cover Image: The clash of the C.S.S. *Virginia* and the U.S.S. *Monitor* at Hampton Roads was provided by the U. S. Department of the Navy, Naval Historical Center.

Front Cover Design by E-Tex Writers Agency, Tyler, TX

This book is dedicated to
My daughters
Kelly Marie Vogl and Julie Elizabeth Czerekowski

And Mr. James Titone

And to the men of the Confederate States Navy

Thank You

Captain Will Dossel, United States Navy, (Retired) for his exhaustive efforts to improve my feeble effort to tell the story of the Confederate Navy

Mr. Chad Madding, Computer Consultants of Paris, Texas
Chad's technical expertise was critical to completion of this illustrated work

Roger Middleton of E-Tex Writers Agency, Tyler, TX for final preparation for publication

God's Will Be Done

About The Author

Mark K. Vogl is a Distinguished Military Graduate of THE CITADEL, THE MILITARY COLLEGE OF SOUTH CAROLINA, Class of 1977, earning a Bachelor's of Science in Education. He served as an officer in the United States Army, where assignments included two commands in Europe and assignment as an Asst. Professor of Military Science at Fordham University.

This is Mark's seventh published book. His first book, *The Military Lessons of the Civil War, 1861-1865* was in 2007 and was recognized by the United Daughters of the Confederacy with the Jefferson Davis Historical Gold Medal. Other books Mark has written include: *The Rebel Mountain Reader, The Confederate Night Before Christmas, Southern Fried Ramblings with Grits and all the Fixin's, Because of Him*, and *The White House Reclaimed, A Deplorable's View of the 2016 Election*.

In 2009 Mark was selected as the Texas Division, Sons of Confederate Veterans.

Mark and his wife Barbara (retired Lt. Col., U.S. Army) live at Rebel Mountain, outside of Gilmer, Texas. Together they have five children, Kelly and Julie — Mark's daughters, and Jennifer, James and John — Barbara's children.

PREFACE

I decided to write this work after reading the *History of the Confederate States Navy* by J. Thomas Scharf. Scharf's extensive history adds a whole new dimension to those who primarily study the land campaigns of the War for Southern Independence. Scharf's personal experiences during the war, and exhaustive research work after, provide the reader with a comprehensive survey of Southern naval war-making capabilities. While the history is at times, in error, it is a great starting place for a journey through the annals of Confederate naval history. I believe J. Thomas Scharf has earned the right to be called the "father of Confederate naval history."

A study of the ocean operations of the Confederate Navy will introduce you to issues and context not considered in land operations. The global reach of the Confederate Navy, and its success in completely reducing the maritime merchant shipping of the United States of America is a story not often told. The daring of Confederate naval commanders easily match the audacity of Generals Stuart, Forrest, and Morgan.

But there are other stories; the exploitation of new technologies, the success of the South's blockade runners, and the complexities of international relations are all interesting aspects of the story. And there is the successful combined arms offensive operations to re-take the South's largest port west of the Mississippi, Galveston, which demonstrates Southern ingenuity. Lastly there are the stories of the ironclads, some operating as squadrons at Charleston, Mobile and Richmond.

The story of the men who developed naval strategy, and built and served in the Confederate States Navy, (C.S.N.) is as inspirational as that of their brothers who brought glory to the Confederacy on thousands of battlefields. Like the land campaigns, there are endless stories of heroism, ingenuity, imagination, leadership and sacrifice connected with the Confederate Navy. In addition, the South made every effort to use technologies in an attempt to even the odds on the world's oceans and America's rivers. The story demonstrates a southern will to meet the challenges of fighting an enemy superior in material resources, with innovation, guile, courage and determination.

My work is intended as an introductory history of the Southern naval war effort with the goal of providing you an appreciation of the size, scope and success of the Confederate naval effort. It is my great hope that once you read this, you will decide to spend more time learning about the South's best kept secret: he Confederate States Navy.

I want to thank Roger Middleton for his work in making the final changes and preparation for publication.

Mark K. Vogl

Table of Contents

Chapter One Introduction 1

Chapter Two Georgia Dictates a Maritime Tradition for both North and South 13

Chapter Three Setting the table for naval power in 1861 23

Chapter Four The Battle at Sea 31

Chapter Five The naval battle at home, along the coasts, in the ports, and on Dixie's rivers 59

Appendix 1 83

Chapter Six Confederate Special Naval Operations 101

Chapter Seven Building the Confederate States Navy 113

Chapter Eight Confederate States Naval Academy 123

Chapter Nine The Confederate States Marine Corps 135

Chapter Ten The Confederate Naval Torpedo Service 139

Chapter Eleven Conclusion 147

Appendix 2 Roll of Confederate Naval Officers 159

Appendix 3 Roll of Confederate Naval vessels 161

Appendix 4 Confederate Commerce Raiders 169

Appendix 5 The Confederate Ironclads 171

Appendix 6 Blockade Runners 183

Appendix 7 Mysteries of the Confederate Submarine Service ... 189

Bibliography 203

Table of Figures 206

Chapter One —

Introduction

The War Between the States, or the War for Southern Independence, 1861-1865 has most often been told through the eyes of infantrymen and cavalrymen. The great land battles hold legendary status in American folklore. As a tribute to those who fought in the American armies of Gray and Blue, people have joined across the expanse of the United States to preserve and protect many of the hallowed fields that saw American kill American. And, if one reads enough, it becomes obvious to even the most novice student that the southern nation fielded armies that bested their opponents in many a battle. Some Confederate commanders, because of their military genius and success on the field of battle (for example Generals Lee, Jackson, and Forrest) are still studied throughout America's military institutions. For four years, the Southern Army leadership offset the numerical and material superiority of an enemy three times the size of the infant Confederacy.

There are countless books, maps, museums and battlefields to assist one in gaining an understanding of the land campaigns. The same cannot be said for the naval aspects of the "late unpleasantness," though interest in the Navy has spurred substantial work in the late twentieth century to tell the story of this side of the war.

For many students of the War for Southern Independence, the naval war seems minor, almost insignificant in comparison to the great land campaigns of the war. Most Americans know of the clash of the ironclads (C.S.S. *Virginia* and U.S.S. *Monitor*) at Hampton Roads. Some know of the exploits of Admiral Raphael Semmes and his ship the C.S.S. *Alabama*. And, a few know about one of the Confederate submarines, the C.S.S. *Hunley*. Until recently, the lack of published and available naval histories left Americans with only a bare awareness that the Confederacy had a navy. Most students of the war are surprised to learn; the Confederate Navy may have had as many as 400 ships during the period 1861 – 1865 and had between 6,500 and 7,000 men in uniform during the war.

At least 18 different Southern shipyards were used to construct all of the submarines, and all but one of the ironclads, and many of the other ships of the Confederate brown water naval forces.

Battles and Commanders, published in 1906 by the U.S. War Department, credits the Confederacy with sinking more than 200 Federal ships, no small feat for a non-existent navy.

It is my intent to provide the reader with a fairly broad introductory overview of the Confederate Navy, from a Southern point of view. I will demonstrate, with facts and stories, that the Confederacy developed a maritime strategy that fit the infant nation's circumstances and worked hard to create a navy to meet the many and various needs of a nation at war. The work is also intended to demonstrate how southern leaders offset the northern advantages of a standing navy, operating shipyards, a large manufacturing base, and a massive economy by embracing technology, innovation, diplomacy, and international commerce as their principal tools. In addition, I hope to clearly demonstrate that the Confederacy possessed a makeshift but highly active naval manufacturing element. And lastly; to show that from the onset of secession, the leaders of the emerging Confederate States of America (C.S.A.) understood the importance of the sea and its tributaries and worked diligently to challenge the Federals.

We will approach the study of the C.S.A. Department of the Navy by dividing it into sections:

Ocean operations
Blockade Running
Commerce Raiding
Defense of the Southern homeland
Port Defense
River operations
Special Operations
C.S.A. Naval Department Infrastructure
C.S.A. Naval Procurement
C.S.A. Naval Academy
C.S.A. Marine Corps
C.S.A. Torpedo Service

While many sources were used, the inspiration for this work began in the pages of *The History of the Confederate States Navy*, written by J. Thomas Scharf and published in 1888. Scharf's comprehensive work helped me design the book with respect to what I believe are the fundamentals of Southern Naval effort. In many cases, I rely on Scharf's work to begin consideration of a subject and then add to it, or counter Scharf's view with writings from other authors. Scharf's work, though lengthy, is understandably incomplete. At the time of its writing, Scharf was doing all the research first hand with few established records to work from. Still, J. Thomas Scharf has done yeoman's work in writing the original Southern naval history, and as such, should be recognized as the father of the Confederate Naval History.

I strongly recommend Scharf's work (as the companion to *The Lost Cause*, by E. A. Pollard) to any serious student of the War Between the States because of the authors' respective roles as Southern patriots during the war, their comprehensive approach to the war, and as an example of the Southern viewpoint of the war.

The purpose of this book is to provide an initial introduction to the size and scope of the effort made by the Confederate States of America to fashion a navy to meet all the various needs of a nation at war and to provide some evidence of the degree of the success of those efforts. This study will explain the structure of the Confederate Navy by identifying its' major components and missions. Individual naval actions will be used to illustrate strategies and help paint the larger picture of Confederate naval capabilities and limits.

"Why was it that there were no preparations?" asks J. Thomas Scharf, referring to the lack of war-making ability in the South upon the commencement of secession. Scharf replies, "The answer must be found in the conviction of all men that none could be needed (emphasis my own) – because secession was a peaceful remedy… and war would not follow separating from the Union…"

It seems fantastic to consider, but many, if not most Southerners believed they would be allowed to leave the Union peacefully. Jefferson Davis wrote, "For my own part, while believing that secession was a right, and properly a peaceable remedy, I had never believed that it would be permitted to be peaceably exercised. Very few in the South at that time agreed with me, and my answers to queries on the subject were, therefore, as unexpected as they were unwelcome."

This first assertion by Scharf, that secession could be done peacefully, is essential to understanding the actions of the people in the Deep South in the winter of 1860-61. The great majority of people in the seven states which voted themselves out of the Union, beginning with South Carolina in December of 1860, did not believe war was imminent. Secession had been discussed as a political option by people in many states since the adoption of the Constitution. It was a fundamental assumption that the states, which voluntarily joined the Union, could just as easily leave. While secession brewed in the South for some time, there is no evidence that Southerners with the power to do so directed war materials south in anticipation for a war. Scharf asserts that Southerners, while the question of secession was still just a discussion, could not believe that war would occur as a result of their decision to leave the Union.

However, after Lincoln's election, men such as Colonel Robert E. Lee, Senator Jefferson Davis, and others clearly saw war clouds on the horizon. The question of the general condition of un-preparedness of the Southern states for war and the lack of pre-emptive action taken by Southerners while in the offices of the Federal government must now seem a mystery. But for the men who fought the American war, honor would not permit treasonous acts against the government of the United States in anticipation of northern aggression.

When South Carolina adopted its Ordinance of Secession on December 20th, 1860, the state stood almost defenseless. As other states in the Deep South passed their respective ordinance, they too found themselves like a newborn babe, with little to protect them from whatever circumstances might arise. As each state moved for independence, state authorities directed the seizure of Federal assets such as forts, arsenals, government mints, and ships.

The first ships of what would become the Confederate States Navy were seized in Charleston, South Carolina, New Orleans, Louisiana, Galveston, Texas, Georgia, and Alabama. Combined, they totaled five ships with nine guns. Another five ships would be captured or purchased, adding six more guns before the Confederate Congress met in Montgomery, Alabama.

On February 4th, 1861, the Congress adopted the Provisional Constitution of the Confederate States. This constitution, and the permanent one subsequently adopted in Richmond, called for the creation of a navy. On February 14th, Congress created the Committee on Naval Affairs to seek out the very best advice concerning naval matters.

And on February 21st, the Congress passed the act that established the Department of the Navy. We will discuss its formation, bureaus, and their responsibilities in Chapter Seven, "Building the Confederate Navy." But it is important here to introduce the Confederacy's two senior naval leaders, Secretary of the Navy, the Honorable Stephen Russell Mallory, and the Confederacy's first admiral, Franklin Buchanan.

Stephen Mallory was born in Trinidad off the coast of Venezuela to a Yankee father and a mother born and raised in Ireland. When Stephen was a year old, the Mallory's moved to Key West, Florida, and settled there. Within a couple of years, Mallory's father would die. At 13 or 14, Stephen was sent by his mother to a school for boys in Pennsylvania, where he remained for three years. He then returned home to Key West. When he was 19, he was appointed Inspector of Customs for Key West. During this time, he studied the Law and was accepted to the Florida Bar circa 1839. After serving a few years as Inspector, Mallory was appointed Collector of Customs at Key West. He also volunteered to fight in the Indian Wars against the Seminoles. By the age of 35, Stephen spoke both Spanish and French fluently.

In 1838, Stephen Mallory married. His law practice grew, and he prospered, gaining a good reputation. In 1851 the Florida Legislature selected Mallory as one of two Senators representing Florida in Washington, D.C. At the time, the Florida Legislature selected Mallory for the honor, he was not even aware he was under consideration. Mallory was sent back to the nation's capital for a second term in 1857. During most of his service in Washington, Senator Mallory would serve as the chairman of the Committee for Naval Affairs. In 1858 Mallory moved his home from Key West to Pensacola.

In 1861, when Florida seceded, Senator Mallory resigned his seat and headed home. Mallory embraced a leadership role in attempting to prevent the arrival of Yankee reinforcements to Ft. Pickens, warning the commander that any reinforcement would be taken as an act of war and would immediately trigger an attack against the fort.

Once Congress acted to create a Department of the Navy, President Davis (who had served with Mallory in the United Senate for almost a decade) immediately called for Stephen Mallory to accept the post of Secretary of the Navy. Throughout the war, Davis and Mallory would work well together. However, Mallory constantly worked to meet the needs of the Navy in a war where the land armies had "first pick'ns" of the South's limited resources.

Scharf writes of Secretary Mallory, "He was a gentleman of excellent sense, unpretending manners, and probably conducted his department as successful as was possible with the limited naval resources of the South."

As we shall see through this work, the Secretary was one of many in the Confederate States Navy who practiced ingenuity, imagination, prudence, and skill to give the South a navy it desperately needed.

Admiral Franklin "Buck" Buchanan was the senior naval officer in the Confederate States Navy and would command the Confederate squadrons in battle at Hampton Roads and Mobile Bay. While Admiral Buchanan did not have the wide breadth of command his army colleagues enjoyed, he was an important figure with more influence, over a wider range of issues, than other officers in the Confederate States Navy.

Buck was born in Baltimore, Maryland. In 1815, when he was 14, Buck was appointed a midshipman in the United States Navy. At this time, newly commissioned midshipmen reported directly to their first ship. When his ship was delayed in sailing, Buck immediately asked the Secretary of the Navy for a furlough so that he could take a seaman's position on a commercial ship. His furlough was approved, and Buck's maritime career began.

Buchanan quickly proved he loved the sea. His early cruises would be in the Caribbean and Mediterranean.

Buchanan had his first command when he was in his mid-twenties. He commanded a frigate, the *Baltimore*, that had been built in the United States and then sold to Brazil. Buchanan's task was to sail the ship from its U.S. port to Brazil and deliver it to the proper authorities. The assignment was something of a plum in that officers of Buchanan's rank were rarely given the command of a frigate. The passage was not without challenge. Just a few days out at sea, the Baltimore ran into a hurricane. As this was the ship's maiden voyage, the stress of hurricane winds and high seas proved to be a true test of the ship's quality. At one point, Buchanan actually believed he might lose the mainmast, and if he did, he would lose the ship. In response, Buchanan worked his crew; continually changing sail through the storm, and eventually working his way out of the hurricane proceeded to Brazil.

Buck was a technically proficient sailor, and a strong disciplinarian. He would not accept poor performance because of human failings such as laziness or drunkenness. And, he was not afraid to use the lash for punishment.

Franklin met Anne (Nannie) Lloyd, daughter of Edward Lloyd, one of the wealthiest men in Maryland. They would have a long courtship, interrupted by several lengthy voyages, finally marrying 19 February 1835. Nannie was the first reason to change Franklin's desire for long sea voyages. Nannie, and later their five daughters, would have a firm hold on Franklin's heart and changed his request for assignments from ones that had been dominated by the search for adventure and career advancement, to shorter overseas voyages and assignments close to home. Buck was a good father and husband. He sometimes spent himself into debt purchasing gifts for his wife and children. Buck's family would eventually grow to eight daughters and one son.

In September 1841, Franklin Buchanan was promoted to the rank of Commander. Also, in 1841, Nannie's brother purchased a home for the Buchanan's on Maryland's eastern shore. A home they would call "the Rest."

Buchanan was accepted into the greater Lloyd family. The Lloyd's owned great swathes of land in Talbot County, Maryland, and hundreds of slaves who operated a number of plantations.

Buchanan got his second command in 1842, when he was assigned to the U.S.S. *Vincennes* an eighteen-gun sloop of war. His time on the *Vincennes* was spent mostly in the Gulf of Mexico and was uneventful. Buck continued to demonstrate his wide knowledge of seamanship and his penchant for discipline. In the summer of 1845, Commander Buchanan was called to the Office of the Secretary of the Navy for a new mission.

Pressure had been building in the United States for the creation of a naval academy similar to that of United States Military Academy at West Point. But, as is always the case with new ideas, there are at least two concerns; cost, and was the idea really justifiable … do we need it? When a mutiny aboard a U.S. naval training ship almost occurred, it was taken as evidence that increased evaluation and training of midshipmen was needed. But to keep the cost of operating a school down, and to attempt to mitigate any appearance of creating senior births for navy officers, the Secretary of the Navy decided to select a seasoned commander, rather than captain, as the commandant of the academy.

Buck's experience at sea, reputation for discipline, and pragmatic decision-making convinced the Secretary that Buchanan should be the first Superintendent of the Naval Academy.

Secretary Bancroft personally notified Buchanan of his selection as Superintendent in a meeting in Washington in July of 1845. And he had just months to organize the curriculum, get the selected site, Ft. Stevens, prepared for accepting students, and to bring aboard the instructors. The first class of 50 midshipmen would arrive in October. Buck did an excellent job of organizing all aspects of preparation of the school. And once the midshipmen arrived, he took deliberate steps to quickly establish a strong disciplinary code. The Secretary praised Commander Buchanan's efforts to Congress in January 1846.

Buchanan's next assignment would be as commander of the U.S.S. *Germantown* during the Mexican War. Buchanan's ship was assigned to the command of Mathew C. Perry. Perry outlined for Buchanan his plan to clear the Mexican coast of hostile forces. Their first target would be on the Tuxpan River. The fort's name was La Peña, three miles inland. The Squadron moved north, and when they got to the mouth of the river, they found it too shallow for the heavier ships. Perry decided to launch an amphibious assault up the river in the small boats available on each of the ships.

Buck led the landing force and overwhelmed the fort quickly. After 32 years in the navy, Buck's first combat experience was in a land battle! But he was successful in taking his objective. Buck's second engagement would be another infantry fight at San Juan Bautista.

This second campaign was a little more difficult. The sailors and marines would land some two miles down-stream from the final objective and would have to fight through a number of defensive positions. In order to have artillery support, some six-pound cannon were brought ashore and had to be towed by the men. Though some fighting occurred on the ground, the fall of San Juan Bautista occurred before the land force arrived. The ships accompanying the land force up the river arrived first and forced the surrender. Though the war would go on for months, Buck had seen all the combat he would see in the Mexican War.

Commander Buchanan would return home for about two years before he received orders to proceed to Asia to assume command of America's newest and largest steam frigate, the U.S.S. *Susquehanna*.

This was quite an honor considering Buck was not a captain, and yet he was given what might be considered the best command in the U.S. Navy!

Naval officers, as a part of their duty and of the mission of the navy, had to interact with both American and foreign diplomats. Showing the flag was often a mission assigned to America's fleet. Buck had had previous experience with elements of diplomacy, but in Asia, he would find himself in the middle of power fights between the Department of the Navy, and the Commodore commanding the Squadron, and in the midst of diplomatic issues in both China and Japan. America saw opening Japan to trade as major commercial goal. Buck would become America's representative in Tokyo, negotiating for Commodore Perry, who had assumed the same behind the scenes approach to diplomatic activity as the Emperor of Japan. Buchanan would be the first American to step ashore in Edo Bay.

In Asia, Buck continued to demonstrate that he could get the job done! But, a problem unanticipated by either Buchanan or Commodore Perry arose. In 1850, the Congress acted to prohibit the use of the lash as a disciplinary tool. Both Perry and Buchanan were advocates of the lash as an essential element of ship discipline, and both saw its end as a real threat to command authority aboard ships. Commodore Perry developed a "carrot and stick" approach as the best alternative to the loss of a very effective punishment. Commander Buchanan did not appreciate the use of the carrot. This difference of view in how to deal with the change caused friction between two men who had been a very effective leadership team. Upon his return from Asia, Buck would spend the remainder of the 1850s on shore, at home.

In January 1855, the Chair of the Senate Naval Affairs Committee, Stephen Mallory offered legislation to establish a retirement provision for naval officers. Buck was a strong supporter, and when it passed, he was appointed to the committee that would evaluate the Navy's senior officers and recommend retirement. This committee became known as "The Immortal Fifteen," and they reviewed more than 700 cases over a five-week period. Buck used this forum to apply his standards with respect to an officer's moral standing, as a part of his evaluation process. The committee identified 201 officers for retirement, most of them senior officers. Coincidentally, Buck and the four other commanders serving on the Board were selected for promotion to captain. The announcement of the promotions being made public a day after the publication of the retirement list, politics heated up.

During the political wrangling which occurred in follow up to the issuance of the retirement letters, Buck had an opportunity to speak with many Senators on this and variety of issues concerning the Navy. He spoke at length with Judah P. Benjamin of Louisiana. Buck who had been an outspoken supporter of the committee was caught, out on a limb, when the Senate demanded a series of boards be established to review the decisions. Some members of "The Fifteen" who had voted to retire officers, suddenly changed their minds, or claimed they had not voted to retire certain individuals. 64 of the original 204 were returned to duty. Needless to say, Buchanan's reputation suffered in the eyes of some officers because of his firm commitment to the retiring of officers who he felt were no longer performing good service.

As war clouds gathered in America, Buck was living in Maryland, a state where slavery was a very controversial issue. As a border state with a large free black population, it was the target of abolitionist literature. Buck, as a landowner, slave owner, and member of a family that owned hundreds of slaves, was not of a mind to accept abolition.

With Lincoln's election Buck faced a situation similar to many of his peers in the Army. He had spent his whole life in the U.S. Navy. His career had been challenging, and he had proven himself. He was on the "inside" or inner circle when it came to all things navy. Further, some believe that service in the navy separated naval officers from their home states and the politics associated with secession. Admiral George Dewey, U.S.N. wrote:

Loyalty (to the United States of America) was stronger in the navy than in the army, for the reason that the naval officer felt an affection for the flag born of sentiment of our splendid record in the War of 1812, and a realization born of his foreign cruises, that our strength before the other nations of the world, who selfishly wished to see our growing power divided, was in unity. Besides, naval life separates one from State and political associations.

Only half of the Southern-born naval officers would resign their commission to go with the Confederacy.

Buchanan, like many from the Talbot County area, expected Maryland to secede. When reports came of the rioting in Baltimore and the firing of United States soldiers on the civilian citizens of Baltimore, Buchanan saw no recourse. Three days after the riots, he entered the Secretary of the Navy's office with his resignation. It was accepted without comment. But Buck then had second thoughts and even attempted to rescind his resignation. But the Secretary would have none of it. Captain Franklin Buchanan, late of the United States Navy, was out.

Buck was not quick to enter the service of the Confederacy. Initially, he hoped the Union would allow the South to leave peacefully. He eventually traveled to Richmond, arriving on September 4th, 1861.

He met with Secretary of the Navy Stephen Mallory and was given a captain's commission in the Confederate States Navy, and appointed as chief of the Bureau of Orders and Detail. Initially, he would act as the Navy's personnel officer and be responsible for officer assignments. Buck would also act as a close confidant to the Secretary on a wide variety of issues pertaining to the infant Navy.

Chapter Two —

Georgia Dictates a Maritime Tradition for both North and South

From its very conception, as a grouping of European colonies, the United States of America was a maritime society. Its entire western character had been transported across a vast ocean and deposited on the Atlantic shores of North America. Initially, its laws, languages, traditions, and religions came from Europe.

The initial purposes of the colonies were to provide religious freedom, evangelism to the Amerindians, economic gain, and social relief for the European nations smart enough to place a flag in the west. The maritime links to Europe and the rest of the world only grew as the colonies developed into the world's first democratic nation. The very issues that drove the southern states to secede from the union emanated from the sea and its relationship to America. Tariffs, the cotton trade, the industrialization of the north, and even slavery all had deep roots in the maritime tradition and commerce of the United States.

And then, there were the river systems and lakes that provided efficient, relatively fast highways for the ever-developing inland portions of the North American continent. Of the Mississippi River, President Lincoln said, "The Mississippi is the backbone of the Rebellion; it is the key to the whole situation."

Before the advent of the railroads, and even after, the inland waterways dictated the location of cities and towns, and acted as the axis of many a trade route. In his work, *The Mississippi*, Lt. Francis V. Greene, Corps of Engineers, explains that the Mississippi was a theatre of war unto itself. He correctly points out that the first objective of the Federals war in the west was to capture and control the entire Mississippi River.

The new Southern government quickly acted to avoid one possible commercial cause for Northern aggression. The Mississippi River was the primary avenue for the movement of agricultural and commercial goods produced in the states of Ohio and west. Loss of access to the Mississippi would cause great economic strain to the American northwest. Acting to ease anxiety in the northwest, one of the first acts of the Confederate Congress proclaimed; "That the peaceful navigation of the Mississippi River is hereby declared free to the citizens of any State upon its borders, or upon the borders of its navigable tributaries."

This act literally allowed free and unchecked passage of northern goods through the very heart of the new Southern nation.

During the War for Southern Independence, the islands of Bermuda, the Bahamas, and Cuba gained great importance to the South. These islands would become way stations for the blockade-runners carrying the South's principal export, cotton, and for the ships bringing war materials, medicines, and goods from Europe. Repeatedly in the reports and diaries of Southern naval personnel, there are clear indications that they felt these islands were very pro-southern in their outlook.

The 3,500 miles of Confederate coastline can be divided into three segments: the Atlantic coast from Hampton Roads to Jacksonville, the Florida coast from Jacksonville to Pensacola, and the Gulf coast, from Pensacola to Corpus Christi. I divide the coast area in three because the factors which are important, the availability of ports, the distance to the different Caribbean islands, the availability of rail or other inland transportation avenues, and the proximity of usable, defensible coastline and ports to strategic inland areas seem to naturally create these three different coasts.

On the Atlantic coast there are at least two significant nautical geographical features, the Hampton Roads area and Albemarle-Pamlico Sound in North Carolina. The Gulf coastline can be sub-divided into two segments east and west of the mouth if the Mississippi River.

Clearly, if the Southern nation were to actually exist, a good amount of effort would be required to not only defend the 3,500 miles of coastline, and the vast waterways that ran through the Confederacy, but to utilize this major transportation complex for military and logistical purposes. Southern needs, in terms of war materials, medicines, and the export of cotton to finance the war effort, all drove elements of Confederate naval and maritime thinking.

Perhaps no body of water was more important, in the early years of the war, than Hampton Roads, Virginia. As the southern entrance to the Chesapeake Bay, any significant Confederate naval and land presence would result in Rebel control of the Roads. Gosport Naval Yard, across from Norfolk, the only complete naval facility in the South was located here. Fortress Monroe, with guns overlooking the Roads and acting as a large secure land base approximately one hundred miles from Richmond, sat at the end of a peninsula formed by the James and York Rivers.

Southern land forces initially made the greatest impact on the Roads when they occupied Norfolk and captured the partially destroyed naval base. In addition, Southern infantry moved down the peninsula to establish a presence in the Yorktown area, closing off the river access to Richmond. The capture of Norfolk and the Gosport Naval Yard on April 17th by the Confederates had the additional bonus of providing the southern nation with the hull of a partially destroyed steam frigate, the U.S.S. *Merrimac*.

The importance of the capture of the *Merrimac* can be measured both by the tremendous engineering success it facilitated, and in the strategic consequences of the presence of the ship it became. Work began almost immediately to convert the hull into the Confederacy's best-known ironclad. The C.S.S. *Virginia's* victory against the U.S.S. *Congress* with 50 guns and U.S.S. *Cumberland* with 30 guns on March 8th, 1862, in the main theatre of the war, proved the value of new technology. The solid performance of the Rebel vessel, against both the best wooden ships of the federal fleet, and the Yankees' own ironclad, the U.S.S. *Monitor*, on March 9th, confirmed for President Davis, Secretary Mallory, and the Confederate Congress the worth of investing money into the production of Southern ironclads. As a result, more than 20 ironclad ships would be ordered by the Confederate government. *(See Appendix 4, Confederate Ironclads)*

And, for the foreign powers, whose ships were present in the Roads on March 8th, their naval officers passed on eyewitness reports as to the performance of the C.S.S. *Virginia*.

In Washington, D.C. the most important men in the Lincoln Administration were in near panic when the *Virginia* appeared. They feared the *Virginia* would sail up the Chesapeake and then up the Potomac to shell the capital. Given the concern expressed in Washington, one would think the Federals had read Secretary Mallory's orders to Admiral Buchanan:

The *Virginia* is a novelty in naval construction, is untried and her powers unknown; and hence the department will not give specific orders as to her attack upon the enemy. Her powers as a ram are regarded as very formidable, and it is hoped, you will be able to test them. Like the bayonet charge of infantry, this mode of attack, while the most destructive, will commend itself to you in the present scarcity of ammunition. It is one also that may be rendered destructive at night against the enemy at anchor. Even without guns the ship would, it is believed, be formidable ram.

Could you pass Old Point and make a dashing cruise into the Potomac as far as Washington, its effect upon the public mind would be important to our cause.

The condition of our country, and the painful reverses we have just suffered, demand our utmost exertions; and convinced as I am that the opportunity and the means for striking a decisive blow for our navy are now, for the first time, presented, I congratulate you upon it, and know that your judgment and gallantry will meet all just expectations.

Action, prompt and successful just now, would be of serious importance to our cause.

On the local scene, as long as the Confederates could hold Gosport Naval Yard, the C.S.S. *Virginia* would remain a factor in any military plans concerning the peninsula. The Union could not attempt to approach Richmond from Fortress Monroe as long as the Confederates controlled the James River.

After the *Virginia* – *Monitor* duel, General McClellan wrote, "The performances of the *Merrimac* placed a new aspect upon everything and may probably change my whole plan of campaign just on the eve of execution."

At a Cabinet meeting the day after the battle, Navy Secretary Welles reported Secretary Stanton as saying:

The *Merrimac* will change the whole character of the war ... she will lay all cities on the seaboard under contribution. I shall immediately recall Burnside: Port Royal (SC) must be abandoned. [I have no doubt] that the *Merrimac* [is] at [this] moment on her way to Washington, ...not unlikely we shall have shell or cannon ball from one of her guns in the White House before we leave this room.

McClellan also telegraphed commanders of forts along the east coast:

… The rebel ironclad steamer *Merrimac* has destroyed two of our frigates near Fort Monroe, and finally retired last night to Craney Island. She may succeed in passing the batteries and go to sea. It is necessary that you place your fort in the best possible condition for defense, and do your best to stop her should she endeavor to run by.

Meanwhile, Secretary Stanton telegraphed to the Governors of New York and Massachusetts:

… The opinion of the naval commanders here is that the *Merrimac* will not venture to sea, but they advise that immediate preparations be made to guard against the danger to our ports by large timber rafts protected by batteries. They regard timber rafts, guarded by batteries, as the best protection for temporary purposes.

One Yankee defense plan, approved by President Lincoln, members of the Cabinet, and General McClellan focused on sinking barges filled with stones at the appropriate place in the Potomac River so as to make it impassable for the *Virginia*.

After the famous engagement of March 9th, the instructions from the respective Navy Departments to their ironclads could not have been more different.

The Confederates sought a second engagement between the two ironclads. Secretary Mallory in a letter on April 4th to Commander Tattnall, the wounded Buchanan's replacement, encouraged immediate action:

Do not hesitate or wait for orders, but strike, when, how, and where your judgment may dictate. Take her (the *Virginia*) out of the dock when you deem best, and this point is left entirely to your decision.

As we have seen above, Lincoln and his senior advisers were fearful of a raid by the C.S.S. *Virginia* on the nation's capital. President Lincoln had personally spoken with the wounded commander of the *Monitor*, who feared losing the ship if the Rebels boarded.

This fear motivated orders issued to the U.S.S. *Monitor*'s commander, which were exactly opposite of Secretary Mallory's:

Navy Department, March 10th, 1862
It is directed by the President that the *Monitor* be not too much exposed and that in no event shall any attempt be made to proceed with her unattended to Norfolk. If the vessels can be procured and loaded with stone and sunk in the channel, it is important that it should be done.

Other instructions for other commanders followed, and Gideon Welles, Secretary of the Navy, signed the orders.

Secretary Mallory not only encouraged offensive action by the *Virginia*, he went so far as to identify the weaknesses of the U.S.S. *Monitor* as they had been identified in *The Scientific American*, and outlined the specific tactics to be used.

Mallory wrote to Commander Tattnall;

But little preparation to resist boarders exists, it would seem; and a wet sail thrown over her pilot house would effectively close down the steerman's eyes. Her grated turret, her smokestack, ventilators, and air holes invite attack with inflammables and combustibles; and it would seem that twenty men thus provided, once upon her deck, as her turret is but nine feet high, might drive everyman out of her.

After the initial battle with the U.S.S. *Monitor*, the *Virginia* was placed in dry dock for repairs at Gosport Naval Yard from 11 March through 4 April. On April 11th, the C.S.S. *Virginia* sailed out looking for another engagement with Monitor. Despite the threat of the *Virginia* to numerous federal transports at anchorage in and around the Roads, and the capture of three small federal ships, the *Monitor* refused to sally out into the deeper water.

The *Virginia* required 23 feet of water, the *Monitor* 12 feet. On May 8th, with the *Monitor* and several other large warships shelling a target ashore, the *Virginia* ventured out again and headed directly for the *Monitor*. Scharf clearly indicates there is a dispute over who avoided the fight. One account had the *Virginia* steaming directly towards the *Monitor* only to have her run. The Yankee version says that *Monitor* stood her ground, and that the *Virginia* acted "cautiously."

While the accounts differ, one thing is clear; the U.S.S. *Monitor* did not attack the *Virginia*. It seems certain that preservation of the force was the essence of the Yankee strategy during this period.

But on the Confederate side, the entire Yankee Army was transferred to the Peninsula while the *Virginia* was present. If the Yankees were cautious about letting the *Monitor* fight, the Confederates seem just as cautious about allowing the *Virginia* to travel out of the Roads into the Chesapeake to attack Yankee shipping en route to Fortress Monroe. And in fact, this timidity ended with the destruction of the *Virginia* by the Confederates as a result of the loss of Gosport Naval Yard as a part of the advance of Yankee armies on the Peninsula.

Scharf wrote,
… *The Sounds of North Carolina were no less important to the defence [sic] of that State than Hampton Roads was to that of Virginia, and that if the blockade of the Southern coast was to be effective indeed, then the sounds, as coaling stations and harbor of refuge, were of prime importance to the United States.*

He goes on to say,
The command of the broad waters of these sounds, with their navigable rivers extending far into the interior, would control more than one-third of the State and threaten the main line of railroad between Richmond and the sea coast portion of the Confederate States.

The importance of the Carolina Sounds might be reflected in the rapidity with which the Federals moved to secure control of them. One of the first Federal amphibious operations would be commenced during the summer of 1861 to secure the Hatteras Inlet, an early assembly area for Southern privateers operating against Federal commercial shipping. As early as August 9th, Yankee insurance companies were already feeling the pain from losses inflicted by the handful of privateers operating off North Carolina.

These companies joined together to petition Secretary of the Navy Gideon Welles to attack the "nest of pirates." By late August, U.S. Naval and Army forces arrived in the area. On the 28th, Col. Martin withdrew the 7th North Carolina Volunteers from Fort Clark and moved to Fort Hatteras. On the 29th, after a bombardment from 70 guns from the broadsides of the U.S.S. *Minnesota, Wabash, Susquehanna, Cumber-*

land, *Pawnee*, and *Harriet Lane* and the three-gun battery already landed on the island south of Fort Hatteras, the Confederates surrendered. The bombardment lasted only three hours, and casualties within the Fort were light, but the Southern commander felt forced to surrender because he could not return effective fire on the Federal ships that were out of the range of his guns.

This victory for the North did not secure the Sounds, but it did demonstrate they could and would project power utilizing a combination of naval and land forces (Combined Arms Operations). The Yankees would be back the following year to expand their presence in this strategic area.

The rest of the Atlantic coast south of the Sounds featured important ports, including Wilmington, Charleston, Port Royal, and Savannah. All but Port Royal would be important destinations for blockade-runners.

The Gulf Coast created a whole second naval theatre, and opportunities for naval operations for both North and South.

The dominant nautical feature on the Gulf Coast is the entrance of the Mississippi River, and upstream about 75 miles the Crescent City, New Orleans. New Orleans was the second-largest city in the Confederacy, and it served as the hub of the cotton trade in the Deep South. When united, the entrance to the Mississippi was the gateway for imports and exports from America's Mississippi-Ohio-Red River complex. As we have discussed earlier in the Chapter, both Lincoln and Provisional Confederate Congress recognized the import of this huge natural communications highway. Lincoln identified it as a strategic theatre of the war. The Confederates at first hoped to eliminate a cause for war by announcing transit would remain unobstructed for goods from any state bordering the Mississippi River. Once war was inevitable, the Mississippi and New Orleans became a priority in the Confederates defense planning. The Confederates occupied two forts, with interlocking fire, south of New Orleans, Fort St. Phillip and Fort Jackson. These twin forts became the centerpiece of the defensive scheme for New Orleans.

The second most important nautical feature on the Confederate Gulf Coast is Mobile Bay. Two rivers, the Alabama River from Selma and Montgomery and the Tombigbee - Mobile River from western Alabama, flow into the Bay from the north. In addition, a rail line links the city of Mobile with the rest of the Confederacy. Mobile Bay is forty miles deep and between 10 and 20 miles wide. It is shielded from the Mexican Gulf by a combination of islands and peninsulas, providing great defensive strength.

Further to the east, Pensacola offered a good harbor, a rail connection, and a protected harbor. Like Charleston, Pensacola was occupied by Federal troops who refused to leave. Biloxi, Mississippi also offered a good harbor. But without a rail connection it was a dead end for goods received.

Galveston and other port cities in Texas offered blockade-runners alternative destinations. But the further west one delivered the goods, the further they had to be transported so that they could have some positive effect on the Confederate war effort.

List of Confederate Privateers
Compiled from *The Confederate Privateers*

Ship	Port
Triton	Brunswick, Ga.
Phenix	Wilmington, De.
Calhoun	New Orleans, La.
Music	New Orleans, La.
Ivy	New Orleans, La.
J. O. Nixon	New Orleans, La.
Savannah	Charleston, S.C.
Jefferson Davis	Charleston, S.C.

(originally named the *Rattlesnake* in its application for a letter of marquis.)

Dixie	Charleston, S.C.
York	Hatteras, N.C.
Mariner	Hatteras, N.C.
Gordon	Hatteras, N.C.
Sallie	Charleston, S.C.
Petrel	Charleston, S.C.
Beauregard	Charleston, S.C.
Rattlesnake	Savannah, Ga.
Manassas	New Orleans, La.

(First ironclad, built by investors in La., taken into C.S.N. prior to its first engagement.)

Pioneer	New Orleans, La.

(First Confederate submarine, built by investors, sank before Yankee attack on New Orleans.)

Pioneer II	Mobile Bay, Al.
Hunley	Charleston, S.C.

Chapter Three —

Setting the table for naval power in 1861

As dependent as the United States was on maritime commerce, the "United States naval register of 1860 shows a navy of only 90 vessels, of which 21 are designated as unserviceable, 27 available but not in commission, and 42 in commission."

Many of the operational vessels were stationed far from their homeport and American waters.

On June 3, 1861, a roster of U.S. Navy personnel in the grades Captain through Third Assistants totaled 1,563 of which 671 were Southerners, or 42.9 percent of the United States Naval Officer Corps. This is an extremely important piece of information because it seems to cast doubt on "Civil War Conventional Wisdom" that Southerners were not especially good seaman. 321 southerners (only 20 percent of the total force) of these officers would resign their commission, but 350 would remain in the U.S. Navy.

Interestingly, of the 102 U.S. Navy officers of Southern birthright in the grades of Captain or Commander, only 50 resigned their commission. The grade where Southerners left the U.S. Navy by the largest percentage was the entry-level officer position of acting midshipmen. In this grade 106 of 129 resigned their commissions.

One officer, Lieutenant J.R. Hamilton resigned his commission and then wrote an address to the "Southern Officers of the U.S. Navy." Lt. Hamilton called on naval officers of Southern heritage to mutiny and bring the ships they served on to the South. This appeal may have influenced some officers to resign, but not one ship of the U.S. Navy was taken by mutiny and brought south.

The Confederate Congress acted in February 1861 by creating an authorization for the following positions in the Confederate Navy: 4 Admirals, 10 Captains, 31 Commanders, 100 First Lieutenants, and positions for various other officers.

To help the Confederate States offset the initial advantages of the Union, the Confederate Congress would appropriate $14,605,777.86 between February 1861 and August 1862, for naval purposes.

During the course of the entire conflict, the federal government would spend 310 million dollars, dwarfing Confederate expenditures.

Northern recognition of the need to rapidly expand their navy is seen in Secretary Welles immediate action to purchase 136 vessels, which when altered, added 518 guns to the U.S. fleet.

These initial purchases would be supplemented with orders to naval contractors for eight sloops of war, ironclads, and river ships.

Another important aspect of naval operations in play in the early days of secession were the naval facilities located in the South, chief among these were Norfolk and Pensacola. At Pensacola, the navy dockyard was not designed for construction of ships, but rather for repair.

Local troops from Florida seized the dockyard for the Confederacy. Union forces retreated to a nearby Fort Pickens, and through political maneuvering and reinforcement, Union forces were able to remain in the vicinity. Within a year, the Confederates would withdraw from the Pensacola area.

The Confederacy also seized the Gosport Navy Yard at Norfolk, including a dry dock worth several million dollars. And within the Navy Yard, the partially damaged hull of the steam frigate, U.S.S. *Merrimac*, launched in 1856 was located and raised. In terms of the war, this seizure of Norfolk, and the reconstruction of the *Merrimac* into the ironclad ram C.S.S. *Virginia* would have important strategic and historic consequences.

British historian John Keegan, in his work *The Price of Admiralty*, in his only reference to the naval aspects of the American War Between the States wrote in 1989, "The first iron gunboat constructed by the South in the American Civil War drove the northern fleet of traditional wooden ships ignominiously into harbour [sic]."

The subtle weight of Keegan's assessment, assumedly based on the eyewitness accounts of the officers of His Majesty's fleet present to view the debut of the C.S.S. *Virginia* against the U.S.S. *Constitution* and *Congress* in Hampton Roads, demonstrates just how important the introduction of an effective ironclad must have been to the European naval officers who witnessed the battle.

In the earliest days of the new Confederacy, ingenuity, courage, and daring had to take the place of iron, steel, and sail. The Confederacy needed a presence on the water, and needed a means to combat the unchallenged power of Yankee shipping. Part of the initial answer was a tactic often embraced by a people with little organized military power. As part of the South's response to Lincoln's call for 75,000 volunteers on April 15th, 1861, the Confederate Congress in special session on April 29th, met to address President Davis' call for the authorization of the issuance of Letters of Marque.

On May 4th, the Congress passed legislation recognizing that a state of war existed between the United States and the Confederate States of America. It then authorized the President "… to issue private vessel communications or letters of marque and general reprisal," and in Section 7 of the same legislation prescribed specific rules and guidelines.

J. Thomas Scharf provides an excellent description of the authority and role of the privateer and the differences between a privateer and a pirate.

A privateer, as the name imports, is a private armed ship, fitted out at the owner's expense, but commissioned by a belligerent government to capture the ships and goods of the enemy at sea, or the ships of neutrals when conveying to the enemy goods contraband of war. A privateer differs from a pirate in this, that the one has a commission and the other has none. A privateer is entitled to the same rights of war as the public vessels of the belligerent. A pirate ship has no rights, and her crew is liable to be captured and put to death by all nations, as robbers and murderers on the high seas.

As an instrument of national power, one can easily see that the privateer is the "poor man's" navy. Since the Confederacy did not have a standing navy and did not have the material resources to build one quickly, the embrace of this form of naval warfare was both fiscally prudent and strategically necessary. Scharf goes on to describe in great detail the reliance of the United States on the privateer during her two wars with Great Britain. Scharf points out that, "During the Revolutionary war this country had 1,500 privateers on the ocean, having 15,000 guns."

During the first year of the American Revolution, privateers captured 530 British vessels carrying cargo valued at five million dollars. And in the War of 1812, American privateers captured 2,000 British vessels!

However, as war clouds gathered between North and South, the government of the United States attempted to block the acceptance of Confederate privateers by the European powers. The European powers (Great Britain, France, Austria, Prussia, Sardina, and Turkey) had already signed the treaty of Paris, in 1856, amongst themselves that forbade the use of privateers in wars involving the signers. The United States had been asked to sign, but declined. Now, the United States wished to enter the treaty. The Europeans seeing the gambit for what it was, and unfair to the Confederacy, declined to allow the United States the protection of the treaty.

The important thing to note is that privateers, operating under a letter of marquis from the government of the Confederate States, had to abide by rules on the open sea. The privateers could not attack just any ship, but only those ships involved in the prosecution of the war against the South. Additionally, the behavior of the ship, its crew, and officers were the responsibility of the Confederacy. But unlike the C.S.S. *Alabama*, the *Florida*, and other commerce raiders who were owned by the Confederate government, the privateer ship was owned by private citizens, investors who had applied to the Confederate government for a license to conduct operations against the enemy at sea.

The *Savannah* was the first of the Confederate privateers. She was originally captured by the C.S.S. *Lady Davis* in Charleston and sold at auction. A crew was gathered, and the *Savannah* was fitted out with an eighteen-pound gun before she put out to sea under the command of Captain Thomas Harrison Baker. After capturing only one prize, the *Savannah* surrendered to the U.S.S. *Perry*. And thus, began the legal and political struggle concerning the real status of privateers in the War for Southern Independence.

On April 19th, through proclamation, President Lincoln asserted:

… if any person under the pretended authority of the said States, or under any other pretence [sic], shall molest a vessel of the United States, or the person or cargo on board of her, such person will be held amenable to the laws of the United States for the prevention and punishment of piracy.

An indictment was written against the *Savannah's* Captain and crew. It was read, and the prisoners were remanded to the Tombs in New York City. While the case was argued in public opinion, the Confederate government, under President Davis, promised retaliation should the Confederate prisoners be harmed.

In England, the situation was important enough to be addressed in the House of Lords, by Lord Brougham, who said, "… it is clear that privateering was not piracy by the law of nations."

It appears President Lincoln took this opportunity to question the legitimacy of secession. The very fact that nations could sign treaties forbidding a former practice of war clearly demonstrated that privateering was different from piracy. But if President Lincoln acknowledged Confederate privateering he would also be acknowledging Confederate nation-hood. Therefore, his allegations of piracy merely reflected the administration's position that the Confederate States of America were not a nation, but rather an illegal formation of states within the Union.

However, President Lincoln was also acutely aware of both the pressure coming from the European states concerning this issue and the feud-like reality and perception that would be created if North and South began executing prisoners of war.

The prisoners were eventually transferred to a prisoner of war status, and negotiations commenced for exchange. For a time, the Union stalled the exchange, but in 1862, as tens of thousands of Union soldiers were captured as a result of Confederate victories in Virginia, the situation was eased, and prisoners from a large variety of Confederate ships were exchanged.

As with many means of war originally condemned by the Union, privateering would eventually be incorporated into the Union war plan. In March 1863, the United States Congress would approve legislation authorizing President Lincoln to issue Letters of Marque! In this case, some northern editors endorsed this idea in the hopes that the incentive of profit would be more effective as a tool to find and destroy the Confederate commerce raiders than the power and might of the newly expanded Yankee navy.

During the earliest months of the war, while the Yankee blockade was still more aspiration than reality, the Southern privateers could return their captures to a Confederate port. The *Jefferson Davis*, a privateer fitted out of Charleston, attempted the return of prizes when it ventured out in July of 1861. The *Avis* captured the *John Welsh*, the *Enchantress*, and the *S.J. Waring* off Long Island, placing a prize crew on each and sending them south. Only the first two prizes made it to Southern ports. The third was recaptured by its original crew and returned north. The *Jefferson Davis* was lost off St. Augustine on the night of August 16th.

Privateers operated from many Southern ports, including Charleston, Wilmington, Savannah, and New Orleans and did great damage to the American commercial fleet in the opening days of the war. Between the commencement of the war and August 1861, Scharf states, "The little privateers, … captured within the same length of time nearly sixty Federal vessels."

On August 10th, the *New York Herald* wrote, "that already $20,000,000 worth of property has been lost in various ways through the operations of these highwaymen of the seas, increasing daily in numbers, and becoming more and more daring in their impunity. The worst effect is not the loss of the vessels and their cargoes, but the destruction of our trade. Our commerce with the West Indies was immense before the pirates commenced their depredations. Now no Northern vessel will get a charter or can be insured for any reasonable premium. English bottoms are taking all our trade."

Early in the war, the issue of privateers and their prizes created an issue of some importance within the Confederacy concerning Mexico. While the European powers had rejected the idea that the Confederates could bring captured prizes to their ports, and subsequently the ports of their colonies, Mexico was a different story. Mexico had never signed the treaty prohibiting privateering, and if the Confederacy could convince Mexico to keep her ports open to the ships captured by the South, a vital link between the two nations would be established and from there, who knows how that relationship could develop? The blockade would be severely damaged if Mexico openly cooperated with the Confederacy. But alas, that was not to be. Mexico's government would decide against allowing Confederate prizes within their ports.

As the Federals expanded their navy, bought and built modern warships, and established, expanded, and sustained the blockade, privateering lost much of initial advantage. The challenge of entering and exiting ports grew and forced those who would attempt the venture, attempt it in ships of very specific qualities. But it is clear in the opening days of the war, this makeshift fleet made itself felt against the largest maritime commercial trading nation in the world.

A variant of privateering which gained some headway within the Confederacy was the idea of a Confederate Volunteer Navy.[1]

One individual, B. J. Sage, of Louisiana worked hard to convince Congress and Secretary Mallory that the inclusion of private investors in the procurement process of vessels operating in conjunction with Southern national interests was an important alternative to the conventional navy.

Sage envisioned a hybrid privateer system where its officers would hold commissions from the Confederate government, separate from but similar to the regular Navy. Sage saw the creation of naval companies as a method of raising money for this new arm of Southern naval operations. The officers would receive a stipend from the government when at sea. And seaman would receive some pay also. Prize money would be calculated similarly to existing privateers, except that a portion of the prize money would be held in a widow's and orphans trust fund for those sailors lost while in operations against Union warships.

Mr. Sage also promoted the idea that these vessels should be, if possible, purchased overseas. He suggested that purchase of these ships overseas was just another means of augmenting the number of naval craft in service to the Confederacy.[2]

Sage also believed investors should be compensated from the government for the loss of their ship should it be lost in an action against Federal warships.

By 1862, some of Sage's ideas were being considered and acted on in Richmond.[3] Many of his provisions would be enacted into law over the years of the war, though the "Volunteer Navy" bill was initially defeated in Congress[4]. By 1863, sentiment in the Congress would change, and the Confederate Volunteer Navy would be created. In 1864 a pay scale would be established.[5]

---

1 *The Confederate Privateers*, Chapter XXV Much of what is written in this section was found in this work.
2 Ibid
3 Ibid, page 321
4 Ibid, page 323
5 Ibid, page 328

Of special note is the fact that the earliest work on submarines in the Confederacy was done as an element of privateering. The first work done, on the *Pioneer* in New Orleans, was done as a result of private investment with the intention of collecting the prize money authorized by the Confederate Congress for the sinking of an enemy warship. Though the three-man submarine *Pioneer* sank before the Battle of New Orleans, the inventor and machinists moved on to Mobile where they built both the *Pioneer II* and *Hunley*. In addition, the first David class torpedo boat was built as a result of the spirit of privateering.[6]

In general then, it appears that the Union held the initial advantage with respect to naval forces, though the initial difference in power between North and South was relatively small as the war began. The real advantage was in the long term. The Federals were able to quickly convert much of an existing large commercial fleet into military use. A little more than a year after the war began, the Federal Navy had grown from 90 ships to 386, carrying 3,072 guns.[7] Over time, U.S. financial strength, and pre-existing manufacturing infrastructure would allow the Federals to implement their blockade, conduct amphibious operations along the coast, combat Confederate cruisers, and build a large river squadron on the Mississippi to seize and operate on the inland waterways of the South.

---

6   Ibid, page 344
7   Ibid, page 192

Chapter Four —

The Battle at Sea

As we have discussed earlier, for both the North and South, the Atlantic Ocean was important as a highway to export domestic goods, and to import much needed war materials. "By 1860 roughly 70 percent of the world's maritime commerce was being conducted aboard American ships."[8] Both American nations looked to Europe for goods, friends, and as the center of the community of nations. Both nations wanted England, France, and the other European nations as allies, a market, and as a source of weapons.

On April 13th, 1861, President Lincoln, recognizing the importance of isolating the southern nation, declared a blockade.[9] Initially Lincoln's declaration was more the articulation of an aspiration and a strategy than a reality. Mr. Scharf, in his *History of the Confederate States Navy*, dedicates a lot of time to the issue of the legality of a non-existent blockade. Scharf asserts that international law requires naval forces be present to enforce the announced blockade, otherwise the ships of neutral nations could ignore the proclamation. This focus on the legality of the blockade is important because merchant ships flying a neutral flag would not be violating their neutrality if they entered a port that was not "effectively" blockaded. As long as Southern ports were not under blockade, the Confederacy was not reliant solely on blockade-runners to provide it with goods from Europe; ships flying neutral flags could enter southern ports.

The Confederacy did win an early diplomatic victory when the nations of Europe recognized the Confederacy on equal terms with the United States as a belligerent at war. This recognition allowed Confederate ships to enter foreign ports and extended the protection of the host nation to the ships while in their ports.[10]

Through the duration of the conflict, the war at sea was essentially about sustaining a lifeline to the Confederacy through a fleet of block-

---

8   *America's Civil War*, January 1993, Book Review by Jon Guttman of *Gray Raiders of the Sea; How Eight Confederate Warships destroyed the Union's High Seas Fleet* by Chester G. Hearn.
9   *Civil War Times Illustrated*, December 1971 "Mr. Lincoln's Blockade" by V.C. Jones
10 *History of the Confederate States Navy*, page 56

ade-runners and attacking the vast northern commercial fleet through another fleet of commerce raiders.

It is estimated some 300 vessels "tested the Federal blockade during the war."[11] Of this 300, 136 ships were captured, and 85 were destroyed during an estimated 1,300 attempts to penetrate the blockade.[12] Another source estimates there were as many as 8,000 violations of the blockade.[13] Even towards the end of the war, a large number of blockade-runners were still operating.

Figure 1 – The blockade–runner, C.S.S. *Robert E. Lee*
Image was provided by the US Department of Navy, Naval Historical Center

A few of the blockade-runners were owned by the Confederate government and operated as a part of the C.S. Navy, most were owned by commercial investors. One of the most inaccurate assumptions, both during the war and today, is that the commercially owned blockade-runners were primarily interested in transporting the most expensive and difficult-to-get commercial items so that profits could be maximized, thus making military needs a secondary consideration. However, the Confederate government controlled exactly how much of the available space on board a ship could be used for non-military items. When a blockade-runner entered a Southern port, Confederate officials at the port met the ship. The inventory of the shipment was checked to ensure that military and medical necessities were present in the appropriate amounts for the hold space available. A relatively small amount of hold space could be used for commercial goods. After

---

11   *Southern Fire, Exploits of the Confederate Navy* Page 188
12   Ibid
13   *The Civil War Archives, the history of the Civil War in documents*, page 617

the goods were offloaded from the blockade-runner, cotton was loaded into the empty hull to earn foreign currency for the Confederacy.

Initially, merchant ships of all types attempted to evade the blockade. But as the Union Navy grew in size, and as newer, faster ships were assigned to guarding the entrances of ports, the successful blockade-runner developed a very specific design. The ship was built low to the water to reduce its' silhouette and painted gray to help minimize the likelihood it would be observed. Blockade-running captains went so far as to purchase certain coals that emitted little or no smoke. The blockade-runners were of relatively shallow draft and were swift, possessing both steam and sail capability.

The improvements in design and the ability of the Confederates to successfully defend ports allowed the lifeline to remain open and effective in providing much needed supplies. As late as 1864, Confederate States government reports indicate blockade runners took out 5.3 million dollars' worth of cotton, and imported 8.6 million pounds of meat, 1.9 million pounds of saltpeter, 1.5 million pounds of lead, .5 million pounds of coffee, 69,000 rifles, 97 packages of revolvers, and 43 cannon, and 2,639 packages of medicine[14]

While the Union blockade had real effect in reducing imports to the South, blockade running only ended when the last Southern ports, Wilmington and Charleston, were closed through capture. 35 runners were waiting in Nassau as the war ended.[15]

The C.S.S. *Robert E. Lee* was a Confederate blockade-runner of the very first class. She was low and lean and ran fast. The ship was owned by the Confederate government and made at least 21 successful voyages against the Union blockade. Her captain, John Wilkinson, had resigned his commission in the U.S. Navy at the commencement of the war. Wilkinson had fought at New Orleans and would command another ship, the C.S.S. *Chickamauga*, later in the war. If commanding a blockade-runner is not sufficient to prove Wilkinson's daring, it should be noted that he was also involved in John Yates Beall's attempt to seize Johnson Island.[16] *(See Chapter Six, Confederate Naval Special Operations)*

---

14 *Civil War Times Illustrated*, December 1971, "Mr. Lincoln's Blockade" by V.C. Jones
15 Ibid
16 "The Robert E. Lee Runs the Blockade," *The Civil War Archives*, page 622

Captain Wilkinson wrote of his adventures with the *Lee*. He describes how his tactics and strategies for avoiding capture changed with the war. For instance, initially, he would attempt to run the blockade on the moonless nights hoping to take advantage of the increased darkness, but changed when he met a British Naval officer who had been mistakenly taken prisoner by the Yankees. The British officer related to Wilkinson that the Yankee squadron commander had told how the blockading squadron was more vigilant on the moonless nights, sleeping when the moon was full. Sometimes, the Federal commander would even send ships for re-coaling on the moonlit nights, figuring no rebel captain would attempt to evade the blockade during "moon bright."

On one such night, Wilkinson writes:

The tide was serving at ten o'clock, we succeeded in crossing the rip at that hour, and as we passed over the New Inlet bar, the moon rose on a cloudless sky. It was a calm night too, and the regular beat of the paddles through the smooth water sounded to our ears ominously loud.

Wilkinson goes on to tell how they left Wilmington, and remained close to land, using the darkened shore to hide his long, low silhouette, and using the sound of the waves breaking on the beach to mask his paddle wheels slapping the water. It was his practice to run the coastline for ten to twelve miles, slipping between the Yankee blockading vessels and the shore. Of course, there was always the chance of running aground or striking an obstacle such as a sunken ship.

Wilkinson had even detected that the federal ships would signal each other once they had spied a runner, and were preparing to fire their broadsides. The Yankee ships would show a light and then fire a number of rockets. The code would change from time to time, but it always included rockets. The rockets were used to point the rest of the blockading squadron towards the blockade-runner. Captain Wilkinson purchased some of the very same rockets being used and kept them on the bridge. When spotted, and his adversary had fired his rockets, Wilkinson would then fire his rockets in a different direction causing confusion amongst the Yankee ships in the dark of the night.[17]

---

17 Ibid page 623

On August 15th, 1863, the C.S.S. *Lee* was beginning another voyage from Wilmington to Bermuda. Captain Wilkinson tells us:

We passed safely though the blockading fleet off the New Inlet Bar, receiving no damage from the few shots fired at us, and gained an offing from the coast thirty miles by day light. By this time our supply of English coal had been exhausted, and we were obliged to commence upon North Carolina coal of very inferior quality, which smoked terribly.

The captain reports that shortly after sun up, a lookout spots a sail. In reply to a call for where away, the lookout "… sang out, 'Right astern, sir, and in chase.'"

Captain Wilkinson went to the masthead, and within 30 minutes saw the … top-gallant sail showed above the horizon. By this time the sun had risen in a cloudless sky. It was evident our pursuer would be alongside of us by mid-day at the rate we were going.

Wilkinson had his men throw over board the cotton loaded on deck, and gave orders for the engineer to make more steam.[18]

As the ship's company added all the canvas on the ship, the engineer reported to Wilkinson that the Carolina coal was filled with dirt and debris and could not be counted upon to raise the steam pressure. In other words, there was no way to increase the speed of the ship.

As the day wore on, the federal ship was gaining. It was only a matter of time.

"A happy inspiration occurred to me when the case seemed hopeless." writes Wilkinson, "Sending for the chief engineer I said, "Mr. S., let us try cotton saturated with spirits of turpentine." They were on board as part of the deck load, thirty or forty barrels of spirits"[19]

The cotton was torn open, and saturated with the turpentine before they were passed down to the "fire room." Almost immediately, the engineer reported that a full head of steam was had. As a result of the Captain's curiosity, the speed of the ship was measured and found first to be at 9 knots, and then at 13 ½ knots. For the time being, the *Lee* had equaled the speed of its pursuer.

About an hour before sunset the engineer reported to the Captain that the residue of the burning cotton was fouling the machinery and

---

18 Ibid page 623
19 Ibid page 624

that they were losing speed. The Captain encouraged the engineer to do all he could until nightfall, when the Captain would issue new instructions. Darkness fell, and while the pursuer had closed to about four miles, the Captain directed that the Carolina coal be used again, thus creating a large trail of black smoke. Wilkinson headed directly for a fog bank. Once inside the fog bank, the Captain had them close the dampers, shutting off the smoke, turned with the wind (about a ninety-degree turn from the course he had been on), and ran in the fog.

Wilkinson had lost the Yankee pursuer.

The second aspect of the war at sea was also strategic in nature, a direct attack on the economy of the North through an assault on their commercial fleet. The Confederate government decided to invest assets into attacking the commercial fleet of the United States. From May 1861 through the conclusion of the war, the South would eventually commission 19 commerce raiders.[20] The Confederacy created their raider fleet through foreign purchase and through the capture of vessels, mostly on the high seas. Eleven of these commerce raiders were cruisers built in Great Britain and Scotland.[21] Those eleven vessels caused an estimated 17.9 million dollars in losses to US trade, in the sinking of ships and their cargoes. Sharf's history identifies each of the 256 ships that were intercepted by the Confederate raiders.[22]

This attack on the Federal commerce fleet had real consequences on the northern economy, the cost of imported goods, and forced the rapid transfer of U.S. merchant ships to foreign owners. "Nearly 350 American ships were sold to British owners during 1863 …"[23] providing solid evidence of the effectiveness of the Confederate cruisers. Records indicate that a total of 715 ships transferred from the American to the British flag during the four years of the conflict.[24] Northern naval planners had to allocate resources to defend their dwindling commercial fleet and pursuing Southern cruisers.

---

20 *History of the Confederate States Navy* See Appendix 1 of this paper for a list of the cruisers and their operational dates.
21 Ibid, page 782 (those cruisers were the C.S.S. *Alabama, Shenandoah, Florida, Tallahassee, Georgia, Chickamauga, Nashville, Retribution, Sumter, Sallie* and *Boston.*) See Appendix 1 for complete list of raiders and their dates of operation.
22 *History of the Confederate States Navy* pages 814 - 818
23 *Civil War Times*, August, 1996, "Reluctant Raider," by John M. Taylor
24 *History of the Confederate States Navy,* page 783

When looking at the Confederate cruisers from a strategic point of view, it is important to note that the C.S.S. *Alabama*, C.S.S. *Florida*, and C.S.S. *Georgia* were all operating during the summer of 1863. The havoc being caused on the sea, simultaneous to General Lee's ambitious campaign in the summer of '63 was either a masterful combined arms strategic plan coordinated in Richmond, or the stroke of greatest fortune by pure coincidence.

Many wars have been won and lost in the minds of the peoples involved. (This is referred to, as the national will by strategic thinkers and military planners.) The essence of a strategy based on defeating the national will focuses on creating a perception that the enemy is winning, and will not quit. In 1863, with Lee in Pennsylvania, riots exploding in the streets of northern cities, and Southern Commerce raiders at their busiest, those who were growing tired of the war in the North had plenty of reasons to consider ending a stalemated war.

As a measure of success, who today, could suppose that the Confederate naval offensive on high seas would destroy, or drive from the American flag, almost 1,000 ships during the War for Southern Independence? When one considers that before 1860 American commercial ships were carrying 70 percent of the world's trade, we can begin to understand how the Confederate success at sea seriously damaged both the Federal economy and U.S. prestige on the world stage.

The results of the depredations of these commerce destroyers upon the American merchant marine were disastrous; not for two generations did the American fleet regain its' place on the high seas, and as late as 1910 American flag merchant ships totaled only one third the tonnage of 1860.[25]

An overview of the Confederate States Navy, and particularly the portion discussing the Southern success with respect to commercial raiding requires an acknowledgment of Admiral Raphael Semmes.

Raphael Semmes was born in Charles County, Maryland in 1809. Semmes entered active service in the United States Navy in 1832. Older than most of his peers, Semmes had delayed his entry into the Navy in order to study law with his brother. In 1837, he was promoted to Lieutenant, and he moved to Alabama in 1842. He served in the Mexican War, gaining some distinction, though his first sea command was lost

---

25 *The Civil War Archive, the history of the Civil War in documents,* page 618

as a result of heavy weather. After the war, he was assigned as inspector of lighthouses along the Gulf Coast, and in 1855, he was promoted to the rank of commander[26].

Semmes would continue his development when in 1858 he was assigned as Secretary of the Light Board in Washington. Semmes resigned his commission upon the secession of Alabama. He traveled to Montgomery, where President Davis immediately dispatched him north to secure whatever mechanics he could recruit south, and machinery he could purchase. He was also to purchase whatever war materials he could.[27] While in the north, Semmes actually witnessed President Lincoln's inauguration, and inspected the machinery of the arsenal located in the nation's capital!

The letter of instructions to Mr. Semmes, from President Jefferson Davis is provided here:

MONTGOMERY, ALABAMA,
February 12, 1861
DEAR SIR: As an agent of the Confederate States, you are authorized to proceed as hereinafter set forth, to make purchases and contracts for machinery and munitions, or for the manufacture of arms and munitions of war.

Of the proprietor of the – Powder Company, in ——, you will probably be able to obtain cannon- musket-powder-the former to be of coarsest grain; and also to engage with him for the establishment of a powder-mill at some point in the limits of our territory.

The quantity of powder to be supplied immediately will exceed his stock on hand, and the arrangement for further supply should, if possible, be by manufacture in our own territory; if this is not practicable, means must be sought for further shipments from any and all sources which are reliable.

At the arsenal at Washington you will find an artisan named ——, who has brought the cap-making machine to its present state of efficiency, and who might furnish a cap-machine, and accompany it to direct its operations. If not in this, I hope you may in some other way be able to obtain a cap-machine with little delay and have it sent to the Mount Vernon Arsenal, Alabama.

---

26 *History of the Confederate States Navy*, page 785
27 Ibid, page 785

We shall require a manufactory for friction primers, and you will, if possible, induce some capable person to establish one in our country. The demand of the Confederate States will be the inducement in this as in the case of the powder-mill proposed.

A short time since, the most improved machinery for the manufacture of rifles, intended for the Harpers Ferry Armory, was, it was said, for sale by the manufacturer. If it be so at this time, you will procure it for this Government, and use the needful precaution in relation to its transportation. Mr. _____ of the Harpers Ferry Armory, can give you all the information in that connection which you may require. Mr. Ball, the master armorer at Harpers Ferry, is willing to accept service under our Government, and could probably bring with him skilled workmen. If we get the machinery, this will be important.

Machinery for grooving muskets and heavy guns is, I hope, to be purchased ready made [sic]. If not, you will contract for its manufacture and delivery. You will endeavor to obtain the most improved shot for rifled cannon, and persons skilled in the preparation of that and other fixed ammunitions. Captain G.W. Smith and Captain Lovell, late of the United States Army, and now New York City, may aid you in your task; and you will please say to them that we will be happy to have their service in our army.

You will make such inquiries as your varied knowledge will suggest in relation to the supply of guns of different calibers, especially the largest. I suggest the advantage, if to be obtained, of having a few of the fifteen-inch guns, like the one cast at Pittsburg.

I have not sought to prescribe so as to limit your inequities, either as to object or place, but only to suggest for your reflection and consideration the points which have chanced to come under my observation. You will use your discretion in visiting places where information of persons or things is to be obtained for the furtherance of the object in view. Any contracts made will be sent to the Hon. L.P. Walker, Secretary of War, for his approval; and the contractor need not fear that delay will be encountered in the action of this Government.

    Very respectful yours, etc.,
(Signed) Jefferson Davis"[28]

---

28 *The Rise and Fall of the Confederate Government*, Volume I, pages 270-271

Mr. Semmes then traveled through New York, Connecticut, and Massachusetts finding no shortage of businessmen willing to sell arms and munitions to the South. Semmes was successful in purchasing both gun powder and the machinery necessary to rifle artillery. All of this was sent south. Secretary of the Navy Mallory sent Semmes a letter while he was in New York asking him to pay particular attention to finding fast, light draft, steam-powered vessels for the Confederate Navy.[29]

Semmes returned to Montgomery, Alabama, where he received his commission as a commander, C.S.N., and was given orders to take command of the lighthouse bureau. That did not last long. Within two weeks, he was on his way to New Orleans to take command of the C.S.S. *Sumter*. Semmes orders were "to do the enemy's commerce the greatest injury in the shortest time."[30]

Figure 2 – Commander Raphael Semmes photo taken in 1862.
Image was provided by the US Department of Navy, Naval Historical Center

---

29 *History of the Confederate States Navy*, page 786
30 Ibid 787

After a narrow escape from the U.S.S. *Brooklyn* while leaving the mouth of the Mississippi River, the Sumter headed for Cuba where they took their first prize, the *Golden Rocket*, on July 3rd. Prisoners were taken aboard, and then ship was burned. Semmes captured two more prizes and headed for a Cuban port with them. He refused entrance, as all the European powers had declared they would allow the entrances of captured prizes into their ports. The *Sumter* took six more prizes but lost all of them because she entered a neutral port with them.[31]

Semmes decided to head for new hunting grounds near Brazil. He took and burned two more ships and then headed for Martinique. At Martinique, he went into port to coal and refit. The Federal warship *Iroquois*, under the command of Captain Palmer, arrived in the harbor and made pleas to the Governor of Martinique opposing their hospitality to a ship that was attacking U.S. commercial shipping. Palmer was told that the Southern ship was welcome, as was the Yankee ship. He was further told that if he remained in port, and the C.S.S. *Sumter* left, he would be delayed by twenty-four hours from departing. The French Governor enforced his decrees with the arrival of a French man-of-war. Palmer left, after arranging for a Union commercial vessel to maintain a watch on the *Sumter* and to arrange for signals should the ship prepare to leave. For eight days, Semmes waited for his chance to depart. During that time, Commander Semmes found out the signals to be used between the two union ships. After dark on 23 October, Semmes headed south. Once he saw that the Yankee ship *Windward* had signaled his direction, he brought his ship to under the shadow of a mountain, giving room for Palmer to speed off to the south. Semmes then headed north, and made his escape.

Semmes headed across the Atlantic, taking prizes and prisoners. When he arrived off Cadiz, Spain he was advised that he would not be allowed to enter the port. After negotiations, he was allowed briefly to enter Caracca, a harbor a few miles east, where he deposited the prisoners with the US counsel and made some minor repairs to his ship. He was ordered to leave before he could pick up coal, and so decided to head for Gibraltar. On the way, the Sumter took two more prizes.[32] The *Sumter* was eventually bottled up in Gibraltar by the three U.S. warships, *Tuscarora*, *Kearsarge*, and *Chippewa*. Semmes, after consultation

---

31 Ibid 787
32 Ibid, page 789

with the Confederacy's representative Mr. Mason, Semmes decided to lay the ship up. Most of the crew was paid off, and the ship was left with a skeleton crew. The *Sumter* was sold. But the result of Semmes first command was the capture of 18 prizes over a six-month period. Commander Semmes was ordered to England where he would prepare to assume command of the C.S.S. *Alabama*.

Possibly Captain Bulloch's most famous purchase, the ship designated No. 290, was built by Mssrs. Laird, operators of the Birkenhead shipyards. Federal agents in England discovered the deal and applied to the British Foreign office to block the transfer. Unfortunately for the United States, the British authorities arrived at the shipyard in late July, after No. 290 had departed. At sea, on August 24th, after a rendezvous with another ship that brought the crew and officers of the *Alabama*, the ship was officially added to the rolls of the Confederate Navy with Captain Rafael Semmes in command.[33]

The C.S.S. *Alabama* was 220 feet long and 32 feet breadth of beam. She was both sail and steam-powered, and her propeller could be lifted from the sea when not in use. Her best-recorded speed was 11 ½ knots. She had six 32-pound cannon, a 100 pounder Blakely, and an 8-inch smoothbore. Her crew numbered 148[34].

Captain Semmes would terrorize Yankee shipping in both the north and south Atlantic from September 5th, 1862 through January 14th, 1864. He would begin his campaign near the Western Islands against the American whaling fleet where he would seize and destroy or bond a dozen ships. He then moved to the Newfoundland Banks in search of American grain ships. He arrived in this area in October 1862, and during this month, made capture of 21 prizes before "falling in" with an unusual amount of neutral ships.

Semmes convened a prize court in his cabin, and after diligent investigation, the Court decided that the neutrality papers of many were fraudulent. The appropriate vessels and their cargo were destroyed. The *Alabama* then turned south, eventually putting in at Port de France in Martinique. The U.S.S. *San Jacinto*, a frigate arrived, but she was too slow to contain the *Alabama*. Semmes then set course for Venezuela, where he received coal from a tender. Once restocked with coal, he

---

33 Ibid, page 796
34 Ibid page 797

headed for San Domingo, where he would settle and wait for additional prey.³⁵

Semmes was looking for the gold ships en route to New York from California. He never sighted one. He did capture the *Ariel*, but finding it loaded with five hundred women and children, he released it.

Semmes then headed into the Gulf of Mexico, where he hoped to intercept ships headed to General Nathaniel Banks, who was then gathering forces for an upcoming campaign. When nothing appeared, he moved further west to Galveston, where a Yankee squadron was bombarding the city. Semmes concealed the *Alabama's* identity and was able to draw off one of the Yankee warships, the U.S.S. *Hatteras*, commanded by Lt. Commander Homer C. Blake.

The action commenced at 9 p.m. on the evening of January 11th, 1863. The *Alabama's* fire was lethal to the hull of the Yankee vessel, and within 15 minutes, the fight was over. 15 minutes later, the *Hatteras* sank, but not before all of the Union sailors, including all the wounded were removed.³⁶

Semmes now made for Jamaica and after a short layover, set course this time for Brazil and then to the Cape of Good Hope. Sitting on this maritime crossroads, Semmes struck a bonanza, taking 24 prizes. He destroyed all but one of those prizes, the *Conrad*. He decided to convert this ship into a commercial cruiser like the *Alabama*. He named the new cruiser, the C.S.S. *Tuscaloosa*, provided it with captain and crew from the existing crew of the *Alabama*, and sent them off to find more Yankee prey.

Semmes then turned east, and headed for Africa. On his way, he took another two prizes before putting into Saldanha Bay on July 28th, 1863. He took one additional prize, before heading into the Straits of Sunsa, the China Sea, and the Bay of Bengal. Returning to the south Atlantic, on April 27th, 1864, the *Tycoon* was the last Yankee commercial ship to be taken prize by the C.S.S. *Alabama*. Semmes then headed for France and the port of Cherbourg.³⁷

Captain Semmes filled a detailed report of the battle to Secretary Mallory, which is provided here:

---

35 Ibid, page 797
36 Ibid, page 798
37 Ibid, page 798

Southampton, June 21st 1864

Sir: I have the honor to inform you, that in accordance with my intention as previously announced to you, I steamed out of the harbor of Cherbourg between nine and ten o'clock on the morning of the 19th of June, for the purpose of engaging the enemy's steamer *Kearsarge*, which had been lying off and on the port, for several days previously. After clearing the harbor, we descried the enemy, with his head off shore, at the distance of about seven miles. We were three-quarters of an hour in coming up with him. I had previously pivoted my guns to starboard, and made all preparations for engaging the enemy on that side. When within about a mile and quarter of the enemy, he suddenly wheeled, and, bringing his head in shore, presented his starboard battery to me. By this time, we were distant about one mile from each other, when I opened on him with solid shot, to which he replied in a few minutes, and the action became active on both sides. The enemy now pressed his ship under full steam and to prevent our passing each other too speedily, and to keep our respective broadsides bearing, it became necessary to fight in a circle; two ships steaming around a common center and preserving a distance from each other of from three-quarters to half a mile. When we got within good shell range, we opened upon him with shell. Some ten or fifteen minutes after the commencement of the fight, our spanker-gaff was shot away, and our ensign came down by the run. This was immediately replaced by another at the mizzen-masthead. The firing now became very hot, and the enemy's shot and shell soon began to tell upon our hull, knocking down, killing, and disabling a number of men, at the same time, in different parts of the ship. Perceiving that our shell, though apparently exploding against the enemy's sides, were doing him but little damage, I returned to solid-shot firing, and from this time onward alternated with shot and shell.

After the lapse of about one hour and ten minutes, our ship was ascertained to be in a sinking condition, the enemy's shell having exploded in our side and between decks, opening large apertures through which the water rushed with great rapidity. For some few moments, I had hopes of being able to reach the French coast, for which purpose I gave the ship all steam, and set such fore and aft sails as were available. The ship filled so rapidly, however, that before we had made much progress, the fires were extinguished in the furnace, and we were evidently on the point of sinking. I now hauled down my colors, to prevent the further destruction of life, and dispatched a boat to inform the enemy of our condition. Although we were not but 400 yards from each other, the enemy fired upon me five more times after my colors had been struck. It is charitable to suppose that a ship of war of a Christian nation could not have done this intentionally. We now directed all our exertions toward saving the wounded and such of the boys of the ship as were unable to swim. These were dispatched in my quarter boats, the only boats remaining to me: the waist boats having been torn to pieces. Some twenty minutes after my furnace fires had been extinguished, and when the ship was the point of settling, every man, in obedience to a previous order which had been given, the crew, jumped overboard and endeavored to save himself. There was no appearance of any boot coming to me from the enemy until after my ship went down. Fortunately, however, the steam yacht, *Deerhound*, owned by a gentleman of Lancashire, England — Mr. John Lancaster — who was himself on board, steamed up amidst of my drowning men, and rescued a number of both officers and men from the water. I was fortunate enough myself thus to escape to the shelter of the neutral flag, together with about forty others, all told. About this time, the *Kearsarge* sent one, and then, tardily, another boat. Accompanying, you will find lists of the killed and wounded, and those who were picked up by the *Deerhound*; the remainder there is reason to hope, were picked up by the enemy, and by a couple of French pilot boats, which were also fortunately near the scene of action. At the end of the engagement, it was discovered by those of our officers who went alongside of the enemy's ship with the wounded, that her midship section, on both sides, was thoroughly iron-coated; this having been done with chains, constructed for the purpose, placed perpendicularly, from the rail to the water's edge, the whole covered over by a thin outer planking, which gave no indication of armor beneath. This planking had been ripped off, in every direction, by our shot and shell, the chain broken and indented in many places, and forced partly into the ship's side. She was effectually guarded, however, in this section from penetration. The enemy was much damaged in other parts, but to what extent it is now impossible to say. It is believed he is badly crippled. My officers and men behaved steadily and gallantly, and though they have lost their ship, they not lost their honor. Where all behaved so well, it would be invidious to particularize, but I cannot deny myself the pleasure of saying that Mr. Kell, my first lieutenant, deserves great credit for the fine condition in which the ship went into action, with regard to her battery, magazine and shell rooms, and that he rendered me great assistance, by his coolness and judgment, as the fight proceeded. The enemy was heavier than myself, both in ship, battery, and crew; but I did not know until the action was over that she was also iron-clad. Our total loss in killed and wounded, is 30, to wit, 9 killed and 21 wounded.[38]

J. Thomas Scharf tells us that Semmes came closer to winning the battle than he knew at the time of writing the above report. Scharf states that one of the *Alabama's* shells did penetrate the *Kearsarge* near the sternpost but failed to explode. Scharf goes on to speculate that had the 8-inch percussion shell exploded; the resulting hole may have been sufficiently large to sink the Yankee ship.

And so, the very effective life of the South's most famous and most dangerous ocean cruiser came to an end. But for Semmes, the war was not over. He returned to the Confederacy, where he was promoted to Rear Admiral and placed in command of the James River Squadron. When Richmond fell, Semmes ordered the squadron destroyed, and with approximately five hundred men, looked for a means to continue the war. (See Chapter 8, *The Confederate States Naval Academy*)

The C.S.S. *Florida* was the first of the steam cruisers built in England for the Confederacy. On March 22nd, 1862, English officers and sailors took her out from Liverpool as the unarmed merchantman, *Oreto*. She sailed for the Nassau where she arrived on April 28th. The *Oreto* was seized twice by British authorities while in port because of allegations by the U.S. counsel that she was going to be transferred to the Confederacy. But both times, there was insufficient evidence to prove the claim.[39] On August 10th, at Green Cay, the *Oreto* met a schooner that carried the guns and Confederate crew. The transfer was complete, and the ship was commissioned as the C.S.S. *Florida* under the command of Captain John N. Maffitt.

The *Florida* had two 7-inch and four 6-inch rifled Blakely guns.

The *Florida's* Rebel career started off with bad luck. The crew contracted Yellow Fever and had to make for a Cuban port seeking medical help. When the Spanish Governor General seemed likely to take possession of the ship, Lt. Commander Maffitt decided to make a run for

---

38 Ibid, pages 799-800
39 *History of the Confederate States Navy*, page 790

Mobile and attempt running the blockade. Maffitt deceived the blockaders, flying British colors until she had come up on the blockade line. But as he passed the blockaders and was called to stop, Maffitt raised the Confederate colors and was instantly blasted by a broadside from the U.S.S. *Oneida*. For two hours, the blockaders fired on the *Florida*, hitting her repeatedly, but she finally made it to the safety of the guns of Fort Morgan.[40] Once within Mobile Bay, recently arrived Admiral Franklin Buchanan had to decide what to do with her. The *Florida* was anchored some fifteen miles from Mobile. The sick crew was transferred to another ship so that the *Florida* could be "cleaned, fumigated, repainted and refitted."[41]

It would take three weeks before the ship could be made safe for workmen. And since the ship was deep draft, she could not be brought into Mobile for the repair work. With winter approaching, delay followed delay. Included in the delays, was the missing equipage for the ship's guns. When the ship's crew rushed to leave Nassau, these important tools had been left behind.[42] In addition, Maffitt himself had been severely worn by the disease. He suffered from the exhaustion of providing medical treatment to the officers who remained on board once in Mobile. In Richmond, Secretary Mallory began to press for a departure date. As time passed, rumors made their way to Richmond that Maffitt was busying himself with Mobile's social life, inviting parties aboard. Tensions grew, and Maffitt was actually relieved of command. Admiral Buchanan found himself as advocate on behalf of Maffitt. The admiral appealed directly to President Davis, and Lt. Commander Maffitt was eventually reinstated to command.[43] On the evening of January 15th, 1863, with 19 officers and 116 men,[44] the *Florida* rested under the guns of Ft. Morgan. A strong northerly gale came up, the temperature dropping as strong winds helped energize the Gulf raising the waves. The blockading squadron had been reinforced from three to twelve ships. Maffitt waited until the storm subsided some, and the sea was covered with a cold mist. At 2 a.m., he called the men to quarters and began his race for the Gulf. The *Florida* passed quietly through the first line of picket ships, only to find a second line comprised of the U.S.S.

---

40 *History of the Confederate States Navy*, pages 790
41 *Confederate Admiral, The Life and Wars of Franklin Buchanan*, pages 181
42 *Southern Fire, Exploits of the Confederate Navy*, page 23
43 *Confederate Admiral, The Life and Wars of Franklin Buchanan*, pages 181
44 *Southern Fire, Exploits of the Confederate Navy*, page 24

Susquehanna and the U.S.S. *Cuyler*.[45]

Maffitt boldly ordered the helmsman to steer between the two ships and seemed to be on his way undetected when a bright flash arose through the *Florida's* funnels. The flash was caused when the engineers were forced to change to a different type of coal and was seen by the watch on both Yankee ships. Maffitt ordered full sail, and full speed from the engine room. The *Cuyler* turned in pursuit. The sun came up, and with the U.S.S. *Cuyler* five miles behind; the race went on all day. The *Florida* was making 14.5 knots bounding over high waves. The two ships remained in view of one another ... the distance between them shrinking and then widening throughout the day. As sunset approached, Maffitt prepared to change tactics. Once all light had left the sky, he had his sail quickly reefed, meanwhile called "all ahead stop" to the engine room. The helmsman swung hard to port, and the ship fell into a deep trough amongst the waves.[46]

The U.S.S. *Cuyler* sped past the *Florida* and on into the night.

Once free, Captain Maffitt set course for hunting waters off the north coast of Cuba. In short order, the *Estelle* was sighted, chased, and caught. Her cargo included rum and molasses for Boston, and she was put to the torch. Maffitt did remove the topsail for use by his own ship. He then made for Havana to replenish his depleted supply of coal. On the 22nd of January 1863, the *Florida* left Havana and the same day sank two more Yankee commercial vessels. However, problems arose with the coal purchased in Havana, and it had to be thrown overboard. Captain Maffitt determined from then on to coal only at British ports. He made for Nassau, reporting that the people there were "decidedly" pro Confederate.[47]

On February 1st, a Union warship was sighted and incorrectly identified as the U.S.S. *Santiago de Cuba* thought to have ten guns. Maffitt wanted no part of a fight with a heavier Union ship and turned to run. The Yankee ship was actually the much less dangerous U.S.S. *Sonoma* of four guns. The *Florida* would lose the Yankee ship after a few days.[48] Later in February, the *Sonoma* would be spotted and identified by the *Florida* crew, and they would attempt to lure the *Sonoma*

---

45 Ibid, page 26
46 Ibid, page 27
47 Ibid, page 29
48 Ibid, page 29

into a fight. But the smaller ship would not bite.[49]

February 1863 had proven to be a busy month for the crew of the C.S.S. *Florida*. On the evening of February 5th, the *Florida* had a close call when the U.S.S. *Vanderbilt* came upon her at top speed. Captain Maffitt, caught at a complete stop, and knowing he could not out run the 3,360-ton steamer, decided to play possum. He had the guns covered over with canvas, lowered the smoke stacks, had all lights extinguished but one, and lay completely still. The *Vanderbilt* circled the *Florida*, snipers poised, but decided this could not be the scourge of the Yankee commercial fleet and sailed off. Maffitt wrote in his log, "To have been rammed by this immense steamer would have closed our career, and all were rejoiced to see her leave us." [50] A week later, on February 12th, the *Jacob Bell* was spotted off the Windward Islands. The *Florida* was cleared for action, turning in pursuit. The clipper ship *Jacob Bell* was out of Foo Chow, China headed for New York. Her hold was full of treasures from the Far East, including tea and silks, 10,000 boxes of firecrackers, matting, and camphor. In addition, the *Jacob Bell* carried 43 passengers, including two women.[51] With his engines at full, and his sail all out, the *Florida* began to close on its prey, though it would take six hours to finally catch the *Jacob Bell*. The boarding party of the *Florida*, commanded by Lt. Hoole, after reviewing the ship's papers would estimate the value of the cargo at one and half million dollars, the largest prize capture of the war. After the passengers, crew, and their baggage were removed, the *Jacob Bell* was set ablaze the following morning.

Captain Maffitt would command the C.S.S. *Florida* until she reached Brest, France on August 23rd, 1863. The *Florida* would remain there, at a government dock, for six months to refit. Captain Maffitt, due to ill health, was relieved of command. His successor, Commander Joseph Barney was also relieved for ill health on the 4th of January 1864. Lt. Charles M. Morris was assigned as her new commander.[52]

The *Florida* would make at least 14 more captures during 1864 until she found her way to Bahai, Brazil on October 4th. Below I provide a copy of Lt. Morris' report to Secretary Mallory concerning the events,

---

49 *History of the Confederate Navy*, page 792
50 *Southern Fire, Exploits of the Confederate Navy*
51 *Southern Fire, Exploits of the Confederate Navy*, page 30
52 *History of the Confederate Navy*, page 792

which occurred in the neutral Brazilian report that ended the career of the *Florida*.

> Bahia,
> SIR:
>
> It is with great pain that I have to report the capture of the C.S.S. *Florida*, lately under my command. I arrived at this port on the 4th instant, at 9 p. m., to procure coal and provisions, and also to get some slight repairs, after a cruise of sixty-one days. Just after anchoring a boat passing around us asked the name of our vessel, and upon reply stated that the boat was from H. B. M. S. *Curlew*. Next morning I found that the U.S.S. *Wachusett* was at anchor near us, but no British steamer, so I at once concluded that the boat which hailed us the evening before was from the *Wachusett*. We were visited on the morning of the 5th by a Brazilian officer, to whom I stated my wants, and was informed by him that he would report the same to the president, and that until his answer was received we could hold no communication with the shore. At noon I received a communication (which was left on board the *Florida*) from the president, stating that he was ready to receive me. At my interview he informed me that forty-eight hours would be allowed me to refit and repair, but that should his chief engineer, whom he would send on board to examine the machinery, deem the time too short, he would grant the necessary extension. He was most urgent in his request that I would strictly observe the laws of neutrality (implying by his manner, and, in fact, almost as many words, that he had no fears on account of the United States steamer, but that I was the cause of uneasiness to him, lest I should attack the *Wachusett* in port), at the same time stating to me that he had received most solemn assurances from the U. S. consul that the United States steamer would do nothing while in port contrary to the laws and that he desired the same from me, which I unhesitatingly gave. The Brazilian admiral, who was present at the interview, suggested that I had better move my vessel between his ship and the shore, as our proximity to the *Wachusett* might cause some difficulty. My assurances to the president seemed to set his mind at rest on the score of any collision between the two vessels, and upon leaving him I immediately repaired on board and moved the *Florida* closer inshore to the position suggested by the admiral. I found the Brazilian engineer on board, and was informed by him that it would take four days to repair the pipe of the condenser.

Feeling now no apprehension of any difficulty occurring while in port, and wishing to gratify the crew with a short liberty, not only on the score of good conduct, but also of health, I determined to permit one watch at a time to go ashore for twelve hours, and sent the port watch off that afternoon. About 7:30 p. m. a boat came alongside stating that she was from the U.S.S. *Wachusett*, with the U. S. consul, who had an official communication for the commander of the *Florida*. The letter with the card of the consul was handed to First Lieutenant Porter, who, after examining it and finding it directed to Captain Morris, sloop *Florida*, returned it unopened to the consul, stating that it was improperly addressed; that the vessel was the C.S.S. *Florida*, and that when the letter was so directed it would be received. The next day (6th) a Mr. de Videky came on board, having received a letter from the U. S. consul enclosing one for me. He requested me, before receiving my letter, to permit him to read the one sent to him. It was a request to Mr. de V. to carry a challenge to the commander of the *Florida* and in case of its acceptance to offer his (the consul's) influence in having the repairs of the *Florida* speedily finished. I informed Mr. de V. that I had heard quite enough, and finding the letter for me still improperly addressed, declined receiving it, but at the same time said to him that I had come to Bahia for a special purpose, which being accomplished I should leave; that I would neither seek nor avoid a contest with the *Wachusett*, but should I encounter her outside of Brazilian waters, would use my utmost endeavors to destroy her. I enclosed a letter, marked 1, since received from Mr. de Videky. That afternoon, the port watch having returned, I sent the starboard watch ashore on liberty, going also myself, in company with several of the officers. At 3:30 a. m. on the 7th I was awakened by the proprietor of the hotel at which I was staying and told that there was some trouble on board the *Florida*, as he had heard firing and cheering in the direction of the vessel, but on account of the darkness was unable to discern anything. I immediately hastened to the landing, and was informed by a Brazilian officer that the U.S.S. *Wachusett* had rammed and captured the *Florida* and was then towing her out of the harbor. I hurried off to the admiral's vessel and was told by him that he was at once going in pursuit. He returned in the afternoon with all his vessels, having been unable to overtake the *Wachusett*. Upon mustering the officers and crew left on shore, I found there were four officers, viz. Lieutenant Barron, Paymaster Taylor, Midshipman Dyke, and Master's Mate King, and seventy-one men, of whom six had escaped by swimming from the *Florida* after her capture. Of the actual occurrences and loss of life on board the *Florida* I have been able to find out very little. The substance of what I have gathered from the six men who escaped is as follows: That at 3:15 a. m. on the 7th, Acting Master T. T. Hunter, Jr., being in charge of the deck, the *Wachusett* left her anchorage, and taking advantage of the darkness steamed for the *Florida*, from which she was not seen until close aboard; that she was hailed by Mr. Hunter, who, receiving no answer, called all hands to quarters. Before the officers and crew were all on deck the *Wachusett* struck the *Florida* on her starboard quarter, cutting her rail down to the deck and carrying away her mizzenmast, at the same time pouring a volume of musketry and a charge of cannister from her forecastle pivot gun upon our decks. The *Wachusett* then backed off and demanded our surrender, to which demand First Lieutenant Porter declined to accede. The enemy then fired again and again into us, which was returned by the officers and crew of the *Florida*. Another demand was then made for our surrender, and Lieutenant Porter answered, "I will surrender conditionally." The enemy then stopped firing, and the commander called for Captain Morris to come on board. Lieutenant Porter answered that Captain Morris was on shore, and that he as commanding officer would come on board as soon as he could get a boat ready. The enemy then sent a number of armed boats to take possession of the *Florida*. As soon as Lieutenant Porter was heard to surrender, fifteen of our crew jumped overboard to escape capture, of whom only six succeeded, the remaining nine having been shot in the water by men on the forecastle and in the boats of the *Wachusett*. Mr. Hunter was wounded, and a number of men killed. The enemy made fast a hawser to the foremast of the *Florida*, and, after slipping her cable, towed her out to sea. I called in person upon the president as soon as possible, but could get no further information from him. On the 8th I sent a protest to the president, of which I send you a copy, marked 2. On the 10th our agent was informed by the interpreter that the president did not intend to answer my protest, as the Confederate Government had not been recognized by Brazil, and that I would find all the official correspondence in the newspaper. I then wrote the letter marked 3, in which reference is made to a letter from the president, marked 4. Just before leaving Bahia, having received no answer, I sent our agent, Mr. James Dwyer, to the president. The result of his visit is contained in his letter, marked 5. My next thought was for the care of my officers and crew then ashore. Finding that it would be impossible to negotiate a bill for an amount sufficient to pay off the crew, all of whom desired to remain in the Confederate service, I deemed it best to secure a passage on some merchant vessel bound to England. Arrangements were made with Captain Bray, of the English bark *Linda*, to take the men at £10 each and the officers at £20 each, we to pay the expense of fitting up the berths, etc., which would cost about £80. The *Linda* is expected to sail for London on the 15th, two days after I leave. I have taken passage for Paymaster Taylor and myself on the English mail steamer, so that on our arrival, such arrangements may be made for the reception and disposal of the men as you deem best. The Bahia papers contain a number of reports as to the killed and wounded on board the *Florida*, all of which I have thoroughly sifted and find no foundation for the same. At the time of her capture there were about 25 tons of coal on board the *Florida*, most of which was dust. The amount of funds and the list of officers captured are contained in the report of Paymaster Taylor, herewith enclosed and marked 6. The enclosed newspaper is an official extra containing all the Brazilian official correspondence in reference to the *Florida*. All of my papers, the signal book, and cipher were captured in the ship, but I hope they were destroyed, as the first lieutenant, the surgeon, and the captain's clerk all knew where they were kept.

I am, very respectfully, your obedient servant,
D. MANIGAULT MORRIS,
Lieutenant, C. S. Navy, Commanding,
Late in Command of the C.S.S. *Florida*

Flag-Officer
SAML. BARRON, C. S. NAVY,
Commanding C. S. Naval Forces in Europe.[53]

The attack by the federal ship on the C.S.S. *Florida* anchored in a Brazilian port demonstrates just how much the ship's captain was willing to risk ending the *Florida's* raid on Union commercial shipping. Clearly this was an illegal act. Clearly the federal commander placed

---

53 *Official Records of the Union and Confederate Navies in the War of the Rebellion.* Series 1, vol. 3 (Washington: Government Printing Office, 1896): 631-633. This report was secured from the Naval Historical Center website, www.history.navy.mil/index.html

his career on the line in conducting the attack. But, the actions of the Federals after the *Florida* was towed north demonstrates that the Commander Collins, U.S.N. desperation was shared by the Lincoln Administration.

The *Florida* was taken prize by the crew of the U.S.S. *Waschusett*, which placed what remained of the Confederate crew, about 18, under irons, and then escorted the famous Rebel raider to Newport News where it arrived on November 12th.[54] Meanwhile, the nation of Brazil began immediately calling for the return of the *Florida* to Bahai. The situation took on global importance when nations from all over the world condemned the Yankee attack in a neutral port. Of course, the Federals condemned the actions of their rogue captain, but were slow to respond to the calls for returning the *Florida*. Commander Collins faced Court Martial, was found guilty and dismissed from the service. (The case would be set aside by Secretary Welles, and he would be restored to rank and placed back on the active rolls.)

In Newport News the *Florida* was accidentally struck on November 19th by a U.S. Army barge causing major damage. Pumps had to be constantly run, and despite orders to keep the *Florida* afloat, she mysteriously sank on November 28th, and thus could not be returned.

The C.S.S. *Florida's* story would not be complete without a discussion of Lt. Charles W. "Savez" Read. Born in Mississippi, Read was 21 when war broke out. He had attended the U. S. Naval Academy and won the nickname "Savez" from his classmates as a joke. It was said savez was the only word Read had learned in his French classes. Midshipman Read was not a scholar. But he did do enough work to graduate.

When the war broke out, Read was commissioned in the Confederate Navy and sent to New Orleans where he joined the C.S.S. *McRae*. When his commander was killed during the battle for New Orleans, Read assumed command and moved the *McRae* to engage the union fleet. He stood his ground until the ship was so badly shot up it had to be surrendered. Read escaped capture and was assigned to the ironclad being built north of Vicksburg, the C.S.S. *Arkansas*. Lt. Read would participate in that ship's heroic fights against two Yankee squadrons on

---

54 *Southern Fire, Exploits of the Confederate Navy,* page 92. More than 70 of the *Florida's* crew escaped, either because they were not aboard when the attack occurred, or because they jumped ship after the attack.

the Mississippi River.[55]

"Savez" would then be assigned to the crew of the *Florida* under the command of Commander John N. Maffitt. Though a veteran of some tough fighting, Read did not initially impress Maffitt. In fact, Maffitt wrote of Read that he was "slow." On the seas, Read would prove that observation less than accurate.

On May 6th, 1863, the *Florida* captured the *Clarence* bound for Baltimore with a cargo of coffee.[56] Read sat down and wrote a letter to Maffitt suggesting that he be given the prize and twenty men. Read further suggested that he would take the *Clarence* up to the Chesapeake Bay and "cut out" a Yankee warship. Maffitt studied the letter and after a brief consult with its author decided to give "Savez" his own command.

Just the boldness of this decision-making process demands some comment and thought. Like Lee and Jackson at Chancellorsville, Maffitt and Read were facing a huge and overpowering enemy. The *Florida* had barely sufficient guns and men for her own needs as a commerce raider. Yet, a subordinate suggested dividing the *Florida's* crew and proposing a mission that literally targeted the most heavily defended piece of naval territory in the war!

And, in brief time, commander and subordinate decided in favor of the proposal! What would be an almost insane decision for a power near equal to its opponent becomes a piece of daring brilliance when the odds against one are so high. Yet it is not desperation but inspiration that is the father of such boldness.

Maffitt gave Read the men he asked for, but he could spare only a six-pounder boat howitzer for Read's new command.[57]

The *Clarence* was not a fast ship, and Read's first attempts to seize prizes were dismal failures. No ship's captain was intimidated by the weakly armed raider and therefore would not submit to the calls for their surrender. "Savez" set about to change the appearance of the vessel. He ordered that the extra masts stored on board be cut and painted black. He ordered gun ports be cut into the sides of the vessel. And he practiced his crew on running the five "guns" forward out the ports, once the howitzer had been fired.

With these changes, the *Clarence* appeared to be a formidable

---

55 *Southern Fire, Exploits of the Confederate Navy*, page 41
56 *Divided Waters*, page 338.
57 *History of the Confederate States Navy*, page 794

raider, and the Confederates quickly saw a change in attitude by the ships they approached. The *Clarence* took six prizes in the mid-Atlantic before Read decided to transfer his flag to the sixth, the *Tacony*. While taking these prizes Read realized, through reading captured newspapers, that his plan to enter the Chesapeake Bay would not work.

The *Tacony* was faster, and once the gun ports had been cut and the Quaker guns transferred, she became an even more dangerous looking raider than her predecessor.

"Savez" turned his ship north and headed for the waters off New England. He took seventeen more prizes before he again transferred his flag, crew, and "guns" to the *Archer*. The New England maritime public was in arms! They called on the Northern government to send out whatever naval ships were needed to put an end to this Confederate raider!

Meanwhile, "Savez" was cooking up an even bolder adventure.

From captured fisherman "Savez" learned of an armed steam revenue cutter, the *Caleb Cushing* anchored in the port of Portland, Maine. "Savez" saw an opportunity to meet part of the objective he had originally laid out in his letter to Commander Maffitt. Though Maffitt's orders had left Lt. Read discretion to do what damage he could; Read must have seen this as a real opportunity to demonstrate the viability of raids on northern ports.

On June 27th, 1863, "Savez" sailed the *Archer* into the Portland harbor. That evening he led most of his crew in small boats across the harbor and onto the *Cushing*. They quickly and quietly overwhelmed the watch and took control of the ship. Because the steam was not up, they had to resort to sail and tide to effectuate their escape. Nature's elements were not favorable, and it took until dawn for the *Cushing* to clear the port entrance and head for open sea.

Coincidentally, the new Yankee captain of the *Cushing* was entering the port as she sailed out. On shore, the Yankees had awakened to find their cutter sailing out. Immediately alarm rang out, and a seagoing posse was organized. Unable to operate the steam engines, the *Cushing* could not outrun the collection of tugboats and steam ships sent out after her. Though "Savez" attempted to drive them off with the few rounds stored aboard the ship, he eventually decided to abandon the ship, destroying it through fire in the process.

The adventure ended when "Savez" and his men were captured, shortly after the *Archer* was taken.

While we will not cover the C.S.S. *Shenandoah*, (the only Confederate vessel to circumnavigate the world), or the *Tallahassee*, *Sumter*, and the other raiders here, it is clear that the Confederate commerce raider fleet was an effective strategic arm of the Confederate Navy. There are many more instances, not covered in this work, where the leaders and crews of the *Alabama* and *Florida* demonstrated great skill, courage, tenacity, and cunning. The impact of the Confederate commercial raiding fleet on American maritime commerce was decisive. The increased insurance rates and unreliability of Yankee shipping forced the literal dismemberment of the American merchant fleet.

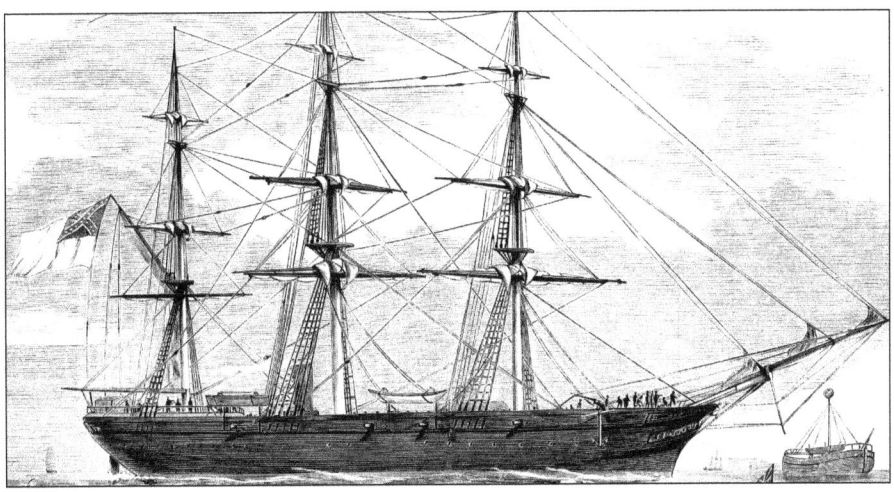

The C.S.S. *Shenandoah*

Figure 3 – Charleston during the great war.
In the upper center you see the initial location for the Military College of South Carolina, The Citadel.
This photo is from the Library of Congress

Chapter Five —

The naval battle at home, along the coasts, in the ports, and on Dixie's rivers

Looking back on the War, the clarity of time allows us to see that defending Southern ports so as to continue international commerce and controlling or obstructing the South's inland waterways were essential strategic elements to any successful prosecution of the Southern war effort. Unlike the war at sea, the battles for the coastline and rivers allowed for the opportunity of cooperation between naval and land forces. The quality of this cooperation many times influenced the outcome of the struggle.

As we have seen above, the South's war effort was reliant on the lifeline sustained by the blockade-runners. The goods that came from Europe traveled through Bermuda or Nassau where they might be transferred from a ship of neutral flag to one of the specialized blockade-runners. But once aboard these fast, sleek ships, there was an obvious need for a Confederate port. Along the Atlantic coast, Charleston, Wilmington, and Savannah seem to have been the favorites. On the Gulf of Mexico, New Orleans, Galveston, and Mobile are mentioned often as destinations for the runners.

Early in the war, New Orleans was seen as an important port for both sides because of its proximity to large quantities of cotton.[58] Admiral Porter wrote, "The most important event of the War of the Rebellion, with the exception of the fall of Richmond, was the capture of New Orleans. ..."[59]

However, Charleston might be the best example of cooperation between the services, and also the South's efforts at technological innovation to offset the huge advantages of the Union forces. Of important note is the fact that two of the Confederacy's most renowned and senior generals, Robert E. Lee and P.G.T. Beauregard, were assigned to command the forces defending Charleston at various times. Both made surveys of the defenses and added their own improvements.

---

58 *History of the Confederate States Navy*
59 "Our Cake is all dough" by Admiral Porter, page 121 in *Battles and Leaders of the Civil War*

In the traditional sense of port defense, we are aware of Ft. Sumter, and to some extent, are knowledgeable of the other land fortifications deployed around the harbor and at its various entrance points. Islands outside and within the harbor provided excellent vantage points for batteries where their combined fires could be effective. The existing defenses would benefit from the keen eye of General Robert E. Lee during the period of November 1861 to March 3rd, 1862.[60]

Beauregard would command the southern coast during the period of August 29th, 1862, through April 20th, 1864.[61] Charleston benefited from the innovative thinking of an army officer on Beauregard's staff who experimented with the design and construction of torpedoes and later with the offensive concept of submerged torpedo boats. This officer was Captain Francis Lee, (no relation to the Lee's of Virginia), supported by Beauregard, designed the torpedo that would be used in the torpedo fields (mine fields) in Charleston Harbor. One Union naval commander identified the torpedo fields as the reason he was hesitant to attack Charleston Harbor.

Captain Lee also worked with the torpedo boat C.S.S. *Torch*, in its unsuccessful endeavor to attack the U.S.S. *New Ironsides* in August of 1863.[62] A second attack would be made by another Confederate torpedo boat, the C.S.S. *David*, on the 5th of October 1863. Though not sunk, the damage caused by the C.S.S. *David* was severe enough to lay up for repairs the largest ship in the Federal Navy for a year.[63]

And, of course, the now famous C.S.S. *Hunley* would also operate in the waters of Charleston Harbor, sinking the U.S.S. *Houstonic* on February 17th, 1864. Unlike the David class ships previously mentioned, the C.S.S. *Hunley* was built with the intention of completely submerging below the water to a depth sufficient to pass under the keel of its intended target while pulling the torpedo into the target's hull. Because of failures in the test phase, costing the lives of the inventor and 23 other men, Gen. Beauregard gave orders that the ship must

---

60   *Gray Fox, Robert E. Lee and the Civil War* Pages 56-64, by Burke Davis,
61   Information found on www.civilwarhome.com which referenced *Who Was Who in the Civil War* by Stephen Sifakis
62   *Southern Fire, Exploits of the Confederate States Navy*, Page 116 by R. Thomas Campbell
63   *Confederate Veteran* magazine, Volume II, 1999, "David and Goliath" by R. Thomas Campbell

remain at the surface. [64]

Given the novelty of the idea of a partially submerged craft and the fact that the Federals had to know of at least three operating in the Charleston Harbor, it must have seemed like a hornets' nest to any Federal ship commander. After the evacuation of Charleston by the Confederates, the Yankees would find a total of eleven "Davids" in the Charleston Harbor.[65] And, these boats were only a single element of the naval defense of the harbor.

A second element of the naval defense of the harbor was the use of torpedoes. Also, a new weapon of naval warfare, these torpedoes, which today would be called mines, were being improved and deployed within the harbor. These torpedoes could be detonated by contact with a ship, or through command via a primitive electric line that ran to the shore and would be touched against an electric battery.

The third element of the naval defense of Charleston Harbor was a squadron of ships, including several ironclads. A Southern naval presence actually occurred in the harbor even before the Confederacy formed.[66] Among the early vessels defending the harbor was the *Lady Davis*. When the Confederacy took over responsibility for Charleston, the squadron had grown to include the C.S.S. *Gordon* and C.S.S. *General Clinch*. Some of the South's most prominent naval officers including Commodore Josiah Tattnall and Lt. J.N. Maffitt were assigned to the waters defending the South Carolina and Georgia coasts.[67]

The Southerners added to their growing fleet when they isolated and captured the 450-ton steamer U.S.S. *Isaac Smith* with nine guns on the Stono River, disabling the ship through cannon fire. The Confederates repaired her and renamed her the C.S.S. *Stono*.[68]

In November 1861, Captain Duncan Ingraham was named commander of all Southern naval forces in Charleston. The Confederacy and South Carolina worked in concert to place ironclads in the defending squadron[69]. The result was the ironclad ram C.S.S. *Palmetto State*. A

---

64 *Confederate Veteran* Volume VI, 1996, "Unraveling the Mystery of the C.S.S. Hunley" by James L. McClinton, Ph.D Special note, the C.S.S. *Hunley* was built in Mobile, Alabama and shipped via rail to Charleston.
65 *Southern Fire, Exploits of the Confederate States Navy* by R. Thomas Campbell, Page 129
66 *History of the Confederate States Navy* page 657
67 Ibid page 664
68 Ibid, Page 670
69 Ibid, Page 37

second ironclad, the C.S.S. *Chicora* joined in August of 1862. In December of '62, another ironclad's keel, the C.S.S. *Charleston*, was laid. Nine months later, she would be commissioned.[70] A fourth ironclad was planned, "but the ship was not completed when Charleston was evacuated."[71]

With this combination of naval and land power, it seems easy to understand why all the serious federal efforts to take Charleston were essentially conducted by the Army forces operating on the islands surrounding the harbor. Though small engagements occurred, the federal Navy did not offer an opportunity to engage the coordinated Confederate defense within the harbor. Only events far larger in scope and very late in the war caused the eventual southern withdrawal from Charleston.

Arriving from Alabama, where he was in charge of naval affairs in that state, Commodore Duncan Nathaniel Ingraham, C.S.N., arrived in Charleston in early 1862. Ingraham was a seasoned sailor with almost fifty years of service. Ingraham's father, Nathaniel, had served with Captain John Paul Jones on the U.S.S. *Le Bon Homme Richard* in the famous battle with the H.M.S. *Serapis* in 1779.[72]

A native Charlestonian, at age ten, Midshipman Ingraham entered the United States Navy in 1812 and was almost assigned to the U.S.S. *Congress* off Brazil. Ingraham's assignments included duty aboard U.S.S. *Madison* on Lake Ontario, the brig *Boxer*, the sloop-of-war *Hornet*, the schooner *Revenge*, and the frigate *Macedonian*. He was present at the ceremony that transferred the state of Florida from Spain to the United States. During the Mexican War, Commander Ingraham commanded the U.S.S. *Somers* and participated in the blockade of Mexican ports.

In 1853, while in command of the sloop-of-war U.S.S. *St. Louis* in the Mediterranean Sea, Commander Ingraham, at the advice of the U.S. Consul to Smyrna, intervened on behalf of a U.S. citizen-to-be who was being held by the Austrians on their warship Hussar. When Ingraham had his ship cleared for action, the Austrians, though manning a much superior warship, decided to heed Ingraham's request, and the situation was diffused. Eventually, the citizen-to-be was released and returned to America. For this action, the U.S. Congress in 1854 awarded Ingraham

---

70 Ibid, Page 670
71 Ibid, Page 670
72 Ibid, Page 674

a Congressional Gold Medal.[73] In 1860, after a tour of duty within the Navy Department in Washington, D.C., he was given command of the flagship of the Mediterranean Fleet, the U.S.S. *Richmond*.[74]

Commander Ingraham resigned from the U.S. Navy in January 1861 and traveled to Montgomery, Alabama, where he served as a member of a board created by the Confederate Congress to study Confederate Naval issues. He was later appointed Commodore and sent to command the Confederate naval station and forces in Pensacola, Florida.[75]

To have a port which was safe from capture was only half the battle. For the port to be of real value to the South, it had to be available for maritime trade and commerce. Of course, blockade-running operations would be an option. But what if the port could be opened to regular commerce?

Lt. Bier of the C.S.S. *Chicora* indicates in a letter he wrote that French and English naval officers planted the idea of breaking the blockade in the mind of General Beauregard:

Beauregard told me that some time since the English and French commanders had told him that if he would send the vessels down and raise the blockade for twenty hours' they would sail out and proclaim the Blockade raised — that he had suggested it to Ingraham and that he was afraid that the motive power of the vessels was not great enough. How the Devil is he going to find that out unless he tries? I suppose he will wait until the Yankees have accumulated three or four of their heavy ironclads and then send us to certain destruction.[76]

In January 1863, General P.G.T. Beauregard and Flag Officer Duncan N. Ingraham, C.S.N. began developing a plan to exercise the power of the Confederate ironclad fleet then on station at Charleston. In a very interesting example of cooperation between the services, General Beauregard "suggested" that Flag Officer Ingraham use his two

---

73 Congressional Gold Medal Recipients, www.congressionalgoldmedal.com/DuncanNIngraham.htm
74 *History of the Confederate States Navy*, page 674
75 Ibid page 675
76 *Southern Fire, Exploits of the Confederate Navy,* page 103 If the foreign naval officers did plant the idea with General Beauregard, was it because they favored the South, or because they wanted to observe the sea worthiness of the Confederate vessels?

ironclads, the C.S.S. Palmetto State and the C.S.S. Chicora to venture out from Charleston harbor, taking advantage of the absence of any Federal ironclads, and attack the remaining blockaders with the intent of destroying them or driving them off so as to open the blockade.[77] If the blockade could be lifted, in the eyes of the international community, even for a day, it would take at least thirty days for the process to officially recognize the re-establishment of the blockade.

Lieutenant Commander John Rutledge commanded the C.S.S. *Palmetto State*, and Commander John R. Tucker commanded the C.S.S. *Chicora*. Both of these ships were built on the lines of the C.S.S. *Virginia* of Hampton Roads fame.[78] The *Palmetto State's* keel was laid in January 1862, and most of her construction occurred under the supervision of Ingraham, who had arrived to command the naval forces of Charleston that winter. She had four inches of iron plating. Her armament included an 80-pound rifled gun forward, a 60-pound rifled gun aft, and two 8-inch shell guns, one on each broadside.[79] An image of the *Palmetto State* depicts three gun ports on the broadside indicating the bow and aft guns could pivot to either port or starboard.[80] The C.S.S. *Chicora* was begun just months after the work started on her sister. The *Chicora* was to be 150 feet by 35 feet at the beam, with a 12-foot depth of hold. She had two inches of iron laid on top of 22 inches of oak and pine. Like her sister, she was given a ram on the bow. Her battery consisted of six guns, two 9-inch smooth-bores, and four rifled 32-pounders.[81]

On the evening of January 30th, 1863, (simultaneous to the seizure of the U.S.S. *Isaac P. Smith* in the Stono River) the Confederate flotilla under command of Commodore Ingraham, comprised of the ironclads *Palmetto State* and *Chicora* and three steam tenders, *General Cinch*, *Etowan*, and *Chesterfield*, left their moorings to launch a surprise attack against the Charleston blockaders. A little after 5 am on January 31st, the ironclads crossed the outer bar and silently approached their prey.

Commodore Ingraham was aboard the *Palmetto State* as she first sighted a Yankee vessel outlined dimly in the distance. The decision

---

77 P.G.T. Beauregard, *Napoleon in Gray*, page 173
78 *History of the Confederate States Navy*, page 672
79 Ibid page 670
80 See image in Confederate Ironclad Appendix, image taken from Naval Historical Center
81 Ibid page 670

was made to head straight for the ship and to ram her. The sun was not yet up as the *Palmetto State* poured on the steam achieving a speed of about 7 knots and headed directly towards the resting ship. The watch aboard the U.S.S. *Mercedita* was just able to get off a warning before the Confederate ram crashed into its target. Just before the ram hit, her forward gun port dropped, and her bow gun extended so as to fire directly into the target after the full impact of the collision had been felt. Thinking his ship was mortally wounded, the federal commander, Capt. Stellwagon struck his colors and sent his executive officer off in a dingy to the *Palmetto State* to confirm their surrender and request assistance to save the crew.[82] The ship did not sink, and was assisted by other federal ships in returning to the naval station at Port Royal, South Carolina.

The C.S.S. *Palmetto State* continued out to sea, following the C.S.S. *Chicora* on a search for more victims. The *Chicora* had engaged two Union vessels. The U.S.S. *Quaker City* was driven off fairly quickly, but a second vessel, the U.S.S. *Keystone State* stayed to fight it out. The *Chicora's* fire was effective. The port wheel on the Yankee vessel was damaged and could not turn. Fires broke out on both the bow and stern. This second Yankee ship lowered her flag in surrender, only to steam away. When three miles away from the Confederate ships, this "surrendered" ship fired a gun at the Confederate, raised her flag, and proceeded to Port Royal.

Meanwhile, the C.S.S. *Chicora* engaged six more blockaders at long range before turning to follow the *Palmetto State* back into Charleston.

As a result of the action, General Beauregard claimed the blockade lifted and took the British, French and Spanish consuls out on an inspection tour of more than five miles from the harbor entrance to prove the success of the attack.[83] Beauregard and Ingraham issued a joint proclamation:

Headquarters Naval and Land Forces
    Charleston, January 31, 1863
At about the hour of 5 o'clock this morning the Confederate States naval forces on this station attacked the United States blockading fleet off the harbor of this city of Charleston and sunk, dispersed, or drove

---

82 Ibid page 676
83 *PGT Beauregard, Napoleon in Gray*, page 174 & *Southern Fire, Exploits of the Confederate Navy*, page 112

off and out of sight for the time the entire hostile fleet. Therefore we, the undersigned commanding respectively the naval and land forces in this quarter, do hereby formally declare the blockade raised by a superior force of the Confederate States from and after this 31st day of January, 1863.

P.G.T. Beauregard, General, Commanding
D. N. / Ingraham, Commanding
Naval Forces, South Carolina[84]

Unfortunately, the Europeans did not follow up on their promise. On two separate inspections of the sea beyond Charleston harbor, the three consuls, on the evening of January 31st, agreed that the blockade had been lifted. However, the declarations of the consuls were less than specific, and the North contradicted the claims made by General Beauregard. Like many a land battle, the naval engagement off Charleston on 31 January 1863 was a decided tactical victory for the South. Alas, the strategic gains, both in terms of lifting the blockade and of creating a foreign perception of the military prowess of the Confederacy, were not to be.

A second Confederate port worth studying is Mobile, Alabama. Mobile was important for two reasons; first, Mobile was second only to Wilmington as a port for the blockade-runners,[85] and second, Mobile acted as the launching point for naval raids on the Mississippi River and at Ft. Pickens and Pensacola, Florida.[86]

Mobile Bay, from a geographical standpoint, is much different from Charleston. Charleston is a relatively small harbor making her numerous land batteries interlocking and effective. Mobile has a narrow entrance of approximately three miles, guarded by two principal islands, but once past those, the bay widens to 15 miles. Inside the harbor, concentrated land defense is not available. Land batteries at the choke point were effective but limited. One other geographical aspect of Mobile Harbor assisted in its defense; the Alabama River served as a link to Selma, "… home of one of the largest naval stations in the Confederacy."[87] The C.S.S. *Tennessee* was built at Selma and arrived to

---

84   *Southern Fire, Exploits of the Confederate Navy*, page 112
85   *The Civil War, A Narrative Red River to Appomattox*, Page 491.
86   *The History of the Confederate States Navy*, Chapter XVIII, Pages 537, 539
87   *The History of the Confederate States Navy*, Page 550

defend the Bay in February 1864. Two other keels had been laid but were unfinished at the time of the battle.[88]

The Confederates worked to take every advantage of the sole geographical aspect in their favor, the narrow single deep-water entrance to the bay. Utilizing existing reef, the Confederates implanted piles whose tips sat just beneath the water at low tide. These piles ran to southeastward from Ft. Gaines. Extending to the eastward from this line of piles were 180 torpedoes deployed in three lines, narrowing the entrance from three miles to several hundred yards under the guns of Ft. Morgan.[89]

Fort Morgan and its exterior batteries equaled 69 guns. Three miles across the main channel on Dauphin Island was Ft. Gaines with 27 guns. A third defensive work, Ft. Powell, on Tower Island sitting astride a shallow backdoor entrance to the Bay, had six guns.[90]

The land defenses were significantly weaker than those of Charleston, and so were the Confederate naval forces available to defend Mobile. The C.S.S. *Tennessee* arrived only days before Farragut's Union fleet would conduct its first attack in January 1864. The *Tennessee* was supported by the C.S.S. *Morgan*, (six guns) C.S.S. *Gaines* (six guns), and the C.S.S. *Selma* (four guns). A second ironclad, the C.S.S. *Baltic*[91] had been assigned to protect Mobile, but because of its poor condition, was dismantled before the battle on August 5th, 1864.

According to Scharf, the federal campaign to seize Mobile began on February 23, 1864. Admiral Farragut sent in his mortar boats and shallow draft ships to attack Ft. Powell. Three days of bombardment resulted in not a single wounded Confederate. The presence of the *Tennessee* eliminated any possibility of Farragut acting without ironclads.

From this point, a race ensued. The Confederates at Selma worked to get more ships completed and sent down the river to Mobile. Admiral Farragut called on the Secretary of the Navy to send him ironclads. When four ironclads (U.S.S. *Tecumseh*, U.S.S. *Manhattan*, U.S.S. *Win-

---

88 Ibid
89 *The Civil War, A Narrative Red River to Appomattox,* Page 496
90 *History of the Confederate States Navy,* Page 553
91 *History of the Confederate States Navy,* Page 550 The C.S.S. *Baltic* was stationed at Mobile according to Scharf, but somehow it was not present for the battle, and Scharf states that there were no records or reports to indicate where it went. According to the Department of Navy, Naval Historical Center website, the *Baltic* was decommissioned in 1863, and stripped of its armor.

nebago, U.S.S. *Chickasaw*) arrived, they added their 12 heavy guns to the 145 guns there with the 14 wooden warships already on station.

On August 2nd, Farragut began the operation by landing 2,000 Federal troops on the western end of Dauphin Island.[92] These troops would move on the rear of Ft. Gaines. Farragut's naval attack plan was simple. The attack would be made in two columns, one ironclads and one wooden. The attack would be towards the Ft. Morgan side of the channel, with the ironclads on the starboard (right) side to accept the fire from Morgan. On the evening before the attack, Farragut sent "grapplers" to attempt to disarm the 180 Confederate torpedoes.[93]

Admiral Buchanan arrayed his flotilla in a line of four just behind the last line of torpedoes with their bows facing east so that each could engage the oncoming federals with a broadside. The *Tennessee* was closest to the open channel so that it could engage and ram the lead ironclad Tecumseh if it made it past the fort's guns.

The federal attack seems to have commenced sometime before 7 a.m., and by 7:15, Farragut's fleet and Ft. Morgan were heavily engaged. Each Federal ship firing broadsides into the fort as they made their way through the gauntlet towards the inner harbor. As the two lines worked their way past the fort and towards the torpedoes and Confederate ships, Buchanan held his fire in the *Tennessee*, ordering his officers not to fire until the ironclads were in physical contact. The *Tennessee* was lying just west of the buoy that marked the eastern end of the torpedo line. The commander of *Tecumseh*, ignoring orders to remain east of the buoy, headed directly for the *Tennessee* and ran smack dab into a torpedo. The explosion was muffled, but the damage fatal, "… a column of water like a fountain springing from the sea shot up beside the Federal monitor; her stern went into the air so that her revolving screw could be plainly seen. …"[94]

Meanwhile, the *Selma*, *Gaines*, and *Morgan* were giving the Yankee wooden ships all they could handle. And, the U.S.S. *Brooklyn*, the lead ship in the federal wooden column, slowed to a stop because of sightings of torpedoes. Seeing the confusion caused when his lead ship stopped in the middle of the entrance leaving the following ships to be ravaged by Morgan's guns, Admiral Farragut directed his flagship,

---

92 *The Civil War, A Narrative – Red River to Appomattox*, Page 497
93 *The Civil War, A Narrative – Red River to Appomattox*, Page 500
94 *The History of the Confederate States Navy*, Page 561

the U.S.S. *Hartford* moved to the front of the line and continued the advance, successfully navigating through the torpedoes and into the harbor.[95] The U.S.S. *Oneida* was severely damaged while passing Ft. Morgan and had to be towed by the U.S.S. *Galena*. But Ft. Morgan could not, by itself, stop the Federal fleet.

Admiral Farragut's courageous decision to drive straight through the minefield, clearing the way for his ships, and removing them from the destructive fire of Fort Morgan was the turning point in the battle.

By 8:20, the battle had moved to within the harbor. The *Tennessee's* escorts went directly for the U.S.S. *Hartford* and raked her, giving their best account of the battle at this moment. The *Tennessee* then attempted to ram the *Hartford*, but the *Hartford* used her speed to easily dodge the attempt and move further into the Bay. Admiral Buchanan then focused on the remainder of the wooden fleet as the Union ships attempted to follow their flagship.

Now, the mere mass of the federal fleet could overwhelm the Confederate ships. *Scharf's History*, quoting Commodore Foxhall A. Parker, U.S.N., explains in his footnotes that the entire federal fleet threw 14,246 pounds of metal in one fleet broadside, compared to about 900 pounds for the Confederate squadron.[96]

The U.S.S. *Hartford* leading struck more than one torpedo, and the primers were heard to click, but they failed to explode. And it is important to note here that the Union's wooden vessels were actually leashed together, by twos. This eliminated their inner broadsides, and made them somewhat more difficult to maneuver. But when running the guns of Fort Morgan, the starboard ship absorbed most of the damage.

The *Brooklyn's* guns hit the C.S.S. *Gaines* at the waterline. She retired to shore, where she was abandoned and lit afire by her crew. The *Richmond*, *Hartford*, and *Metacomet* turned on the C.S.S. *Selma* and C.S.S. *Morgan*. The *Morgan* withdrew under the guns of Ft. Morgan; later she would withdraw to Mobile and the Dog River. The C.S.S. *Selma* was run-down by the *Metacomet* and, after suffering heavy fire and casualties, surrendered.[97]

After engaging most of the Federal fleet with at least one broad-

---

95 *Confederate Admiral, The life and Wars of Franklin Buchanan*, page 212
96 *The History of the Confederate States Navy*, Page 559
97 *The Civil War, A Narrative   Red River to Appomattox* Page 502

side each, Admiral Buchanan turned back into the Bay to seek out the *Hartford*. Buchanan attempted to ram the *Hartford* again, but lack of speed and agility prevented any success. The *Tennessee* then turned on the three surviving Federal monitors exchanging broadsides with each before returning to the vicinity of Ft. Morgan. Like another Confederate ironclad, the C.S.S. *Arkansas* on the Mississippi River, the *Tennessee* was fighting even an entire federal fleet.

At this point, the battle was still in doubt. Ft. Morgan was still very much able to defend itself. Ft. Gaines had not been engaged at all. Buchanan would not wait to see what Farragut would do. He moved directly toward the *Hartford* in the midst of the thirteen union vessels, including the three remaining ironclads. The next round of the engagement commenced about 9:20 am. The U.S.S. *Monongahela* and *Lackawanna* both rammed the *Tennessee* with little effect as she made her dash towards Farragut's flagship. Finally, the *Tennessee* crashed into the bow of the *Hartford*.[98] The heaviest guns of the Union fleet now had only one target. First, the *Tennessee* lost her smokestack, reducing her ability to make any speed. The battle raged on, but eventually, the Yankee ships found the exposed rudder chain that ran above the stern deck of the *Tennessee*. With her rudder out of action, she was without ability to maneuver. Still, she continued to fight; her one advantage being there was enemy in every direction and no friendly ships to strike accidentally. But then the Union bolts began to hit and jam the gun ports, thus reducing the *Tennessee's* battery each time they were successful. After the *Tennessee* lost the ability to answer her attackers with even one gun, she surrendered at ten o'clock.

In three hours of battle, the Confederacy lost 12 men killed, 20 wounded, and 243 captured. The *Tennessee* and *Selma* were captured, the *Gaines* burnt. The Federals lost 172 killed and 170 wounded. The *Tecumseh* was sunk, and most of the wooden fleet sustained significant damage. Ft. Morgan had fired some 500 shot and shell into the wooden fleet as it passed.

The Confederates abandoned Fort Powell, which guarded the backdoor to the Bay, the afternoon of the battle. Fort Gaines also surrendered the same day. Fort Morgan held out for two weeks under the Federal bombardment. On August 22, more than 3,000 shells were fired into the fort by the Union fleet. The following day, 546 Confederates

---

98 Ibid Page 505

surrendered. The battle for the entrance of Mobile Bay was over.

The battle for Mobile demonstrates how much it took to overcome the Southern defense. In the case of Mobile, the Confederacy failed to complete and commission the C.S.S. *Nashville*. This was a double side-wheeler ironclad that had been constructed in Montgomery and moved to Mobile for fitting out. However, it was not completed, and this vital weapon was not ready to help in the defense of Mobile.[99] Imagine how much more difficult it would have been for Farragut if there had been two ironclads waiting for his line as it approached Ft. Morgan.

Charleston and Mobile were selected as ports to demonstrate the use of technology, the integration of land and naval defenses, and the importance of natural geography in defending a port. Of course, Savannah and Galveston, and the other ports of the Confederacy were important to the Cause. A study of these ports and their defenses during the war would be found to be as interesting as the two chosen here to illustrate the South's efforts in defending their ports to sustain their lifeline.

The rivers of the Confederacy are well known to students of the War. The rivers proved to have at least two purposes: one as highway and another as an obstacle to be used in the defensive, or crossed when conducting offensive and defensive operations. For this work, I have decided to consider two campaigns because of their overall impact on the war: the Battle for New Orleans and the fall of Forts Henry and Donelson. The latter campaign is important because of the lack of Confederate naval ability to respond to the naval threats and huge strategic gains, which greatly benefited the Union Army, though the instrument for the success was the Union Navy. But let's consider New Orleans first.

"The most important event of the War of Rebellion, with the exception of the fall of Richmond, was the capture of New Orleans and the forts Jackson and St. Phillip ..." proclaimed Admiral David Porter.[100] Service and personal pride aside, Admiral Porter may not be too far from the truth. President Davis wrote, "New Orleans was the most im-

---

99 Department of the Navy, Naval History Center Web site
100 "Our cake is dough" *Battles and Leaders of the Civil War*, Page 121, by Admiral Porter

portant port in the Confederacy, being the natural outlet of the Mississippi Valley, as well as to ports of Europe as to those Central and South America."[101] As the largest city in the Confederacy, with the inherent financial and manufacturing assets, and as a hub for the international cotton trade sitting astride the central artery of transportation within the Confederacy, New Orleans was undoubtedly of strategic importance to the Southern Cause.

So what actions were taken from early 1861 to the spring of 1862 to protect this prize? In May 1861, the Confederate Congress passed an act which authorized "privateers" to attack U.S. shipping, and the privateers would be paid 20 percent of the value of any shipping they destroyed. As a result, a private investor and long-time labor organizer in New Orleans built the first ironclad, the C.S.S. *Manassas*. Scharf's work indicates the *Manassas* engaged the federal ships blockading the Mississippi in October 1861 and successfully drove the Yankee ships off, temporarily opening the blockade.[102] The C.S.S. *Virginia* was launched on February 24th, 1862, full four months later.[103]

The ram C.S.S. *Manassas* was constructed from the Enoch Train built in Boston in 1855 and is unique to the ironclads of the war. First, a real effort was made to keep it a low-profile ship, presenting a very small target to opponents. Secondly, its armor silhouette featured curves instead of flat sides and hard angles. These soft angles were designed to help deflect cannon shot. In addition, the smokestacks could be lowered so as to reduce their vulnerability in battle.[104]

The ship's sole cannon was in the bow and was revealed when its protective hatch was raised. The only entrance into the ship was through a trap door. And, the designer had included a system based on steam and boiling water to repel borders. Piping inside the ship ran from the steam boilers to small ports along outer walls of the ship. Should there be an attempt to board, steam and boiling water could be showered outside the ship through the ports.[105]

The Confederate Congress appropriated $800,000 dollars in July 1861 to be used to help purchase naval craft necessary for the defense

---

101 *The Rise and Fall of the Confederacy*, Page 177
102 *History of the Confederate States Navy*, Page 265
103 *Duel of the Ironclads*, page 29
104 *History of the Confederate States Navy*, Page 264
105 *History of the Confederate States Navy*, Page 264

of New Orleans.[106] In Richmond, the Secretary of the Navy, Stephen Mallory, worried about possible Yankee advances from both the north and south on New Orleans.

Two ironclads, much larger than the *Manassas*, the *Louisiana* and *Mississippi* began construction in October, 1861.[107] In addition, 26 fire-boats were prepared.[108] These boats were to be lit afire and set adrift, sent against a Yankee fleet coming from the south, down-stream of New Orleans. This tactic would help break up formations, provide illumination at night, and give Federal commanders another set of problems to deal with.

"The Ordnance Bureau at Richmond sent to New Orleans from May 1861 to May 1862, 220 heavy guns."[109] The land component of the naval defense to the south of New Orleans was based on two forts, Fort Jackson (69 guns) and Fort St. Phillip (45 guns), located "approximately 70 miles below New Orleans"[110] near the mouth of the Mississippi. General Beauregard suggested that a boom be constructed to slow the federal fleet.[111] The boom was constructed "of eight half-sunken hulks, long rafts, and chains" and "… stretched across the river …" to block passage.[112]

Commodore Hollins, in command of Confederate Naval Forces in New Orleans, had by February 1st, 1862 the General Polk, Ivy, Livingston, and McRae (seven guns), were supporting the *Manassas*. Work continued on two floating batteries, *Memphis* (18 guns) and *New Orleans* (20 guns), and *Maurepas* (six guns) and *Pontchartrain* (six guns) and the *Pickens* and *Morgan*, both three guns each. The *Carondelet* was completed March 16th, 1862. The *Bienville* was joined on April 5th.[113]

Much hope was placed on the completion of the C.S.S. *Mississippi*. This ship was designed to be the most powerful naval weapon on either side. It was planned to be over 4,000 tons. It was 270 feet long and 58 feet wide and was intended to have three engines, move at a speed of

---

106 Ibid Page 266
107 Ibid Page 265
108 Ibid Page 265
109 Ibid page 49
110 Pathways of the Civil War Web site
111
112 *The Civil War, A Pictorial Profile* Page 86-87 The number of sunken hulks was provided in "Our cake is all dough," by Admiral Porter
113 *History of the Confederate States Navy* Page 266

14 knots, and it would carry 20 guns.[114] The mission of the *Mississippi* was to clear all enemy ships from the Mississippi River and then put into the Gulf of Mexico to lift the blockade.[115] Admiral Porter wrote of the *Mississippi*, "… the most splendid specimen of a floating battery the world has ever seen (a sea-going affair) had she been finished and succeeded in getting to the sea, the whole American navy would have been destroyed."[116]

The problem for the *Mississippi* was that there was one mill in the entire Confederacy capable of casting the 50-foot-long central drive shaft, the Tredegar Iron Works in Richmond. Delivery would take weeks.[117] She wouldn't be ready.

The C.S.S. *Louisiana* was further along. She had been launched, though her engines were not working. Work had been delayed on this ship, in part due to a three-week strike by laborers who would not accept Confederate bonds as pay! She mounted 16 guns.[118] The *Carondelet* was completed March 16th, 1862. The *Bienville* joined on April 5th.[119]

The Confederate fleet was joined by two ships from the Louisiana State Navy, the *Governor Moore* mounting two 32 pounders, and the *General Quitman* and six armed, small towboats under the command of Captain Stephenson. Seven additional unarmed steamers were cooperating with the Confederate fleet.[120] The *Louisiana* was towed downstream and anchored just west of Fort St. Phillip, where it could be used as a floating battery.[121]

The first phase of the Union attack against the forts began with a bombardment by Porter's Mortar boats on April 18th. The boats lay around a curve in the river and were camouflaged next to the bank. Over five days, the Federals poured 16,800 13-inch shells into the forts but with little outward result.[122] Meanwhile, the forces of nature, in the form of unusually high floods, created large gaps in the boom the

---

114 *The Civil War, A Narrative - Ft. Sumter to Perryville* Page 362
115 Ibid
116 *History of the Confederate States Navy,* Page 267
117 Ibid
118 Ibid Page 363
119 *History of the Confederate States Navy,* Page 266
120 *History of the Confederate States Navy,* Page 279
121 *The Civil War, A Narrative - Ft. Sumter to Perryville,* Page 364
122 *The Civil War, A Pictorial Profile,* Page 87

Confederates had spent 100,000 dollars to build. Efforts were made to repair the obstacle but were less than complete when Admiral Farragut sent Captain Bell, with two steamers forward to find a way through on the 20th.[123] With the support of Porter's Mortar boats, to suppress the Confederate gunners in Ft. Jackson who had spotted the Union ships and were attempting to drive them off, Captain Bell was able to remain at the boom and cut enough of the chain loose to open a passage on the left bank.[124] On the 22nd, Porter reported to Farragut that the forts had been significantly hurt by five days of bombardment.

Farragut then determined on a tactic he would use repeatedly during the war. Instead of fighting the battle at the enemy's strongest point, the forts, the Admiral determined to make a run past the forts and sail up the Mississippi to the real objective, New Orleans. His initial plan was to go on the morning of the 23rd, but the weather prevented any attempt.[125] The effort would be made on the 24th. At 2 a.m. on the morning of April 24th, the Federal's line of 17 ships (mounting 126 guns)[126] began to move forward for a run past the forts and the water batteries. The Mortar boats would focus their fire on Fort St. Philip.

Admiral Farragut organized his ships into three divisions. His ship, the *Hartford*, was in the lead of the second division. At 3:40 a.m., Confederates spotted the lead ship of the first division as it breached the boom. The Yankee ships were channeled into a tight space, a perfect target for the guns of both Jackson and Philip, and yet not a shot was fired until after the eight ships of the first division were through. But as the *Hartford* entered the gap, the one hundred guns of the two forts opened, and the fire rafts began to descend. Farragut's ship ran aground, pinned by a fire raft that threatened to consume her.[127] For a time, the crew fought to sink the fire raft so that the fires on board could be contained.

Meanwhile upstream, the Federals' first division moved past the blaze of the land-based cannon and onto the Confederate vessels wait-

---

123 "Our cake is dough," Page131, by Admiral Porter, *Battles and Leaders of the Civil War*
124 "Our cake is dough" page 132, by Admiral Porter, *Battles and Leaders of the Civil War*
125 *The Civil War, A Narrative – Ft. Sumter to Perryville*, Page 365
126 "Our cake is dough" page 129, by Admiral Porter, *Battles and Leaders of the Civil War*
127 *The Civil War, A Narrative – Ft. Sumter to Perryville*, Page 367

ing for them. The *Louisiana* could bring only six guns to bear as she was anchored close to shore. The *McRae* was literally blown to pieces by the converging fire of several Federal ships, but somehow remained afloat. The *Manassas*, under the command of Lt. Warely, charged forward firing her bow gun as she rammed the *Brooklyn*.[128] She backed off from her first target and moved downstream, looking for another when she was bombarded by the guns of both forts that mistook her for a Yankee ship. Apparently, the damage by the forts' guns was significant, as she turned about, to head upstream. She ran into four Federal ships that emptied their broadsides at the *Manassas*. Smoking heavily and damaged, she then turned to avoid a collision with a fifth Yankee ship, the U.S.S. *Mississippi*[129], running aground close to the shore. The crew abandoned her as she sat a motionless target for Federal ships in her vicinity.

The C.S.S. *Governor Moore*, with only two guns, was moving down-stream near the east bank[130] towards the oncoming Federal fleet. In the distance, the 1,300-ton U.S.S. *Varuna*, with ten guns, and the fastest ship in Farragut's fleet, was spotted. Captain Kennon of the *Moore* turned her toward midstream to intercept the *Varuna* from the flank. Approaching in the darkness, when the *Moore* opened with her bow gun, the Federal ship was caught totally unawares. Unfortunately, the shot flew high completely missing the target. The *Varuna's* reply swept the *Moore's* deck, killing and maiming many Confederate sailors. However, the *Moore* came on, firing her one bow gun as she charged. As the *Moore* closed, she lost the ability to fire over her deck to hit the *Varuna*, so the captain ordered the gun depressed so that it would fire down through the *Moore's* deck! The second shot fired in this fashion hit the *Varuna's* pivot gun, causing an explosion and killing many of the gun's crew. The third shot came just as the *Moore* rammed her target amidships.

The *Varuna* replied with a broadside as the *Moore* backed away. But the *Moore* came on again, ramming a second time with her bow gun still firing down through a hole she had blown through her deck. The *Varuna* was mortally crippled. She broke off the fight and made for the shore but was struck by another Confederate gunboat, the *Stonewall*

---

128 *History of the Confederate States Navy*, Page 295
129 *History of the Confederate States Navy*, Page 295
130 *History of the Confederate States Navy*, Page 286

Jackson[131] before she reached it. The U.S.S. *Varuna* sank fast.[132] The *Moore* sailed on looking for another fight, but when she ran up against five Federal warships, their broadsides completely destroyed her. 74 of the C.S.S. *Moore's* crew of 93 were killed or wounded. The battle was over by the time the sun rose at 5 a.m.

The Southern New Orleans squadron was destroyed. The bulk of Farragut's three divisions moved upstream out of the range of the forts. The C.S.S. *Louisiana* fired on the entire Federal fleet as they passed individually; but unable to move, Admiral Farragut treated her more like a fort than a dangerous ironclad and simply bypassed her.

When word reached New Orleans of the action down-river and the approach to the city by the Yankee ships, the people within the city boiled in anger, wanting somehow to continue the resistance. Products in warehouses and along the docks were burned by mobs to prevent them from falling into the hands of the Yankees. And when Confederate authorities were unable to tow the uncompleted C.S.S. *Mississippi* upstream, and were forced to set her afire and adrift, the people along the wharves protested, shouting treason and betrayal.[133]

Downstream, Southern loyalties were not quite as fervent. Despite a lack of pressure by the Union naval components left in their vicinity, the men within both forts, some of Northern birthright, others of foreign origin, mutinied. The guns were spiked, and the men forced their officers to ask for surrender terms. Captain Mitchell of the *Louisiana*, seeing the forts surrender and without any means of escape, decided to blow up his ship. While the terms of the forts surrender were being discussed aboard a Union vessel, the C.S.S. *Louisiana* was destroyed.

One account, provided in Scharf's work on page 539, seems to indicate that the engines for the C.S.S. *Louisiana* were placed in working condition just prior to her destruction. On the morning of the 28th, "Chief Engineer Youngblood stepped up and reported that the auxiliary propeller engines were ready and the whole machinery in running order. Lieut. Wilkinson, who had already received orders to destroy the ship asked Mitchell, "What shall I do?" And the commodore, after some hesitation, replied, "Go on with the work."

---

131 *History of the Confederate States Navy*, Page 286
132 *The Civil War, A Narrative – Fort Sumter to Perryville* Page 368, the general description of *Moore – Varuna* fight was taken primarily from this source. *History of the Confederate States Navy*, Page 286.
133 *The Civil War, A Narrative – Fort Sumter to Perryville*, Page 369

If the *Louisiana* were operational, the decision by Commodore Mitchell seems suspect. This may be one of those questions which can never be adequately answered: Could the *Louisiana* have been taken to Mobile under her own power?

Mr. Scharf is very critical of Secretary Mallory and the Confederate high command for the loss of New Orleans. He attacks the Secretary for misunderstanding the real threat to New Orleans would come from the south. He believes the Secretary overrated the defensive strength of the forts and diverted resources from the Southern defenses. He also states, "The divided command at New Orleans, by which the army and navy were responsible to no common authority, contributed to a want of concert which hindered and embarrassed the fighting capacity of both arms when the hour came needed all the efforts of each."[134]

President Davis explains that the fear of a northern assault on New Orleans was primarily based on the Federal success at Fort Henry and secondarily at Fort Donelson.[135] It appears the Administration was focused on those Yankee forces that had demonstrated their effectiveness, rather than speculating on the actions of an untried force. Davis goes on to point out that a sand bar at the entrance of the Mississippi was expected to cause the Yankees to have to reconfigure or leave behind their most powerful warships.

Clearly, all accounts indicate that the defense was uncoordinated. Few of the 26 fire ships that had been prepared were used. A good portion of the Yankee fleet passed the forts before the Confederates fired their first shots. And lastly, the obstacle intended to block or delay the attacking ships was ineffective for the most part. This left the two forts supported by an odd collection of vessels to defend the most important port in the South.

The Henry – Donelson Campaign came to a conclusion months before the fall of New Orleans in February 1862. No Confederate naval forces were present in this campaign, and that is the point of mentioning this campaign in this work. The Federals demonstrated in this campaign the great potential of cooperating land and naval forces. Fort Henry on the Tennessee River fell to the Union fleet with little real assistance to Grant's land forces.[136] Once Henry fell, Grant turned on Fort

---

134 *History of the Confederate States Navy*, Page 301
135 *The Rise and Fall of the Confederacy*, Page 178
136 *The West Point Atlas of the Civil War*, Map 26

Donelson on the Cumberland River. And as MG Lew Wallace, U.S.V. wrote, "… its navigability for large steamers, its offer of a highway to the rear of the Confederate hosts in Kentucky and the State of Tennessee…"[137] made the Cumberland River key terrain[138] in the center of the western theatre.

For General Albert Sidney Johnson, leading a Confederate Army in central Kentucky, word of Ft. Henry's surrender was the harbinger of disaster in Tennessee, and is a classic example of how "maneuver" on the strategic level can gain more in terms of land and advantage than "mass" and the associated casualties connected to desperate fighting. Johnson recognized immediately that if Fort Donelson were to fall, the Federal fleet would be days from Nashville, his main supply depot and main line of retreat for his forces in Kentucky. The front line of the Confederate western Army, which Johnson had maintained through the winter of 1861-62, collapsed because of the anticipated victory at Donelson and the ability of the Union Navy to move on Nashville. The Confederate line was thus displaced from central Kentucky to Nashville, and then below to Murfreesboro.[139]

I include this action in an overview of the Confederate States Navy because it is an excellent example of the great need for a Southern river defense force and the impact of the Union Navy operating in a vacuum. The Confederacy worked very hard in its ports, on the rivers, and in Europe to buy, build or capture a navy. As we have seen, they made tremendous efforts and had some real successes. But both New Orleans and Nashville fell because the Southern nation could not match the North in production of naval forces. Had either the C.S.S. *Louisiana* or *Mississippi* been fully operational at the time of Farragut's assault on New Orleans, it is conceivable they could have successfully defended New Orleans in April of 1862. And had the South been able to defend New Orleans and keep it open to trade, Admiral Porter felt the South could win the war.[140]

Where the South was working on building a naval defense force for

---

137 "It was not possible for brave men to endure more," Page 61, by General Lew Wallace *Battles and Leaders of the Civil War*
138 A reminder, the military definition of the term "key terrain" is that it is of central military importance to either belligerent.
139 *The Civil War, A Narrative – Ft. Sumter to Perryville*, Page 193.
140 "Our cake is dough" *Battles and Leaders of the Civil War*, Page 121, by Admiral Porter

New Orleans, it is not so for a river defense force in Tennessee. General Grant's great military talent here was seeing what was possible with a relatively small land force complimented by a naval force the Confederacy could not counter.

Another great disappointment with respect to the Confederate Navy was what I call the "strongest Southern squadron never to fight." By 1864, the Confederacy had a squadron of four ironclads on the James River defending Richmond. These were strong ships with armor and a compliment of good guns. However, because the James River had been so effectively blocked with obstacles by the Confederates, and because of the prudence of local Union naval commanders, there was little opportunity for these ships to be employed. The squadron had to be destroyed by the Confederates when Lee's Army of Northern Virginia was forced to abandon Richmond.

Could one or more of these ships been dismantled and shipped, in part or in whole, to some point of greater need or use, say Mobile or Wilmington? Could the South have conducted such an operation, in a timely manner, so as to possibly alter the outcome of the war is a point worthy of discussion. However, one very important point is revealed when you consider a key strategic problem for the South's Navy Department, and that is their reliance on "point defense."

Had the Confederate States been able to mass several of their more powerful ironclads, like the C.S.S. *Virginia* and the C.S.S. *Arkansas*, (whose combat effectiveness as individual ships, was proven against powerful Union fleets), and then employed them in a fight against Farragut's or Porter's ships, there is real reason to believe that their combined strengths would have been too much for the Union fleets. However, the Union Naval Commanders did not test either the James River Squadron of four ironclads, or the Charleston defenses where three ironclads operated together, in concert with extensive land defenses and complimented by the "Davids" and torpedoes.

The South, during the war, used the railroad sometimes very effectively to mass or shift troops. At First Manassas, Shiloh, and Chickamauga the Confederate high command demonstrated they could move forces to change the tactical balance in a theatre. With the exception of moving "Davids" from Mobile to Charleston via rail, the Confederacy was unable to move major naval assets from one theatre to another. Each port or point of naval significance was greatly reliant on itself for its own defense. And without the ability to move around manufacturing assets, the Southern naval forces were left to their ability to cooperate with any Southern land forces in the area and their own ingenuity. Each domino stood alone, and with few exceptions, was eventually overwhelmed once the North could mass its resources on a target.

Appendix 1
Important Confederate Naval Events, Actions and Engagements 1861 – 1865 Time Line

Date	Location	Confederate Forces	Union Forces	Remarks
1861				
8 Jan.	Charleston, South Carolina	Members of THE CITADEL Corps of Cadets	*U.S.S. Star of the West*	Lincoln attempts to reinforce Fort Sumter, first shots of the war are fired to prevent Northern aggressive act. Ft. Sumter is not attacked until April 12th, surrendering that day.
12 Jan.	Pensacola, Florida	Alabama and Florida Troops	Federal soldiers	Confederates seize Pensacola Naval Yard but Yankees retain control of Fort Pickens at the mouth of the harbor.
21 Feb.	Montgomery Alabama			Confederate Congress passes Act which formally creates Confederate States Navy
16 Mar.	Montgomery Alabama			Confederate Congress passes Act which formally creates Confederate States Marine Corps
13 Apr.	Washington, D.C.			President Lincoln declares the intention to establish a blockade of southern ports.
20 Apr.	Norfolk, Virginia	Land Forces	Land and naval forces	Confederates seize Norfolk and Gosport Naval Yard. The partially destroyed hull of the *U.S.S. Merrimac* is recovered, and later transformed into the *C.S.S. Virginia*.

Mark K. Vogl

18 May	Charleston, South Carolina	*Savannah*	Brig Joseph	The *Savannah* was the first ship to receive a Letter of Marque authorizing her to act as a privateer on behalf of the Confederate government. Her first prize is the *Joseph*.
3 Jun.	Atlantic	Raphael Semmes commanding first commercial raider *C.S.S. Sumter*	Yankee commercial ship *Golden Rocket*	After the crew is removed, the *Golden Rocket* is destroyed.
27-18 Aug.	Forts Hatteras and Clark, North Carolina	Flag Officer Samuel Barron, C.S.N. commanding Ft. Hatteras had 25 guns. 7th NC Vols. *C.S.S. Winslow, Forrest and Curlew*	General Butler commanding task force of seven Federal ships and ground troops. Naval units commanded by Commodore Stringham; *U.S.S. Minnesota, Wabash, Monticello, Pawnee, Harriet Lane, Peabody,* and *Adelaide*	Yankees conduct amphibious landing and capture both forts. Control of coastal North Carolina could threaten rail lines from the South into Richmond

12 Oct.	Head of the Passes, Mississippi River, Louisiana	Captain Hollins commanding C.S.S. *Manassas, McRae, Ivy, Calhoun, Tuscarora*, total of 9 guns.	*U.S.S. Richmond* 22 guns and *Preble* 10 guns, *Vincennes* 20 guns, *and Water Witch* 4 guns	**First engagement** where a **Confederate Ironclad** is employed. Confederates drive off Federal blockaders out of the mouth of the Mississippi.
7 Nov.	Port Royal, South Carolina	Commodore Tattnall commanding C.S.S. *Savannah*, and *Resolute*	Admiral Farragut, Commander Porter commanding *U.S.S. Pensacola, Mississippi*, total of 17 warships, plus mortar boats.	Yankees seize Port Royal as a base of operations for blockading ports in Florida, Georgia and South Carolina.
8 Nov.	At sea off Havana, Cuba	Trent "a British mail steamer" carrying a Confederate diplomatic delegation, Commissioners Mason and Slidell	*U.S.S. San Jacinto* after being advised by the U.S. Consul, lays in wait and fires on the Trent. Under protest, the Mason and Slidell party is removed.	"The Trent Affair" as it became known almost brought England into the war as a Southern ally. Britain deployed 8,000 soldiers to Canada. The Yankees eventually released the Commissioners and their party. But this would not be the only infraction of international law by the U.S. Navy during the war.

1862				
6-7 Feb.	Roanoke Island, North Carolina	Gen. H.A. Wise commanding Forts Huger, Blanchard, Bartow, and Forrest. 45 guns, 1,024 troops, Commodore Lynch commanding C.S.S. *Seabird, Curlew, Ellis, Appomattox, Beaufort, Raleigh, Fanny*	Gen. Burnside commanding 17,000 troops, Admiral Goldsborough commanding 17 warships with 48 guns.	At first, for a day, the Confederates repelled the Yankee attempt to land troops on Roanoke but the Union ships re-arranged their alignment so as to mask some of the Rebel guns on the island. The Yankees landed in force capturing the northern most works first, then working their way down the island. Meanwhile the weak Confederate fleet was engaged and completely destroyed
8 Mar.	Hampton Roads, Virginia	Captain Buchanan commanding the *C.S.S. Virginia, Beaufort, Raleigh, Patrick Henry, Jamestown, Teasar,* and *W.A. Webb,* totaling 27 guns.	*U.S.S. Cumberland, Congress,* and *Minnesota* totaling more than 100 guns.	In front of foreign naval ships of war, the *C.S.S. Virginia* destroyed two of the Yankees most powerful warships without suffering apparent damage. However, Captain Buchanan was wounded and replaced by his Executive Officer, Lt. Catesby Jones.
9 Mar.	Hampton Roads, Virginia	Lt. Jones commanding the *C.S.S. Virginia*	Captain Worden commanded the *U.S.S. Monitor*	The battle in Hampton Roads was inconclusive.

Date	Location	Confederate Forces	Union Forces	Notes
6-8 April	Island Number 10, Mississippi River, Tennessee	39 guns 7,000 Confederate soldiers. Commodore Hollins commanded the Confederate flotilla: *C.S.S. Pontchartrain, Maurepas, Ivy,* and *Polk* with 17 guns.	Commodore Andrew Foote, commanding seven ironclads, 11 Mortar boats	Located near the Tennessee – Kentucky state line this was the northern most Confederate defensive position on the Mississippi and western anchor of the Confederate defense in the western theatre. Once two Federal ironclads slipped below Island No. 10, the fight was over.
15 Apr.	New Orleans, Louisiana	*RIVER DEFENSE FLEET* River boat Captains Montgomery and Townsend – Confederacy purchased 14 vessels		The Confederate government, President and Congress adopted a special Act that formed the RIVER DEFENSE FLEET. They spent 1.5 million dollars to create this force outside the authority of the C.S.N. Its intent was to defend New Orleans, using the special knowledge and skill of riverboat captains and crews.
18 – 24 Apr.	Forts Jackson and St. Phillip, Mississippi River, Louisiana	Commodore Mitchell commanding *C.S.S. Manassas, Governor Moore, McRae, Louisiana, Resolute*	Admiral Farragut commanding *U.S.S. Varuna* (sunk), *Hartford*, a total of 17 warships and 6 gunboats and Captain Porter commanding 19 mortar boats	Confederate defense relied upon the forts and manmade obstacles in the form of a chain, sunken ships reaching across the river. Farragut was able to cut his way through the obstacles, once passed the forts, the Confederate flotilla could not hold the much larger force. New Orleans is taken the next day.

9 May	Pensacola, Florida	BG Thomas Jones orders the evacuation of Pensacola and the surrounding facilities.	D.D. Porter takes the surrender of Pensacola from the Mayor the next day.	Confederate forces were withdrawn from Pensacola as a part of the constriction of forces in the west to provide soldiers massing at Corinth to attack the Yankees at Shiloh. Two ironclads being built had to be destroyed because of the evacuation.
10 May	Fort Pillow, Tennessee	Captain Montgomery commanding *C.S.S. Bragg, Sumter, Sterling Price, Van Dorn, Jeff Thompson, General Lovell, Beauregard,* and *Little Rebel*	Commodore Davis commanding seven vessels	Confederates, part of the River Defense Force, sank the *U.S.S. Cincinnati* and *Mound City,* and *the U.S.S. Pittsburgh* was caught in friendly fire. The Confederates suffered minimal damage to the *Price* and *Van Dorn.* Ft. Pillow evacuated 4 June 1862 opening the Mississippi all the way to Memphis.
6 June	Memphis, Tennessee	Captain Montgomery commanding *C.S.S. Bragg, Sumter, Sterling Price, Van Dorn, Jeff Thompson, General Lovell, Beauregard,* and *Little Rebel*	*U.S.S. Queen of the West, Monarch, Benton, Louisville, Carondelet, Cairo, Mound City* (raised after being sunk at Ft. Pillow), and *St. Louis.*	Seven of eight Confederate ships were destroyed, only the *Van Dorn* survived.

15 July	Yazoo River, Mississippi	Commander Isaac N. Brown commanding the *C.S.S. Arkansas*, 10 guns, 2 fore and aft, and 3 in broadside on each side.	Captain Henry Walke commanded the *U.S.S. Carondelet, Tyler*, and *Queen of the West*.	The *C.S.S. Arkansas* was begun with her sister ship the *C.S.S. Tennessee* at Memphis. When Ft. Pillow fell the *Tennessee* was destroyed and the *Arkansas* was moved to Pinehill, Mississippi for completion. In this opening engagement the *Carondelet* was severely punished, the *Arkansas* then continued down to the Mississippi.
15 July	Mississippi River, between Yazoo River and Vicksburg, Mississippi	Commander Isaac N. Brown commanding the *C.S.S. Arkansas*, 10 guns, 2 fore and aft, and 3 *in* broadside on each side.	Admirals Farragut and Davis commanding 33 vessels (over 100 guns) including the *U.S.S. Kineo, Lancaster, Benton, Winona, Hartford, Iroquois, Richmond, Sumter, Louisville,* and *Oneida*	The *C.S.S. Arkansas* fought itself through the entire Union fleet causing great damage and havoc before finally reaching Vicksburg. That evening Farragut ordered the fleet to attack the *Arkansas* while it was moored to the river-bank. A heavy firefight occurred, but only minor damage was caused. The *Winona* was almost sunk.
16 July	Mississippi River at Vicksburg, Mississippi	*C.S.S. Arkansas*	Federal Mortar Boats.	Federals attempt to sink their target through a daylong mortar attack.

Mark K. Vogl

22 July	Mississippi River, at Vicksburg, Mississippi	*C.S.S. Arkansas*	*U.S.S. Essex, Queen of the West,* and another ram.	When the drums beat the roll only 41 men stood to for *C.S.S. Arkansas.* The Federals attempted to ram their target against the shore, but to no avail. Farragut's fleet departed for New Orleans on the 25th, Davis fleet returned north six days later.
6 Aug.	Mississippi River, vicinity Baton Rouge, Louisiana	Lt. Stevens commanding the *C.S.S. Arkansas*	*U.S.S. Essex*	The machinery of the *Arkansas* broke down while engaged with the *Essex,* she was directed ashore, where her crew abandoned ship and she was set fire, later to explode.
10 Aug.	Green Cay, sixty miles off Nassau.	Captain Maffitt commanding the *C.S.S. Florida*		The *Florida* is commissioned; she made her initial voyage heading into a blockaded Mobile on September 4th because of Yellow Fever. She leaves Mobile until Jan 15, 1863 to begin a successful career as a commerce raider.
24 Aug.	Azores Islands, Atlantic Ocean	Captain Rafael Semmes commanding the *C.S.S. Alabama*		The *Alabama* is commissioned and begins her legendary career as the South's most effective commerce raider.

Oct.	Richmond, Virginia	BG G. J. Rains commands the Torpedo Bureau, and Captain M. F. Maury, C.S.N. commands Naval Submarine Battery Service		An Act of Congress establishes the Torpedo Bureau. Stations are established in Richmond, Wilmington, Charleston, Savannah and Mobile.
12 Dec.	Yazoo River, vicinity Haines Bluff, Mississippi	Lt. Commander Selfridge commanding the *U.S.S. Cairo, Pittsburgh, Marmora, Signal, Queen of the West*		The *Cairo* was struck by a Confederate mine and sank in 12 minutes. First instance of a warship being sunk by a mine.
1863				
1 Jan	Galveston, Texas	Gen. Magruder, commanded Sibley's brigade, and *C.S.S. Bayou City*, *Neptune*, *Lady Gwinn*, and *John F. Carr*	Col. Burrill commanded 42nd Mass. Regt. Commodore Renshaw commanded the *U.S.S. Harriet Lane, Westfield, Clifton, Oswaco, and Sachem*	Coordinated land – naval attack retakes Galveston for the South. The *Harriet Lane* is captured. The *Westfield* ran aground and exploded.

Despite a flag of truce, the *Oswaco* and *Clifton* sailed out in the Gulf while their surrender was being discussed. |

4 Jan.	Galveston, Texas	Gen. Magruder, commanded Sibley's brigade, and *C.S.S. Bayou City, Neptune, Lady Gwinn,* and *John F. Carr,* and *Harriet Lane*		Gen. Magruder proclaims the blockade open for Galveston.
11 Jan.	Gulf of Mexico	Captain Semmes commanding the *C.S.S. Alabama*	*U.S.S. Hatteras*	*Alabama* sinks US warship.
16 Jan.	Mobile, Alabama	Captain Maffitt commanding the *C.S.S. Florida*	*U.S.S. Cuyler, Pembina, Susquehanna,* and *Oneida*	Maffitt departs Mobile at two in the morning in a storm. After losing the *Cuyler*, the *Florida* is free to attack Yankee commerce.
30 Jan.	Stono River, South Carolina	Gen. P.G.T. Beauregard	*U.S.S. Isaac P. Smith*	Beauregard who advised Ingraham to attack the Charleston blockaders also engineered the captured of the *Smith*.

31 Jan.	Charleston, South Carolina	Commodore Ingraham commanding the *C.S.S. Palmetto State* and *Chicora*	*U.S.S. Mercedita, Quaker City, Keystone State, Ottawa, Unadilla, Agusta, Stettin, Flag,* and *Memphis*	The two Confederate ironclads sail out to attack the blockading fleet before dawn. The *Mercedita* and *Keystone State* are badly damaged.
24 Feb	Red River – Mississippi River	*C.S.S. Webb* and *Queen of the West*	*U.S.S. Indianola*	Confederates attack and severely damage *Indianola*. She is driven ashore where she sinks and surrenders. Confederates begin salvage operation but are driven off by a Yankee Quaker gunboat. The *Indianola* is blown up!
6 May	Atlantic Ocean	Lt. Read commanding *C.S.S. Clarence, Tacony,* and *Archer*		Capt. Maffitt of the Florida gives Lt. Read his command, which includes one 12-pound gun. With a "*Quaker battery*," he takes 22 prizes
17 June	Savannah, Georgia Wassaw Sound	Commander W. A. Webb commanding the *C.S.S. Atlanta*	*U.S.S. Weehawken* and *Nahant*	An attempt to break blockade at Savannah and then move up and down the coast is defeated in less than 20 minutes. *The Atlanta* surrenders to the two *Monitors*.

Date	Location	Confederate	Union	Notes
13 July	Near Yazoo City, Mississippi, Yazoo River		U.S.S. Baron De Kalb	Destroyed after being struck by a Confederate torpedo. 40 Yankee ships were damaged or sunk by Confederate Torpedoes during the war.
5 Aug.	Off the coast of South Africa	Captain Rafael Semmes commanding the C.S.S. Alabama	Yankee commercial ship Sea Bridge	On its way to the Pacific, ship is taken as a prize and destroyed. Spectators from South Africa watched the chase and kill.
15 Aug.	Wilmington, North Carolina	Lt. Wilkenson commanding C.S.S. Robert E. Lee		A blockade-runner owned by the C.S.A., she is making another run to Bermuda. From June to July 1863, 148 vessels departed Nassau for Confederate ports. 106 made it.
8 Sep.	Sabine Pass, Texas	C.S.S. Uncle Ben, and Ft. Griffin	U.S.S. Sachem, Clifton, Cayuga, Arizona, and Granite City	41 defenders repel Yankee invasion lead by four gunboats. The Clifton was seriously damaged and run aground, where the Confederates captured her. The Sachem was disabled but escaped.
Oct.	James River Richmond, Virginia	Lt. William Harwar Parker commandant C.S.S. Patrick Henry		Confederate Naval Academy opens to the first class of 50.

Date	Location	Commander	Target	Result
5 Oct.	Charleston, South Carolina	Lt. Glassel commanding the C.S.S. David	U.S.S. New Ironside, the largest Yankee warship.	The David detonates a torpedo 6 ½ feet below the waterline of the New Ironsides. She is seriously damaged and knocked out of the war for more than a year
24 Dec.	Straits of Malacca, near Singapore	Captain Semmes commanding C.S.S. Alabama	Star of Texas, a Yankee commerce vessel	Star of Texas is captured and destroyed.
1864				
17 Feb.	Charleston, South Carolina	Lt. Dixon, 21st Alabama Volunteers commanding the C.S.S. Hunley	South Atlantic Blockading Squadron, Admiral Dahlgren, U.S.S. Housatonic	The Housatonic was a large ship of ten guns and a crew of 300. She sank in three minutes after being struck by the Hunley's torpedo. Only three men died as a result of the attack.
19 Apr	Roanoke River, Plymouth, North Carolina	Commander Cooke commanding the C.S.S. Albemarle	North Atlantic Blockading Squadron, U.S.S. Miami and Southfield	The Southfield sank. The Miami was damaged. The Albemarle establishes itself as a force to be reckoned with in the North Carolina Sounds.

5 May	Albemarle Sound, North Carolina	Commander Cooke commanding C.S.S. *Albemarle* and *Bombshell*	Commodore M. Smith commanding U.S.S. *Mattabessett, Sassacus, Wyalsing, Whitehead, Miami,* and *Commodore Hull*	The *Mattabessett* was seriously damaged. The *Albemarle* was able to fend attacks from all these ships, though the *Bombshell* was re-captured by the Yankees.
19 June	Cherbourg, France, English Channel	Captain Semmes commanding the *C.S.S. Alabama*	Captain John A. Winslow commanding U.S.S. *Kearsarge*	The *Alabama* captured 69 prizes in 22 months. However, on this date she would be sunk. Semmes and many of the crew would escape when English and Frenchmen picked up survivors.
20 July	Wilmington, North Carolina	Commander J. T. Wood commanding the *C.S.S. Tallahassee*		Originally built in England, as the blockade-runner *Atlanta*. She made several runs before being converted to a ship of war. The *Tallahassee* was successful. Her name was changed to the *C.S.S. Olustee* under the command Lt. Ward. After additional success she was converted to a blockade-runner. Eventually taken by the British on April 9th, 1865

2 Aug.	Mobile, Alabama Fort Gaines and Fort Morgan	Admiral Buchanan commanding the *C.S.S. Tennessee, Selma, Morgan*, and *Gaines*	Admiral Farragut commanding 31 warships including the *U.S.S. Hartford, Tecumseh, Brooklyn*, and *Chickasaw*.	Farragut leads 19 warships in an attack through the channel between the Forts. The Tecumseh is sunk when it strikes a torpedo. After a ferocious battle, the Tennessee is finally completely surrounded, and battered into submission.
19 Sep.	Lake Ontario, Canada, Ohio, and New York	Lt. John Yates Beall and 20 Confederates	Philo Parsons, *U.S.S. Michigan*	Beall takes the *Philo Parsons* lake steamer as step one in a plan to release thousands of Confederate Prisoners. The plan is foiled when the officers on the *U.S.S. Michigan* prevent the Rebels from seizing the only U.S. warship in the Great Lakes.
6 Oct.	Bahai, Brazil	Lt. Charles M. Morris commanding the *C.S.S. Florida*	Captain Napoleon Collins commanding *U.S.S. Wachusett*	The *Florida* was anchored, guns unloaded per port regulations. At 3 a.m. the *Wachusett* rammed and fired two guns into the *Florida* who surrendered. She was towed out before sunrise.

17 Oct.	Roanoke River, Plymouth, North Carolina	*C.S.S. Albemarle*	Lt. Cushing and 13 men	Lt. Cushing, U.S.N. led a daring night raid in a small boat armed with a torpedo which sunk the *Albemarle*. Only two of the 13 men involved in the raid survived. The *C.S.S. Neuse*, the *Albemarle*'s sister, being constructed in Kinston, N.C. had to be destroyed when Yankee raiders approached before the ship was *able to get down river. The naval war in North Carolina was over.*
20 Oct.	Las Desertas Island	Captain James Waddell commanding the *C.S.S. Shenandoah*		Commissioned on the 20th. Her target was the U.S. whaling fleet in the Arctic.
1865				
23 Jan.	James River, Trent's Reach, Virginia	Commodore Mitchell commanding the James River Squadron comprised of the *C.S.S. Richmond, Virginia II, Fredericksburg*, and torpedo launches *Drowry, Wasp, Hornet* and *Scorpion*.	Captain Parker commanding the *U.S.S. Onondaga*.	This Confederate Navy attempted to break the encirclement of Richmond with an offensive down the James River. Unfortunately, the level of the river, the emplacement of obstructions in the river and the combined strength of Union naval and land forces prevented success.

Date	Location	Confederate	Union	Notes
12 Apr.	Mobile, Alabama	Commodore Farrand commanding C.S.S. *Huntsville* and *Tuscaloosa*		Two unfinished ironclads are sunk when the capture of Mobile becomes imminent.
24 Apr.	Red River to the Mississippi River, between New Orleans and Fts. Jackson and St. Phillip	Lt. "Savez" Read commanding the *C.S.S. Webb*	*U.S.S. Manhattan, Lafayette, Choctaw*, and three ships on the Red River. Passed a gunboat every five miles on the Mississippi. At New Orleans the *U.S.S. Lackawanna, Port Royal,* and *Fearnaught* were engaged. Finally, the *Hollyhock* and *Richmond* finished the *Webb*	One more time Lt. Read attempts the impossible. His plan is to take the *Webb* through the Union fleet on the Red River and the Mississippi to enter the Gulf of Mexico to raid Yankee shipping. He is finally caught south of New Orleans.
4 May	Tombigbee River, Sidney, Alabama	Commodore Farrand commanding C.S. Naval units	Admiral Thatcher commanding Federal naval elements.	Surrenders Confederate Naval forces
19 May	Cuba	Captain Thomas Jefferson Page commanding *C.S.S. Stonewall*		*Stonewall* is sold to Spanish authorities for 16,000 dollars. The U.S. will eventually gain possession through a Claims Court.

22-18 June	Arctic Ocean	Lt. James I. Waddell commanding the *C.S.S. Shenandoah*	24 Yankee whalers taken as prizes.	Not knowing the war was over, the *Shenandoah* destroys the Yankee whaling fleet in the Arctic Ocean.
5 Nov.	Liverpool, England	Lt. James I. Waddell commanding the *C.S.S. Shenandoah*		The *C.S.S. Shenandoah* sails into Liverpool and turns over the vessel to British authorities. The last Confederates surrendered to the officers of the *H.M.S. Donegal*.

Chapter Six —

Confederate Special Naval Operations

Southern naval personnel would be used for a wide variety of missions above and beyond those considered traditional. For example, Confederate naval personnel manned land batteries along the James River and helped repel Federal naval attempts to secure Richmond in 1862.

There was no year of the war during which Confederate seaman did not find upon the broad expanse of the Chesapeake Bay and its many tributaries between the Potomac and the ocean, opportunities for naval raids and skirmishes that included numerous daring exploits and inflicted much annoyance upon the enemy.[141] writes J. Thomas Scharf in his second chapter about naval warfare in the Virginia waters.

Earlier, in a discussion of the James River in 1862, Scharf sites a newspaper ad in the *Richmond Dispatch* under the heading "Save Richmond":

I will be one of 100 to join any party, officered by determined and resolute officers, to board the whole fleet of gunboats and take them at all hazards, to save our beautiful city from destruction. I am not a resident of this state, but of the Confederate States, and of such a scheme can be got up, my name can be had by applying at this office.[142]

This advertisement would pre-date Confederate operations by only a matter of months. John Yates Beall, a graduate of the University of Virginia, would spend most of the war fighting through unconventional methods. Beall was a handsome, medium-sized man, with blue eyes, light-colored hair, and a moustache.[143]

John Beall was commissioned as a Captain in the Second Virginia Infantry Regiment[144] and served in Stonewall Jackson's command for a

---

141 *History of the Confederates States Navy* Page 718
142 Ibid Page 713
143 "The Execution of John Yates Beall, C.S.N.", *The Richmond Examiner*, March 1, 1865, http://hub.dataline.net.au/~tfoen/beall.htm
144 Ibid.

brief time before he was seriously wounded in the lungs.[145]

Captain Beall devised a plan to operate against Federal commercial shipping in the Chesapeake Bay. He approached the Confederate States Department of the Navy with a proposal to raise a company of privateers to operate in Virginia's rivers and in the Chesapeake Bay. Beall's naval operations were to be modeled on those of partisan fighter, Colonel John Mosby. Beall's objective was to raise general havoc and mischief with Yankee commercial vessels. In addition, he planned to attack maritime assets such as the telegraph cable that spanned the Bay, and the lighthouses used for navigation. Beall's force would not be paid through the Department of the Navy, but rather through the earnings made by the sale of any ships or cargo they were able to capture and bring to the Confederacy.[146] Beall's plan was approved and he was transferred to the C.S. Navy and given the rank of Acting Master's Mate. Unofficially, Beall's outfit would come to be known as the "Confederate Volunteer Coast Guard."[147]

Beall's small force of ten men initially began operating out of Mathews County in April 1862. His force grew to approximately twenty, and in August 1862, he led his men across the Chesapeake Bay to Virginia's eastern shore, where they conducted a successful raid on the lighthouse at Cape Charles.[148] They then returned his force to Mathews County in preparation for a more daring enterprise.

In the middle of September, utilizing two small boats, the *Swan* and *Raven*, Beall's small force ventured out into the Bay to seize the Northern sloop *Mary Anne* and two fishing vessels. They then sailed those vessels to Watchapreague on Virginia's eastern shore. On September 21st, they boarded and captured the schooner *Alliance* bound for Port Royal, South Carolina, with a hold filled with $200,000 worth of sutler's stores.[149] Leaving the *Alliance* under guard, on the 22nd, Beall led his reduced force out in his two boats and took three more prizes, the *Horseman*, *Pearsall*, and *Alexander*, over the next two days. Removing the prisoners, all three captures were scuttled, and he returned to the *Alliance*. Beall dispatched a small detachment with the *Swan* and *Raven*

---

145 "President Lincoln and the Case of John Beall," www.geocities.com/Athens/5568/jyb.html
146 *History of the Confederate States Navy*, Page 720
147 "Dictionary of American Naval Fighting Ships," www.history.navy.mil/danfs
148 *History of the Confederate States Navy*, Page 719
149 *Dictionary of American Naval Fighting Ships*, See Swan

to take some of the prisoners back to Mathews County. Beall had determined to sail the *Alliance* and its cargo home as a prize. The *Alliance* never made it, as the Piankatank River pilot[150] ran her aground. Beall salvaged what he could, about ten thousand dollars' worth of goods, before burning the *Alliance*.

In the north, the reaction was furious. The Yankees, assuming large forces had been used to capture so many vessels in such a short time, sent four gunboats, and three other ships, along with the 4th U.S. Colored Infantry, two cavalry regiments, and a battalion of artillery to Mathews County to destroy this new threat in the Chesapeake.[151] The Yankees captured three of Beall's raiders, but the rest escaped and were re-assembled in Richmond.

In November, Beall's force returned to Mathews County to find the *Raven* and *Swan* still safely hidden away. Crossing the Chesapeake, Beall's boys captured another schooner. Beall split his force, sending about half to shore to hide while he and the remainder stayed aboard the captured prize. The U.S. Coast Guard captured the Confederates headed to shore on November 14th. One of the men was hanged, and the others, terrified, gave away Beall's location, causing his entire group to be captured.[152]

Beall and his men, all members of the Confederate Navy, were transported to Ft. McHenry, where they were shackled and to be tried as privateers. When President Davis heard of this, he ordered a like number of Federal seamen to be shackled and held as hostages. The Federals reconsidered, and no charges were filed. Beall and his men were then treated as Prisoners of War. Beall would be exchanged on May 5th, 1864.[153] His war was not over.

Others took up the fight on the Chesapeake while Beall was in a Yankee prison. Lt. John Taylor Wood, on March 6th, 1864, operating

---

150 Throughout my readings many of the pilots who were used in specialized waters were responsible for decisions or outcomes which were not beneficial to the Southern war effort. One can't help but wonder if treason by some pilots and sabotage was not a part of the counter operations plan by the Federals.
151 Ibid.
152 Department of the U.S. Navy, Naval Historical Center Homepage, "Dictionary of American Naval Fighting Ships" See Swan
153 *History of the Confederate States Navy,* Page 720

from Mathews County, led 15 men on a sail across the Bay to Cherrystone Harbor on the eastern shore. Once there, they cut the telegraph wires that ran under the Bay and captured some Federal cavalry pickets before they turned to wait for an opportunity on the water. When the U.S. dispatch boat *Iolas* came into the harbor from Fortress Monroe, Wood's men were able to overwhelm the crew. When another arrived, the *Titan*, it too, was seized. In each case, the raiders were outnumbered, and in each case, they took their prisoners without firing a shot. They then burned a Yankee warehouse filled with commissary stores and were about to burn the *Iolas* when the captain and owner offered to bond his ship for $10,000. The Confederates aboard the *Titan*, with their cavalry prisoners, sailed for the Piankatank River where they burned the ship.[154]

The last operation in the Chesapeake Bay would occur more than a year later, in April 1865. Lt. Commander John C. Brian, C.S.N. led another group that seized and burned a schooner, the *St. Marys*.[155]

After being exchanged in May 1864, Acting Masters Mate John Beall,[156] C.S.N. departed Virginia for Canada and a new adventure.

Once in Canada, Beall went to Toronto, where he met with Colonel Thompson, C.S.A. The mission they discussed was larger than anything John Yates Beall had attempted previously.

Johnson's Island was off the Ohio coast in Lake Erie. It had been chosen because of its unsettled, wooded character as a good place for a Union prison camp. In 1862, the Federal authorities had designated Johnson's Island Prisoner of War Camp as a Confederate officers camp.[157] Thompson wanted Beall, working with Captain Charles H. Cole, C.S.A. (a Confederate spy working in the Lake Erie Region) to attack Johnson's Island with the objective of liberating the Confederate prisoners there.[158] Cole had successfully escaped from Johnson's Island and thus had extensive knowledge of the camp.[159]

---

154 Ibid, Page 722
155 Ibid Page 724
156 The Photo of John Yates Beall was secured at the Web site "President Lincoln and the Case of John Yates Beall, www.geocities.com/Athens/5568/jyb.html, by Isaac Markins
157 http://johnsonsislandmemorial.homestead.com/History.html
158 *Dictionary of American Naval Fighting Ships*, at the Department of the Navy – Naval Historical Center www.history.navy.mil/danfs/m10/michigan-i.htm
159 http://sunnsite.unc.edu/pub/academic/history/marshall/military/civil_war_us-

To accomplish this task, Beall would be given twenty men. His intermediate objective was to be the capture of the Federals' only warship on the Great Lakes, the U.S.S. *Michigan*. The *Michigan* had 14 guns, and it was believed that would be sufficient power to overwhelm the camp guard.

Beall traveled to Windsor, Canada, where he "collected his men,"[160] and then all booked passage on the *Philo Parsons* for September 19th, 1864 at Malden, Ontario.[161] Once the ship was out on Lake Erie, the Confederate raiders shed their civilian clothes and seized the ship. Beall then turned the ship for Johnson's Island, but had to stop at Middle Bass Island for wood to fuel the furnace of the steam engine. While there, "another small steamer, the *Island Queen*, 'with a large number of passengers and 32 soldiers' tied up alongside of…"[162] the *Philo Parsons*.

Beall felt compelled to seize the *Island Queen*. After collecting the passengers, crew, and soldiers, Beall placed them on the island, securing a pledge that the Yankees would not attempt to leave the island for 24 hours. He then took the *Island Queen* out into Lake Erie, where it was scuttled and sent to the bottom.[163]

Finally, the Acting Masters Mate was ready to commence the operation intended to liberate hundreds, if not thousands, of Southern officers.

Captain Charles Cole, late of Nathan Bedford Forrest's cavalry command, had preceded Beall to Johnson's Island, where his task was to gain entry onto the U.S.S. *Michigan*, create a distraction and then provide a pre-arranged signal to Beall's force. Captain Cole succeeded in getting onto the *Michigan* and had even gained access to the ship's officers. Cole and the officers were sharing a drink when something occurred, which tipped off the Federal officers. Cole was arrested and placed in the brig. Thus, Captain Cole was unable to send the message Beall expected when he got within sight of the prison camp and the *Michigan*.[164]

---

a/C.S.N./p.txt
160 Ibid, from an article written by Beall to a Canadian Newspaper.
161 Beall Home Page, www.geocities.com/Athens/5568/philoparsons.html by Kim Beall
162 Ibid
163 Ibid
164 http://sunnsite.unc.edu/pub/academic/history/marshall/military/civil_war_us-

John Beall was undeterred and wanted to proceed with the mission, but 17 of his men mutinied and refused to allow Beall to continue the mission. The *Philo Parsons* turned away, and the ship was taken to Sandwich, Ontario. On the 20th, the *Parsons* was set adrift after having been damaged. Most of the Confederate raiders made their way into the United States and then to the South. For his part in the affair, Col. Thompson was expelled from Canada and returned to the Confederacy.[165]

But John Yates Beall was not through.

If Beall could not liberate the Confederate officers while they were at Johnson's Island, he decided he would attempt to release them while they were in transit from Johnson's Island to Fort Warrens in Boston Harbor. Beall moved his operations into New York near Buffalo. On three separate occasions, he attempted to derail passenger cars. Each attempt failed. And Beall was finally captured near Suspension Bridge, New York on December 14th, 1864.[166]

Beall was to be tried for espionage. He selected a prisoner to defend him, but the Judge Advocate General ruled that a Prisoner of War could not practice law in the defense of a spy, and an attorney was appointed for him. While the prosecution brought forth five witnesses, the defense brought none. Beall was convicted on February 17th, and sentenced to death. But John Yates Beall was not without friends; even in the Union he had spent so much of his energy to defeat.

During the month of February 1865, a massive effort was made to have Beall's sentence commuted. Eventually 91 Federal Senators and Congressmen would sign a petition to the President asking for mercy for John Yates Beall. Important people, including the Librarian of Congress, Governor John Andrew of Massachusetts, former Postmaster General Montgomery Blair, would all appeal directly to President Lincoln, but to no avail.

Now, in these late months of the war, some Confederates, in desperation, had been captured in the midst of conducting terrorist acts (one such attempt in November 1864 focused on burning New York City). Some members of the Administration felt that the President had

---

a/C.S.N./p.txt

165 Beall Home Page, www.geocities.com/Athens/5568/philoparsons.html by Kim Beall

166 "President Lincoln and the Case of John Yates Beall," www.geocities.com/Athens/5568/jyb.html, by Isaac Markins

to hold firm, to send a strong message.[167]

Beall's mother was allowed to visit him in his last days. In his final hours, John Yates Beall would take the sacrament twice and would be visited by two Catholic Priests and Rev. D. Weston of the Episcopal Church. Though clearly shaken, patriot Beall displayed great courage as he was prepared for execution, stating, "I die in defense of my country." John Yates Beall was hanged on Governor's Island, in New York Harbor, at 13 minutes past one p.m., on February 23rd, 1865.[168]

Another center for Confederate Special Naval Operations was Mobile, Alabama. Its central location on the coast of the Gulf of Mexico made it a convenient launch point for raids against the Mississippi River and Pensacola, Florida.

Admiral Raphael Semmes, in his book *Memoirs of Service Afloat*, describes the spirit and activity of Mobile in the spring of 1861.

... In a great state of excitement. Always one of the truest of Southern cities, it was boiling over with enthusiasm; the young merchants had dropped their day-books and ledgers and were forming and drilling companies by night and by day, whilst the older ones were discussing questions of finance and anxiously casting about them to see how the Confederate treasury could be supported.[169]

Scharf reports that Mobile was an epicenter of naval activity, especially special naval operations. He writes,

... Scores of gallant exploits of seamanlike skill and daring; of marine raids by adventuresome hunters and fisherman of these semi-tropical sounds and bayous upon the enemy's transports and tenders ... were based out of Mobile.[170] In April and May 1863, two raids demonstrate the potential of Mobile as jumping off point for raids against the mouth of the Mississippi.

In April, Captain G. Andrews and 15 men set out in a small open boat for their hunting area. These men were armed with nothing more than revolvers, knives, and spirit. They had no specific target in mind instead, operating on the concept of opportunity. The first ship they crossed paths with was a Federal warship with several hundred sailors

---

167 Ibid
168 "The Execution of John Yates Beall, C.S.N.", The Richmond Examiner, March 1, 1865, http://hub.dataline.net.au/~tfoen/beall.htm
169 "The History of the Confederate States Navy," Page 534
170 Ibid, Page 533

aboard. Andrews choose not to engage this opportunity. But on the evening of April 8th, the steamer *Fox* came along, and the Confederates decided this was the perfect prey. They guided their small boat up to their target's side, boarded the *Fox*, and seized her without firing a shot.

They returned to Mobile on the morning of the 9th, being fired on only as they approached the back door entrance to the harbor. Besides the capture of a fine prize, the Confederacy gained 1,000 barrels of coal.

Then in the last week of May, Captain James Duke and 18 volunteers set on another raid in the same general vicinity. Once in the Mississippi, the force landed along the marshy banks, laying in wait for a ship. Eventually, the *Boston* came along, towing a ship behind her. Duke and his men made for the target, and like Andrews were able to take the ship without firing a shot. The captain and crew of the *Boston* were surprised to be boarded by Confederates so deep in an area constantly patrolled by Union warships.

Duke cut loose the ship in tow, and set about looking for other potential prizes. He would capture and scuttle two more ships, the *Lenox* and the *Texana*, before turning for Mobile. The estimated loss in terms of cargo and ships was reported as $200,000 dollars. Again, a few brave hearts with nothing more than small arms, knives, and courage had ventured into Union-held waters and made away with yet another ship.[171]

These raids and those in the Virginia waters demonstrate how a few daring men, who were lightly armed, could conduct operations that could result in the loss of valuable ships and cargo. Since many of the vessels taken or sunk, and much of the cargo on these ships were in the hands of merchants, the cost of commercial shipping was adversely affected by these operations. And like the ocean cruisers raiding Federal commercial fishing fleets, insurance rates rose for all shipping operations.

Two brothers, serving in Mobile on two Rebel ships, were developing another operation with the potential for far larger gains in the Mobile area.

As we discussed earlier, Pensacola was an important port in the Gulf. The Confederates made an early attempt to seize this harbor but

---

[171] Ibid, both Andrews and Duke's raids are described in Scharf's work. Pages 535 -537

failed and were driven off. The Baker brothers believed they could put together an offensive to seize Ft. Pickens, the bastion guarding Pensacola. They believed once the Confederates had seized the fort, the Yankee Navy anchored in Pensacola Bay could be captured, destroyed by the fort's guns, or compelled to withdraw.[172]

Lt. James Baker had been on the C.S.S. *Louisiana* during the battle for New Orleans at Ft. St. Phillip and Ft. Jackson. On April 25th, he had been in command of the C.S.S. *Burton*, where he and his crew had successfully evacuated the officers and men preparing the *Louisiana* for destruction. Baker was then captured but escaped and traveled first to New Orleans and then to Mobile.[173] Baker was then transferred to Columbus, Georgia for a period of time, until he returned to Mobile.

Masters Mate Page Baker, brother of James, forwarded a plan to seize Ft. Pickens to Gen. Butler, C.S.A. in March of 1864. The plan was relatively simple in design; a force of 150 men would be transported via open boats the approximately 35 miles to the Perdido River, where they would go ashore, rest, and wait for night. The next night they would row to the head of the Grand Lagoon, carry the boats across a stretch of land 35 yards wide, and enter Pensacola Bay in vicinity of Ft. Pickens.[174] They would then proceed to land near Ft. Pickens. Masters Mate Baker went on to explain his plan once ashore:

Having landed we would proceed as cautiously as possible to the east face of the fort, and endeavor to effect [sic] our entrance through the embrasures, which are generally left open. Should they be closed, by means of ladders carried with us, in sections, we would mount to the parapet and descend to the center of the fort by the stairways very fortunately at this point. Once inside, would be our objective to secure the garrison, consisting of from 150 to 200 men. For this purpose we would send a large detachment to the men's quarters on the west side of the fort where they sleep with their arms stacked. Another detachment would seize the relief guard just inside of the gate (also asleep,) and a third the officers in their quarters on the south side of the fort. You will observe there is no boat on the east or south side of the fort. There are usually between 18 to 20 vessels lying off the yards, and I have understood by letter recently from

---

172 Map provided by "Florida in the Civil War, 1861 – 1865" website, *Harper's Ferry Weekly*, Feb. 9th, 1861 http://dhr.dos.state.fl.us/museum/civwar/03.html
173 Ibid Page 541
174 Ibid Page 540

Pensacola that Farragut had removed most of their crews to man his fleet off Mobile; be that as it may, they would fall an easy prey with the fort once in our possession. At and around the navy yard there is a force of about 3,500 men, including one Negro regiment. Should Gen. Canby move down with the force under his command and invest the yard, they being cut off from all relief must surrender. As we would need men who can be relied on in any emergency, I would request permission to select volunteers and men who have been tried under fire. We would necessarily need a number of men accustomed to heavy artillery in order to man the guns. It would be necessary also to take several days provisions.[175]

Admiral Buchanan must have been impressed by the degree of detail in the intelligence provided in Baker's plan, and with the audacity of the plan. Baker's belief that he could hold off 3,500 men while holding almost 200 prisoners, with only 150 men is, well difficult to accept. But, if Baker could execute the first two phases of the plan, the secret transit to the area, and the seizure of the fort, it might be possible to have a larger force prepared to cooperate. And if the intelligence was correct, the Confederate Navy could be expanded by up to twenty vessels if plans were made for this contingency.

The Admiral demonstrated interest in the plan by ordering Lt. Baker to fit out a boat for a reconnaissance of the proposed route and Fort Pickens. Baker was ordered to take his Masters Mate brother and ten men.

On the evening of April 25th, 1864, the Bakers with eight other men entered the Gulf some 16 miles east of Fort Morgan. A gale came up, nearly swamping the boat and driving past the Perdido. By 3 a.m., they were near a beach east of the fort. It was decided they would capture a fishing smack, the *Creole*, out of New Orleans. Once done, the crew was sent below, and the force took up the identity of the fishermen.

The *Creole* was then turned toward Ft. Pickens for a closer look. The ship was brought so close that men actually talked with guards, taking copious notes of all they saw and heard. Once the reconnaissance was completed, the *Creole* was turned out into the Gulf and headed east. A sail was identified on the horizon, and Lt. Baker initially decided to make this new sighting a prize. Preparations were made. But then, as

---

175 Ibid 540-541

the ships closed on one another, Lt. Baker was able to identify the ship as a Federal cruiser, armed. Immediately, the plan was changed. The *Creole* could not hope to outrun the steamer, so Baker ordered that the identity of the fishing boat be re-assumed. The Stars and Stripes were raised. A meal was even served as the Federal ship closed on the *Creole* to inspect her.

With Yankee sharpshooters perched in the masts, officers on the Yankee ship used spyglasses to look over the fishing vessel. Satisfied, they moved on.

Baker wanted to try to return to Mobile with his prize, and so sailed for two weeks looking for a means to get by the blockade. But when none could be found, he anchored in St. Andrews Bay where he burned the *Creole*. He now had to find another way to get back to Mobile. The route he took was less than direct. Using an ox wagon provided by locals, the cutter they had first set out on was transported 80 miles to Marianna. From there they went to the Chattahoochee River where they boarded a steamer to Columbus, Georgia. With the cutter still in tow they boarded a train for Montgomery, Alabama. Once there, they launched the cutter and made their way downstream to Mobile.[176]

With Admiral Buchanan lost to the Federals in the Battle of Mobile, an important advocate of the proposed Pensacola offensive was lost.

The results of the reconnaissance were submitted to Farragut's replacement, in command of all naval forces remaining in the area of Mobile, Commodore Farrand. Farrand quickly dismissed the idea.

But the Bakers forwarded the plans and reconnaissance report to Naval Secretary Mallory, who took it to President Davis. Davis liked the idea and approached General Bragg, then his senior military adviser, who ordered that the plan be executed. Farrand, then ordered the Bakers to make preparations, and even allowed them to begin the operation, before calling them back because of fabricated intelligence that the size of the garrison at the fort had been increased.

Thus, ended the plans for one of the most ambitious naval raids to be considered by Confederate naval leaders during the war.

Another special operation was conducted, in part, by seven of the cadets at the Confederate Naval Academy. This complex and daring operation combined naval and marine forces from three different states and was conducted in North Carolina, in conjunction with land opera-

---

176 Ibid, page 543

tions being conducted by General George Pickett, on detached service from the Army of Northern Virginia. *(see Chapter 8, The Confederate States Naval Academy)*

Confederate Special Naval Operations comprised a very important component of the South's naval war. Especially in the earliest days of the war, the South's sole ability to respond on the seas and waterways was through this form of warfare. And even when the South possessed ironclads, and submersibles, and large ocean-going warships, the men of the Confederate States Navy continued to operate in the gray areas of special operations.

As can be seen, by these raids described above, some Confederate Naval Officers were the equal of Generals Stuart and Forrest, and Colonels Mosby and Morgan in boldness, ingenuity, courage, and patriotism. The Confederate sailors proved, through their operations, to be second to none in their ardent patriotism and willingness to expose themselves to great danger.

Chapter Seven —

Building the Confederate States Navy

As we have seen in the earlier chapters, the Confederate States Navy was much larger and much more effective than we may have understood from our previous readings on the War for Southern Independence. When we remember that the Confederate States of America was born with few federally organized resources, we come to rapidly understand that every facet of the new nation's defense had to be created from nothing. In the case of the army, rifles, cannon, munitions, and uniforms had to be gathered, purchased or manufactured, and then, distributed to the units organizing throughout the South. In the case of the navy, most of the same needs were present, plus the need for various types of ships, coal, and the equipage for vessels. Our previous understanding of the fledging nation has made us aware of the South's limited manufacturing base. So how did the Confederate Navy come to exist?

First, the organization.
After Secretary Mallory was appointed to head the Department of the Navy, he immediately went to work to create an organizational structure, identify personnel to fill the leadership posts, and establish responsibilities. He had one early advantage, a surplus of experienced, talented officers. Because there was a lack of ships to assign them to, these officers were available to meet the challenges of creating a navy from scratch. For example, Raphael Semmes, the future legendary cruiser commander, was given authority by President Davis to go north and attempt to purchase ships and any other equipment necessary for the building of a navy.[177] He was literally given a blank check.

Secretary Mallory, as the former Chairman of the United States Senate Committee on Naval Affairs, had extensive knowledge of the organizational structure of the Union Navy. His knowledge of this structure was reflected in the manner in which he created the Department of Navy. The Department would be broken up into four bureaus. These four bureaus, called offices, would be responsible for outfitting, manning, and supporting the operational aspects of the Navy. This organi-

---
[177] *The Rise and Fall of the Confederate Government*, Volume I, page 270-271

zational structure mirrored that of the United States Navy.

The Office of Orders and Detail was principally responsible for the personnel aspects of the Navy. The Office assigned officers to their respective posts, maintained officer and enlisted personnel records, was responsible for recruiting and promotions, and for courts martial. Early in September 1861, when Franklin Buchanan arrived in Richmond and went to meet Secretary Mallory, he was "at once offered ... a commission as a C.S. Navy captain," and "... a plum job as well, chief of the Bureau of Orders and Detail — the highest administrative post in the infant Confederate Navy."[178]

Acting in this capacity, Buchanan had been sent south after the loss of Port Royal Sound, South Carolina, and Hatteras Inlet, North Carolina, to review the situation and attempt to help evaluate what actions could be taken to prevent further Federal advances along the coast. During his tour of the southeast coast, he met with General Robert E. Lee and they agreed that heavy guns on the Federal ships had been the essential reason behind the Union successes. Agreeing the Confederacy could not arm the entire coast, the two considered a strategy that would require the selection of certain ports to defend, while leaving the remainder of the coast virtually unprotected.[179] This strategy reflected the principle of "economy of force." described by Clausewitz in *On War*.[180]

Buchanan took this operational concept back to Richmond and discussed it with Secretary Mallory. Essentially, both agreed that Lee was correct. But which ports to defend and how to do it with the naval resources available was the rub. And more, there does not seem to have been any follow up inter-service discussion of which ports to defend, and an integration of those ports into an overall land strategy. As the war progressed in 1862, both Pensacola and Norfolk would be surrendered without a serious fight.

Still, there were positive outcomes from this initial consideration of Southern maritime strategy. Secretary Mallory would come to believe that because the Confederate Navy could not hope to match the Feder-

---

178 *Confederate Admiral*, page 146-147
179 Ibid, page 151
180 *On Strategy: the Vietnam War in Context*, page 79, Economy of Force was defined in a sentence: "The time and place of the main effort having been determined, men and means are conserved by reducing their employment in other directions."

al Navy in numbers, that the Confederacy must rely on the technological superiority of its ships to be able to defeat a much larger foe.[181] Thus Secretary Mallory quickly embraced the idea of the need for ironclads, and his early decisions gave him a short but important lead on the Federal Navy in that area. This strategy of technological superiority also explains Confederate experiments and efforts with torpedoes and the partially submersible, and submersible vessels intended to deliver them.

This leads us to the second office, the Office of Ordnance and Hydrography. This office was responsible for "… preparing for the manufacture of ordnance, ordnance stores, and naval supplies. …"[182] The office would be under the command of Commander George Minor, assisted by Lt. Robert D. Minor and Commander John Brooke. Later in the war, Commander Brooke would assume command of this office. The work of these men, and other patriots working in this office would be nothing less than Herculean.

Brigadier General Josiah Gorgas, Chief of Ordnance for the Confederate States of America has written a brief summary describing the challenges, and outlining the successes of those involved with ordnance in the CSA:

We began in April 1861, without an arsenal laboratory or powder mill of any capacity, and with no foundry or mill-rolling except at Richmond, and before the close of the of 1863 within a little over two years, we supplied them.

Gorgas goes on to describe the hardships associated with the conduct of the war; the lack of money, the lack of technical expertise, the interruption of raw materials and machinery because of the ever-expanding blockade, and the loss of vital natural resources as a result of Yankee advances. But he writes:

— Against all these obstacles, in spite of all these deficiencies, we persevered at home, as determinedly as did our troops on the field against more tangible opposition; and in that short period created, almost literally out of the ground, foundries and rolling mills at Selma, Richmond, Atlanta, and Macon, smelting works at Petersburg, chemical works at

---

181 Interestingly, the United States would make the same strategic decision when facing the Soviet Union eighty years later. The US realized it could not sustain large conventional armies on the European Continent to balance those of the Soviets. The alternative was to rely on enhanced technology to offset the numerical superiority of the enemy.

182 *The History of the Confederate States Navy,* page 49

Charlotte, North Carolina; a powder mill far superior to any in the United States and unsurpassed by any across the ocean, and a chain of arsenals, armories, and laboratories, equal in their capacity and improvements to the best of those in the United States, stretching link by link from Virginia to Alabama.[183]

The Office of Ordinance and Hydrography was also given responsibility for development and operation of the Confederate States Naval Academy.[184] (See Chapter 7)

The employees of the Ordnance Office in Richmond enrolled in a naval battalion, thus giving up their rights as laborers and donning the Naval uniform. They worked round the clock at their manufacturing jobs but were from time to time called out to perform military duties as circumstances dictated.

As a result of the fall of New Orleans in 1862, the loss of the Norfolk Navy yard and the destruction of C.S.S. *Virginia*, the Confederate Congress felt compelled to investigate the Department of the Navy to root out the inefficiencies and graft, which caused a perceived lack of preparedness in the defense of the Crescent City. A joint select committee of both Houses was convened August 27th, 1862. What they found was a Department which;

… Erected a powder mill which supplies all the powder required by our navy; two engine-boiler machine shops, and five ordnance workshops. It has established 18 yards for building war vessels and a rope walk, making all cordage, from a rope yarn to a nine-inch cable, and capable of turning out 8,000 yards per month.

Of vessels not ironclad the Department has purchased and otherwise acquired and converted to war vessels … 44

Has built and completed as war vessels … 12

Has partially constructed and destroyed to save from the enemy ……………….. 10

Of ironclad vessels, it has now completed and has now in commission …………….…… 12

Has completed or lost by capture … 4

Has in progress of construction, and various stages of forwardness ……………..… 23[185]

---

183 Ibid page 49
184 *Rebel Reefers, The Organization and Midshipman of the Confederate States Naval Academy*, page 9
185 *History of the Confederate States Navy*, page 47

The Department of the Navy had gotten off to a very ambitious start. Mallory's quick decision to initiate 32 contracts for 40 warships between 28 June 1861 and the 1st of December 1862 was beginning to bear fruit. And to think, all of these orders were for ships to be built within the Confederacy! The Confederacy would operate 18 sites where naval construction would occur.

The Confederacy also had to identify and integrate into the naval logistical system the source of steam power, coal.[186] Three major sources would be identified in North Carolina, Alabama, and near Richmond. And they would need to create powder mills for both army and navy uses.

In addition to operations within the Confederacy, the blockade-runners owned by the Department of the Navy were operated out of this office.

Mallory had even been imaginative enough to send Southern mechanics to St. Louis to sign up for work on the building of the Yankees' ironclad fleet.[187] These individuals provided excellent intelligence on the progress of the building program, the characteristics of the vessels and other information.

Despite all these impressive accomplishments, the South would continue to suffer from a lack of raw materials and from insufficient heavy industrial machinery to produce items it needed. These deficiencies would include rolled iron plate that was used to shield the ironclad ships and the ability to manufacture sufficiently powerful steam engines to drive these heavy ships. Repeatedly, the problems with completing the production of ironclads, or with operating them once completed, involved a lack of powerful steam engines to move the vessels once fully armored and loaded with their complete armament.

List of Confederate Naval Facilities — Shipyards
Source of Information: Confederate States Navy Museum, Library and Research Institute, Mobile Alabama, www.csnavy.org
Selma, Alabama
Auburn, Alabama
Montgomery, Alabama
Yazoo City, Mississippi

---

186 Ibid, page 51
187 Ibid, page 44

Wilmington, North Carolina
Berry Shipyard
Cassidy Shipyard
Tarboro, North Carolina
Kinston, North Carolina
Edwards Ferry, North Carolina
Charlotte, North Carolina, ordinance manufacture
Florence, South Carolina
Charleston, South Carolina
James Eason Shipyard
FM Jones Shipyard
James Marsh Shipyard
Purysburg, South Carolina
Richmond, Virginia
Rockett's Landing Shipyard
Graves Shipyard
Tredegar Iron Works
Columbus, Georgia
Savanah, Georgia
A. N. Miller Foundry
Willinks Shipyard
Midgeville, Georgia
Krenson and Hawkes Shipyard
Algiers Point, Louisiana
Shreveport, Louisiana

Secretary Mallory also had wasted no time in starting to work on finding overseas sources for ships. He had immediately selected James D. Bulloch to act as a Confederate purchasing agent and sent him to Europe, where he arrived on June 4th, 1861. Agents were also sent to Canada and to Philadelphia, Baltimore, and New York to identify existing commercial ships that might fit the bill as a warship for the Confederacy.[188] Later, Lt. James M. North would be sent to Europe to purchase ironclads.[189]

James D. Bullock, a graduate of the United States Naval Academy at Annapolis, would prove to be one of the great "finds" for Secretary

---

188 *History of the Confederate States Navy*, page 43
189 Ibid, page 44

Mallory and the Confederacy. Over the next four years, Captain Bulloch would be almost single-handedly responsible for the procurement of the Confederate Cruiser Fleet, which would so successfully punish the U.S. commercial fleet. Among the ships he would procure would be the C.S.S. *Alabama,* C.S.S. *Florida,* and the C.S.S. *Shenandoah.* Bulloch would also purchase blockade-runners. One of the more famous of these was the C.S.S. *Deer.*[190] Bulloch's success is hard to understand given the efforts of the British government to prohibit the manufacture and sale of warships to the Confederacy. And not all of Bulloch's transactions were successful. One can't help but wonder if the British government were somehow less diligent in blocking transactions which would adversely affect the American commercial fleet, at the time the most dominant commercial fleet in the world, while at the same time increasing her vigilance concerning ships which might prove very effective in combating the Federal fleet in American waters and possibly altering the course of the war.

Clearly, one very successful source for procuring quality, effective, ocean-going ships was through the work of Captain James. D. Bullock, C.S.N. When you consider the significant damage done to the U.S. commercial fleet during the War Between the States, and the cost of that damage to both the Federal economy and the nation's prestige around the globe, the real worth of Captain Bulloch's efforts become self-evident.

How important were Confederate efforts to purchase warships and blockade-runners overseas? Battles and Commanders, published in 1904 by the U.S. War Department, states;

The destruction of American shipping was not the most important effect of this surreptitious supply of war vessels by English builders. Except for them, the American Navy need not have been half as large as it was forced to be. A few vessels would have sufficed to blockade the Southern ports and to capture the seaboard cities. There were no facilities in the South for building even one considerable sea-going war vessel.

The author goes on to write,

But, supplied as they were with cruisers, English built, English armed and equipped, and even English manned, the Confederacy became suf-

---

190 Dictionary of American Fighting Ships, www.history.navy.mil/danfs/cfa3/deer.htm

ficiently powerful at sea to force the United States to vastly increase its naval establishment.[191]

Confederate agents were also active in other nations in Europe. Though very late in the war, the Confederacy purchased a seagoing ironclad vessel intended to break the blockade. The C.S.S. *Stonewall* was built in Bordeaux, France and when the national government moved to block the sale, the builder tore up the contract with the Confederate States of America and attempted to sell the ship to the Danes. When that deal collapsed, the builder returned to the Southerners and the deal was consummated.[192]

The Confederate Department of the Navy would also include the Office of Provisions and Clothing and a Medicine and Surgery Bureau. There was also a Chief Clerk, Edward Tidbell, and a Pay Master.[193] Later in the war, the Confederate Congress divided the Torpedo Bureau, giving the Army and Navy control of their respective efforts. The Navy created the Naval Submarine Battery Service headed by Captain M.F. Maury. (See chapter 10)

This extensive system, established to build and sustain the Southern Navy, was composed of three sources of the procurement of ships and equipage; southern construction, the purchase of ships and equipment from overseas, and the capture of Federal vessels.

With respect to strategy and command of the various elements of the operational navy, it appears there were two most common avenues for exercising command. In ports like Charleston, Savannah, Mobile, and New Orleans, the ships on station were organized into squadrons, and commands came from the Secretary of the Navy, or possibly the President to the Squadron Commander. In other instances, ships operated alone and communicated directly with Department of the Navy for instructions.

---

191 *Battles and Commanders*, page 269
192 Department of the US Navy, Naval Historical Center, www.history.navy.mil/photos/sh-us-cs/csa-sh/csash-sz/stonewll.htm See the Ironclad Index at the back of the book for a photograph and description.
193 *History of the Confederate States Navy*, page 25

The official records of war reveal the Confederate Navy commissioned 214 ships during the conflict. However, this count could be significantly short of the actual number of ships which participated in naval operations against Federal forces, or whose keels were laid but never made it to completion to fight against the Northern invaders. I believe that number could substantially add, and possibly even double the number reported in the records. Clearly, the Confederacy exerted tremendous effort and resources to construct and operate a navy of this size.

Figure 4 – Piece of North Carolina currency featuring a Confederate blockade runner
Image from the personal collection of the author.

ORGANIZATIONAL TABLE OF THE CONFEDERATE NAVY

THE DEPARTMENT OF THE CONFEDERATE STATES NAVY
RICHMOND, VIRGINIA
SECRETARY STEPHEN MALLORY

CLERKS

OFFICE OF ORDERS AND DETAILS	OFFICE OF ORDINANCE AND HYDROGRAPHY	OFFICE OF PROVISIONS AND CLOTHING	OFFICE OF SURGERY AND MEDICINES

C.S. Naval Stations

Overseas Station
  Paris, France

Richmond, Virginia
Norfolk, Virginia
Wilmington, North
  Carolina
Charleston, South
  Carolina
Savannah, Georgis
Mobile, Alabama
Pensacola, Florida
New Orleans, Louisiana
Galvaston, Texas
Columbus, Georgia
Selma, Alabama

C.S. Shipyards

<u>Alabama</u>
Auburn
Montgomery
Selma

<u>Florida</u>
Pensacola

<u>Mississippi</u>
Yazoo City

<u>South
  Carolina</u>
Florence
Charleston
Purysburg

<u>Georgia</u>
Columbus
Milledgeville
Savannah

<u>Louisiana</u>
Algers Point
Shreveport

<u>North
  Carolina</u>
Wilmington
Tarboro
Kinston
Edwards Ferry

<u>Tennessee</u>
Memphis

Torpedo Bureau
Naval

Submarine Service

Stations
Richmond, Virginia
Charleston, South
  Carolina
Savannah, Georgia
Wilmington, North
  Carolina
Mobile, Alabama
Houston, Texas
Shreveport, Louisiana

NAVAL ACADEMY
Richmond, Virginia

Shipyard Source of Information: Confederate States Navy Museum, Library and Research Institute, Mobile, Alabama, www.csnavy.org

Chapter Eight —

Confederate States Naval Academy

J. Thomas Scharf, the author of *History of the Confederate States Navy*, was a midshipman at Confederate States Naval Academy in Richmond, beginning his studies in 1864 and participated in some of the cadets' most exciting "scholastic" experiences. The author, therefore, personally knew many of the faculty and cadets. He dedicates a short chapter, Chapter XXV, near the end of his 800-page history of the Southern Navy, to the founding and activities of the institution. As Scharf explains, the authority for the establishment of the C.S. Naval Academy can be found in the section of an Act approved by the Confederate Congress on March 16th, 1861 "which provided that the naval laws of the United States not inconsistent with the act be applied to the navy of the Confederate States. ..."[194] However, the pressing demands commensurate with building the Navy of a new nation and of conducting the naval aspects of ongoing war delayed the actual opening of the academy until 1863. In March, Secretary Mallory laid the foundations of the school by an order for the examination by a board of officers of the acting midshipman at the several stations in seamanship, gunnery, mathematics, steam engineering, navigation, English studies, French, drawing and drafting.[195]

These exams were given to determine who among the 106 acting midshipmen would be chosen for entrance into the first class. Only fifty could be accepted because of the limiting space available to house the cadets.

The Academy was to be located in Richmond, on the C.S.S. *Patrick Henry* in the James River. The *Patrick Henry,* then the Yorktown, was built and launched in New York City in 1853 as a commercial paddle-wheel steamer. She was seized by the State of Virginia in 1861, along with her sister the *Jamestown*,[196] renamed the *Patrick Henry*, and transferred to the Confederate States Navy. She was moved to the Rockett's Navy Yard in Richmond, where an extensive refitting was done. Be-

---

194 *History of the Confederate States Navy*, Page 773
195 Ibid page 773
196 *Rebel Reefer, The Organization and Midshipman of the Confederate States Naval Academy*, page 7

Mark K. Vogl   123 —

sides, clearing the upper decks of commercial cabins, "one-inch iron plates [were] bolted to her sides extended two feet below the waterline…"[197] She mounted eight cannon in broadside and two pivot guns. After being converted to a warship, she was assigned to the James River Squadron and placed under the command of John Randolf Tucker.[198]

The C.S.S. *Patrick Henry* served with the C.S.S. *Virginia* during her engagement with the Yankee fleet on March 8th, 1862. The *Henry* suffered casualties when she attempted to accept the surrender of the U.S.S. *Congress*. The damage was so severe she had to be towed back to port. But she was repaired and back in action with the *Virginia* the following day, during the famous battle of the ironclads in Hampton Roads.[199] The C.S.S. *Patrick Henry* would be in several engagements and serve as the squadron flagship before being selected as the school ship for the Confederate Naval Academy in October 1863.

Lieutenant William Parker, C.S.N. was selected as commandant of the school, and wrote the regulations, approved by C.S. Naval Secretary Mallory, which would govern the academy. Lt. Parker was one of two brothers who served with United States Navy before secession. While Parker's brother remained in the Federal service, William H. Parker resigned his Federal commission, and sought his fate with the fledgling Confederacy.

William Parker had a successful and distinguished career in the US Navy. After entering at age 14, he attended Annapolis in 1841. He quickly gained recognition as a good officer and instructor and was assigned as the assistant professor of mathematics at the U.S. Naval Academy. His written works included Elements of Seamanship, Harbor Routine and Evolutions, Naval Tactics, and Remarks on the Navigation of the Coasts between San Francisco and Panama which were used as textbooks for both the Federal and Confederate naval academies.

During the opening years of the War for Southern Independence, Lt. Parker had served aboard ships fighting in the North Carolina waters, then commanded the gunboat C.S.S. *Beauregard* during the battles in Hampton's Roads, and finally as executive officer on the ironclad, C.S.S. *Palmetto State*, in Charleston.[200] Lt. Parker had a war record and

---

197 Ibid, page 8
198 Department of the Navy, Naval Historical Center, www.history.navy.mil/photos/sh-us-cs/csa-sh/csash-mr/pat-hnry.htm
199 Ibid
200 *The History of the Confederate States Navy*, page 773

a knowledge of academic life that well suited him to the task he had been assigned.

The rest of the staff included:[201]

Lt. W.B. Hall	Commandant of Midshipmen
Lt. Oscar F. Johnston	Professor of Astronomy, Navigation and Surveying
Lt. Thomas W.W. Davis	Assistant Gunnery
Lt. C. J. Graves	Professor of Seamanship
Lt. James W. Billups	Assistant
Lt. Wm Van Comstock	Instructor of Master George M. Peek
	Professor of Mathematics
Master George Armistead	Professor of Physics
Master Pepley	Professor of French and German
Mr. Sanxey*	Infantry Tactics
	**Sword Master
W.J. Addison	Assistant Surgeon
E.G. Hall	Second Asst. Engineer
James G. Bixley	Assistant Surgeon
Wm M. Ladd	Paymaster
Andrew Blakie	Boatswain
E.R. Johnson	Gunner
William Bennett	Sail Maker

* Mr. Sanxey is not provided a rank
** Information not provided

In addition, a number of Army officers were assigned to teach the liberal arts classes. With only minor changes, the staff of the academy remained intact for the last two years of the war.

The course work was extensive and divided into four parts, which under normal circumstances would have taken four years to complete. The studies included mathematics, sciences, geography and history, some languages (French and Spanish), navigation, surveying, classes on seamanship, gunnery, and a study of both infantry and naval tactics. Academic boards, sometimes comprised of visiting officers, held examinations in December and June. Midshipmen were moved along as quickly as they could grasp the skills being taught. The necessities of

---

201 List is provided in *The History of the Confederate States Navy*, page 774

war sustained a constant pressure for trained leaders. More than 180 cadets would attend the Confederate Naval Academy.[202]

To the extent possible, the organization and daily operation of the Richmond academy were modeled after the U.S. Naval Academy. Candidates could be nominated to the C.S. Naval Academy by either their respective Congressman or by President Davis. Prospective appointees had to be at least 14 years old but not more than 18. After passing physical and academic examinations, the nominee was accepted and designated an acting midshipman.

When the first fifty midshipmen reported in the fall of 1863, they represented some of the most respected families in the South. Among them would be the brother-in-law of President Davis, the sons of Admiral Raphael Semmes and General Breckenridge (former U.S. Vice President and future C.S. Secretary of War), and a nephew of General Robert E. Lee.

These acting midshipmen would be called "reefers," a term first used in the federal navy to identify those midshipmen who were new to the navy and had not yet passed their examinations. The new cadets were required to purchase their uniforms, bedding, and personal kit. All told, at least 184 cadets would become reefers at the Confederate States Naval Academy.[203]

The cadets would find a very structured daily routine. This routine, which guided almost every minute in a day, was established to mirror the routines on board a warship. A strict set of punishments for violations of discipline and regulations, ranging from demerits to confinement, were established and enforced. Midshipman could be dismissed from the Academy for either academic or disciplinary reasons.

The United States Naval Academy was removed from its location in Annapolis, Maryland to remote Rhode Island when the war started, but the southern Corps of Midshipmen lived, studied, and when necessary, fought in the eye of the hurricane. Many times, over the latter two years of the war, the midshipmen, as individuals, in groups, or as a Corps, they were called upon to defend Richmond, and to participate in a wide-ranging group of combat operations. The cadets would man some of the guns at Drewry's Bluff. They were also called upon to join

---

202 *Rebel Reefers, The Organization and Midshipman of the Confederate Naval Academy*, pages 111-118, Appendix A.
203 *Rebel Reefers, The Organization and Midshipman of the Confederate Naval Academy*, appendix A as compiled from several sources by James Lee Conrad.

the crews of the C.S.S. *Fredericksburg* and C.S.S. *Virginia II* in the James River Squadron. J. Thomas Scharf tells us that it was not uncommon for the midshipmen to be busily working at their academic studies one moment, and the next moment be manning a gun, either on land or aboard ship, facing a real enemy.

As 1864 began, Commander John Taylor Wood, nephew of President Davis, approached General Robert E. Lee with a daring plan designed to change the balance of power on the waterways of coastal North Carolina. This strategic area, which had been a target of Federal operations since 1862, was important because of its proximity to the rail lines feeding the Confederate capital and the Army of Northern Virginia. In response to Federal successes there, the Confederacy had begun an ironclad building program in the backwaters of North Carolina. The C.S.S. *Albemarle*, C.S.S. *Neuse*, and a third ironclad were being built there to challenge Federal naval supremacy in the area.

Commander Wood proposed to General Lee that a naval force be assembled in the vicinity of Kinston, North Carolina, with the purpose of traversing the rivers, to approach by stealth a Federal naval warship and capture it. The presumption was that the Federal sailors would be unprepared for a boarding party assault to take over the ship. This force would work in cooperation with a land assault against New Bern, a Federal operational and logistical center in eastern North Carolina. The plan was approved, and orders were sent to the Richmond, Wilmington, and Charleston Naval Squadrons to provide both the men and appropriate naval craft for the operation. The Confederate rail system would transport troops and the boats to the assembly area in North Carolina.

Commodore Forrest of the James River Squadron tasked the Confederate Naval Academy to provide eight midshipmen to participate in this operation. J. Thomas Scharf would be one of the eight. The others were Richard Slaughter, Paul H Gibbs, John B. Northrop, William F. Clayton, Henry S. Cooke, Daniel M. Lee, and Palmer Saunders.[204] Lt. Benjamin Loyall of the *Patrick Henry's* faculty was assigned as commander of the 40 men and four boats that would represent the James River Squadron's contribution to the mission. The men would take

---

204 *Rebel Reefers, The Organization of Midshipmen of the Confederate States Naval Academy*, page 61

their boats down the James River, then up the Appomattox River to Petersburg, where the men and boats would be loaded on a train and shipped south to Kinston, North Carolina, where they would meet the detachments from Wilmington and Charleston.

The force from Richmond arrived at Kinston on January 31, joining the forces from Charleston and Wilmington already in the assembly area. The boats were offloaded from the train and taken down to the river. The force from Charleston brought wide, flat-bottom boats and two cannon. These larger boats were difficult to transport from the railhead to the river, and Commander Forrest decided to leave with the twelve smaller boats and told Lt. Gift to come along as fast as he could. A meeting place for the two forces was established at Bachelor's Creek. Their objective was sixty miles down-stream.

When Gift's force finally caught up to Wood, the entire force was told the mission. This force was to attack and seize the U.S.S. *Underwriter* in support of General Pickett's attack on the Union forces in New Bern.[205]

The *Underwriter* was 325 tons, the largest Federal warship in the vicinity of New Bern. Her four guns included two eight-inch guns, one thirty-pound rifled cannon, and another twelve-pounder. The ship's complement was seventy-two.[206] The plan was to quietly approach the ship, board her, and capture her. Once captured, she would be maneuvered so as to use her guns against Federal fortifications in the area. She was presently anchored only a short distance from two Federal forts.

The operation began sometime after midnight on February 1st. Midshipman J. Thomas Scharf was present for the attack, and the following description is taken from his *History of the Confederate Navy*:

> ... Col. Wood had again launched his boats in the Neuse, and arranged them in two divisions, the first commanded by himself, and the second by Lt. B. P. Loyall. After forming parallel to each other, the two divisions pulled rapidly down-stream. When they had rowed a short distance, Col. Wood called all the boats together, final instructions were given, and this being through with, he offered a fervent prayer for the success of the mission. It was a strange and ghostly sight, the men resting on their oars with heads uncovered, the commander also bareheaded,

---

205 Ibid page 63
206 Ibid page 64

standing erect in the stern of his boat; the black waters rippling beneath; the dense overhanging clouds pouring down sheets of rain, and in the blackness beyond an unseen bell tolling as if from some phantom cathedral. The party listened- four peals were sounded, then they knew it was the bell of the Underwriter, *or some other of the gun boats, ringing out for two o'clock. Guided by the sound, the boats pulled toward the steamer, pistols, muskets and cutlasses in readiness. The advance was necessarily slow and cautious. Suddenly when about three hundred yards from the* Underwriter, *her hull loomed up out of the inky darkness. Through the stillness came the sharp ring of five bells for half-past two o'clock, and just as the echo died away, a quick nervous voice from the deck hailed,* "Boat ahoy!" *No answer was given, but Col. Wood kept steadily on.* "Boat ahoy! Boat ahoy!" *again shouted the watch. No answer. Then the rattle on board the steamer sprang summoning the men to quarters, and the Confederates could see the dim and shadowy outline of hurrying figures on deck. Nearer Col. Wood came shouting,* "Give way!" "Give Way, boys, give way!" *repeated Lieut. Loyall and the respective boat commanders, and give way they did with a will. The few minutes that followed were those of terrible suspense. To retreat was impossible, and if the enemy succeeded in opening fire on the boats with his heavy guns all was lost.*[207]

There had been a plan that one division of boats would board the *Underwriter* forward, the other division aft. But as happens so often in tactical operations, the plan was modified by the river current, the dark, the different speeds of the boats, and movement of Underwriter which caused the majority to reach the forward section, a smaller group to come up on the ship aft, and Col. Wood's boat to strike the ship amidship.

As the Confederates approached, Midshipman Scharf, who was in command of one of the boat howitzers, was ordered to commence fire. Scharf's crew got one shot off before his comrades closed on the ship and began boarding.

As the Confederates climbed aboard, the Federals had massed near the wheelhouse and [208] poured a volley after volley into the boarders rowing toward them.

In spite of the heavy fire, the boarders were cool and yet eager, now

---

207 *History of the Confederate States Navy,* page 398
208 *History of the Confederate States Navy,* page 398

and then one or more were struck down, but the rest never faltered. When the boats struck the sides of the *Underwriter* grapnels were thrown on board, and the Confederates were soon scrambling, with cutlass and pistol in hand, to the deck with a rush and a wild cheer, that rung across the waters, the firing from the enemy never ceasing for one moment. The brave Lieut. B. P. Loyall was the first to reach the deck, with Engineer Emmet F. Gill, and Col. Wood at his side."

The firing at this time became so hot that it did not seem possible that more than half the Confederates would escape with their lives. Col. Wood, with bullets whistling around him, issued orders as coolly and unconcerned as if the enemy had not even been in sight. All fought well. There was no halting, no cowardice; every man stood at his post and did his duty.[209]

Scharf cites the C.S. Marine Detachment under Captain Thomas S. Wilson with conspicuous gallantry. Scharf says they worked as a team securing the hurricane deck. The shattering clang of cutlasses and empty pistols engaged in hand-to-hand combat filled the entire main deck. As more and more boarders got on the ship, the Confederates began to take control, though the fighting was vicious. The decks were slippery with blood. Exhausted men fell, not from wounds but for need of rest. Once broken, groups of Federals would be pushed pell-mell down the gangways to the lower decks. The Federals did not surrender easily, the fighting continued through steerage, the wardroom and even the coalbunkers. But eventually the numbers of the Confederates simply overwhelmed the resistance. The Confederates lost six killed, including Midshipman Saunders, and twenty-two wounded.

The *Underwriter* was taken, but Federals in the Forts Anderson and Stevenson had been alerted, and the heavy guns were only a short distance away. The Confederates scrambled to slip their cables and get the ship underway. The Yankee guns began firing, one round exploding on the deck. Yankee wounded were exposed to the fire. The ship was anchored both aft and stern, and the Rebels were unable to slip the cables. The steam was down; the machinery was partially damaged due to the fight and then the shelling by the Yankee guns. Col. Wood determined they could not get the ship out of range before she would be blown to pieces, so he decided to fire the ship and abandon it.

---

[209] *History of the Confederate States Navy*, page 398 - 399

Scharf writes:

The Confederate wounded and those of the enemy were carefully removed to the boats alongside, the guns were loaded and pointed towards the town, fire was applied from the boilers, pointed towards the town, fire was applied from the boilers, and in five minutes after the boarders left, the Underwriter *was a mass of flames from stem to stern. ...*[210]

The Confederates, using the burning ship to hide them from the Yankee guns, withdrew the way they came, up river. They moved eight miles upstream to Swift Creek, where they pulled in to lick their wounds. While at this location, they learned that Pickett's attack had failed, and he had withdrawn from the field. The force would continue back to Kinston where they would return to their various posts.

As the fall of Richmond approached, the midshipmen of the Confederate States Naval Academy were about to begin their most important assignment. At 10:40 a.m. on April 2nd, 1865, a telegram arrived in the C.S. War Department. General Lee had written to Secretary of War Breckenridge:

I see no prospect of doing more than holding my position here till night. I am not certain that I can do that ... I advise that all preparations be made for leaving Richmond to-night. ...
R. E. Lee[211]

President Davis and his Cabinet were not prepared to surrender the Confederacy as a result of the loss of Richmond. Plans were executed to move the government west, possibly to the Department of Trans-Mississippi. Relocating the government required moving the actual assets of the Confederate Treasury Department. And, moving the gold, silver, and other assets required a guard that could be trusted. On April 2nd, 1865, Lt. Parker was directed to move his Corps of Midshipmen to the Danville train depot.[212]

When the Corps arrived, they found "eight wagonloads of money in chests, bags, and barrels, all with fresh official Confederate seals affixed

---
210 *History of the Confederate States Navy*, page 400
211 *The Long Surrender*, page 19
212 *History of the Confederate States Navy*, page 777

by Quarles."[213] The estimate of the amount at the time was about half a million dollars. In addition, there were millions in Confederate bonds and notes, and 16 to 18,000 pounds sterling in "Liverpool Acceptances". And, there were deposits from Richmond's banks also placed on the same train. The private monies were kept separate, on a different train car, from the government assets that were all placed in one car. The "treasure train" was to follow immediately behind the President's.[214] The middies now took control of the security for the entire depot while the trains awaited departure.

President Davis waited near the telegraph at the depot office. He still hoped that Marse Robert would pull off just one more miracle and somehow turn back the Yankee tide. But alas, the telegraph was silent, and at 11 p.m. on April 2nd, the President of the Confederacy boarded his train. It departed almost immediately.

In the distance could be heard the sound of explosions. The cordon around the depot maintained by the Naval Corps was collapsed on order of Lt. Parker so that a tighter circle around the remaining train, more easily observed and reinforced, was created. A crowd began to grow, made up mostly of the South's less-desirable elements. Government storehouses were being looted. Chaos ruled the City of Richmond.

Just before midnight, a crowd made a half-hearted attempt to seize the "treasure train," but when the midshipmen held their ground, and Parker ordered them to prepare to fire on the crowd … well, ambitions and late-night courage evaporated, and the crowd dispersed.

At about midnight, the treasure train began to lurch forward and the middies jumped aboard as the train pulled out of the depot.

But this was not to be the last train to leave Richmond, nor was it to be the last train carrying the Confederate States Navy. Admiral Raphael Semmes who had returned from England after losing the C.S.S. *Alabama* in an uneven fight with the U.S.S. *Kearsarge* off the coast of France, had been given command of the James River Squadron in the final days of the war.

---

213 *The Long Surrender*, page 25 Quarles, refers to Mann S. Quarles, the youngest of the Treasury Clerks, and the only one to remain with the Confederate Treasury as panic resulted from the news that the government would be abandoning Richmond.
214 Ibid

Admiral Semmes had seen personally to the details of destroying the squadron and had stepped ashore only moments before his flagship exploded. With some 500 sailors and officers, Semmes was determined to escape the Yankees. But he knew his men were no match for a long march. So, he went to the depot looking for transport. What he found were a few scattered cars. He was told the last train had just departed carrying the Confederate government.

But then an old steam engine was found by some of his sailors. Semmes, quick to action, ordered his sailors to clear all the civilians off the scattered cars, by bayonet if must be, and then by hand roll the cars together to form a train. The marines that were with Semmes were directed to cut down wooden fences to make firewood for the engine. The Admiral and a few more mechanically-minded fellows went to the old engine to see what could be done. All the while the sounds of a dying city, rampaging populous, and an approaching victorious Yankee Army filled the night air.

It took some doing, but finally, the engine was coaxed into action. The cars were first loaded with Semmes' 500, and then civilians were allowed as space provided. The engine began to move … and another train, the last Confederate train, left Richmond. The train crossed a bridge placing a river between Semmes and the blue columns that were engulfing Richmond. The fires of the city provided sufficient illumination to see the progress of the occupying forces. But then, as the train began to approach its first slope, its movement slowed and then stopped. No amount of stoking could provide sufficient power to the little locomotive to haul the weight of those cars up that first hill. Again, it seemed as if the end were near.

A little way down the track, miraculously another engine was found. It had been hidden by some engineers before they fled Richmond. It was backed up to Semmes train, hooked, and together the two engines pulled the train away. As the trained peaked the hill and began down-hill, it gained speed. Admiral Semmes had escaped again![215]

In the late afternoon of April 3rd, the Confederate government reached Danville, 140 miles from Richmond. On the 4th, the offices of the Confederate treasury opened with the Parker's middies still providing the security. Three days later, the Treasury with its escort re-board-

---

215 Ibid page 39

ed its train to head south through Greensboro for Charlotte, North Carolina, its new home. Before leaving Danville, an inventory of the funds was completed and it showed $327,022.90, a far cry from the estimated 500,000 – 600,000 that was supposed to be aboard. While some disbursements had been made in Danville, the tally seemed false.[216]

Meanwhile, in Danville, on about 5 April, Admiral Semmes had finally arrived with his sailors. President Davis immediately commissioned Semmes a brigadier general in the Confederate States Army so that he could take charge of the defenses of Danville. President Davis was still convinced the war could be fought and won. He received encouraging news from General Lee as to the condition and progress of his Army.

For Admiral Semmes, it was a special day as he was re-united with his 13-year-old son, who was a midshipman.

In Charlotte, Lt. Parker would pick up Mrs. Varina Davis, the First Lady of the Confederacy, and move on to Chester. Here, the Treasury and Mrs. Davis would be offloaded onto wagons for the next phase of the journey. Lt. Parker and the middies would remain with the Treasury as the guards.

For almost a month, Lt. Parker and the midshipmen would remain as guards for the Confederate Treasury and Mrs. Davis. They would move through North Carolina, South Carolina, and into Georgia, where they would finally part with what was left of the Confederate treasury on May 2nd, 1863. Each midshipman was given forty dollars in gold as they started for their homes.[217]

---

216 Ibid page 53
217 *History of the Confederate States Navy*, page 779

Chapter Nine —

The Confederate States Marine Corps

The Confederate Congress authorized the formation of the Confederate States Marine Corps (C.S.M.C.) on March 16th, 1861, and amended the authorization on May 20th so as to authorize the following force structure:

1 Colonel, Commandant of the C.S.M.C.
1 Lieutenant Colonel
1 Major
1 Quartermaster with the rank of major
1 Adjutant with the rank of major
1 Sergeant Major
1 Quartermaster Sergeant
10 Captains
10 First Lieutenants
20 Second Lieutenants
40 Sergeants
40 Corporals
840 Privates
10 drummers
10 fifers
2 musicians [218]

The Corps was to have the same duties as that of the Yankee Marine Corps. Detachments would serve aboard Confederate ships and provide security for naval stations and harbor facilities.

Just as in the army and navy, Southern men serving in the United States Marine Corps tendered their resignations and headed south. The following officers offered their service to the Confederate government:[219]

Major Henry B. Tyler (Virginia)
Brevet Major George H. Terret (Virginia)
Captain Robert Tansill (Virginia)

---

218 *History of the Confederate States Navy*, page 769
219 Ibid page 770 All but Captain Tansill and Lt. Turner served in the C.S.M.C.

Captain Algernon S. Taylor (Virginia)
Captain John D. Simms (Virginia)
First Lieutenant Israel Greene (Virginia)
First Lieutenant John K. H. Tatnall (Georgia)
First Lieutenant Julius E. Meire (Maryland)
First Lieutenant George P. Turner (Virginia)
First Lieutenant Thomas S. Wilson (Missouri)
First Lieutenant Andrew J. Hayes (Alabama)
First Lieutenant Adam N. Baker (Florida)
Second Lieutenant George Holmes (Florida)
Second Lieutenant Calvin L. Sayre (Alabama)
Second Lieutenant Henry L. Ingraham (South Carolina)
Second Lieutenant Baker K. Howell (Mississippi)

These men gathered in Richmond and were joined by about 100 enlisted men who had left the Yankee Marine Corps to serve their Confederacy. This group of men and all but two of the officers comprised the foundation of what would become the C.S.M.C. Scharf writes,

> *There had been no concert of action by which so many of the former men and officers of the U.S. marine corps were assembled at Richmond, but it was not an unfortunate accident for the Confederacy that they did come together at this time.*[220]

Colonel Lloyd J. Beall, formerly of the United States Army, was appointed as Commandant. Richard Taylor Allison was commissioned as a major and appointed paymaster. Henry R. Taylor was commissioned as a Lieutenant Colonel. The Corps was organized in Richmond and remained whole until the summer of 1862. Detachments from the Corps were then made to various ports and ships. One of the Marine Companies under Captain Thom was sent to Pensacola to provide the installation guard. When the Confederates withdrew from Pensacola, Thom's company was re-assigned to Virginia.[221]

One squad of marines was assigned to the C.S.S. *Virginia* and manned one of the guns during the two-day battle in Hampton Roads.

---

220 Ibid page 770
221 Ibid page 37

The squad, along with Captain R. Thom, remained aboard the *Virginia* until its demise.[222]

A detachment of marines under the command of 1st Lt. Howell was assigned to the C.S.S. *Sumter* under the command of Captain Rafael Semmes. J. Thomas Scharf credits the *Sumter* with 18 captures before she was finally bottled up in Gibraltar. Howell and his detachment would then be transferred with Captain Semmes and many of the officers and crew to the C.S.S. *Alabama*. Upon the sinking of the *Alabama* on June 14, 1864, Howell returned to the Confederacy where he served along the southern coast.

Marines served with Admiral Buchanan on the C.S.S. *Tennessee*. Commanded by Lt. David G. Raney, the marines worked one of the guns and were credited with "quick and efficient work. ..."[223] A second group of marines under the command of Lt. J. R. T. Fendall served on the C.S.S. *Gaines* during the Battle of Mobile.

In October 1864, Colonel Beall submitted a report to the Confederate Congress. In that report, he stated that the Confederate States Marine Corps included a total strength of 539 men, of which 64 were presently prisoners of war. Colonel Beall went on to report:

The marine corps is distributed at the following naval stations; Mobile, Savannah, Charleston, Wilmington, and Drewry's Bluff; also on board three iron-clad steamers in the James River, and as guards at the Richmond navy yards. Marine guards have been assigned to the Tallahassee *and* Chickamauga, *destined to operate against the enemy's commerce on the sea.*[224]

Marines, under the command of Captain A.C. Van Bethuysen, served at Ft. Fisher, North Carolina during the battles of December 24th and 25th, and January 5th, 1865.[225]

In the final days of the Confederacy, the marines stationed in and around Richmond were incorporated into the Naval Brigade, which was then assigned Lee's Army of Northern Virginia. The Naval Brigade

---

222 Ibid 771
223 Ibid 772
224 Ibid, page 779
225 Ibid 772, also serving at Ft. Fisher were Lts. Henry H. Doak, and J. Campbell Murdoch

as a whole, and the marines specifically, were mentioned for their bravery at the Battle of Saylors Creek.

Because of the unique missions of the C.S.M.C. and the loss of Colonel Beall's records due to fire, it is impossible to provide a complete summary or accurate portrayal of the work done or the sacrifices made by these brave patriots. Suffice it to say, their history and valor as an organization is interwoven within both the Confederate States Navy and the Confederate States Army.

Flag of the Confederate States Marine Corps

Chapter Ten —

The Confederate Naval Torpedo Service

The pursuit of the technologies required to deploy effective torpedoes is an excellent example of Secretary Mallory's strategy of embracing developing technology as a counter-balance to the mass which the Federals could bring to bear in the naval battle. This area of Confederate military operations has been called the most secret of the entire war effort.[226]

Initial efforts by Confederates to use torpedoes in the Potomac River and in Hampton Roads in 1861 failed. But the idea of using a floating bomb with a variety of fusing devices was here to stay.

In January and February 1862, in places as far apart as Savannah Harbor and Columbus, Kentucky, the Federals discovered different types of Confederate torpedoes. Generally speaking, a torpedo was a device composed of a container filled with an explosive and some type of fuse. Torpedoes could be used as either land or sea mines. If the torpedo were deployed in water, the container had to be waterproof. Normally, the torpedo was detonated either by percussion cap or through an electric device. Torpedoes could be stationary, held in its position by some kind of anchor, or free-floating, moving with the tide. Torpedoes could be above the surface or just below. Torpedoes could also be carried by submarines, partially submerged ships, and light, small boats on extended spars.

The use of torpedoes was a controversial topic within Confederate ranks. When General Rains attempted to deploy torpedoes on land, along roads etc., Generals Joseph E. Johnston and Longstreet opposed the use of torpedoes because of their remoteness to actual combat and their deceptive character. Confederacy policy allowed the use of torpedoes on parapets or on roads, and in rivers and harbors to drive off Federal ships.

October 1862, the Confederate Congress established two agencies to supervise the development and use of torpedoes. Though instrumental in the first use of mine technology on the Yorktown Peninsula against McClellan's forces, Brigadier General G.J. Rains was not immediately appointed head of the Confederate Torpedo Bureau. In

---

226 Phillip Van Doren Stern, *Secret Missions of the Civil War*, page 207

December 1862, Rains was appointed Chief of the Bureau of Conscription, though he was placed on special duty and sent to assist with the preparation of defenses of Vicksburg. From there, he was sent to Savannah, Charleston, and Mobile to assist with the integration of torpedoes in their defensive schemes.[227] And, Captain M.F. Maury was selected to head the Naval Submarine Battery Service.[228] Richmond, Charleston, Savannah, Wilmington, and Mobile were selected as locations for Torpedo stations. Sub-stations were established at other locations.

The Confederate Congress approved legislation that rewarded the inventor of a torpedo that successfully sank an enemy vessel. The reward was 20 percent of the value of the ship sunk.[229] The monies were to be disbursed through the Department of the Navy. The men who entered the Torpedo Corps were sworn to secrecy. Scharf tells us that because of the hazardous nature of the work, the men were "granted extraordinary privileges."[230]

Union Ships attacked by Confederate torpedoes
Source: *History of the Confederate States Navy*, page 768

PLACE	VESSEL	DATE	REMARKS
Yazoo River, Ms.	U.S.S. *Cairo*	Dec. 12, '62	Sunk
Ogeechee River	U.S.S. *Montauk*	Feb. 28, '63	Serious Damage
Yazoo River, Ms.	U.S.S. *Baron De Kalb*	Jul. 22, '63	Sunk
James River, Va.	U.S.S. *Com. Barney*	Aug. 8, '63	Damaged
James River, Va.	*John Farron*	Sep. 8, '63	Damaged
Charleston, SC	U.S.S. *New Ironside*	Oct. 5, '63	Damaged
Charleston, SC	U.S.S. *Housantonic*	Feb. 17, '64	Sunk
St. John's River	*Maple Leaf*	Apr. 1, '64	Sunk
Newport News, Va.	U.S.S. *Minnesota*	Apr. 9, '64	Damaged
St. John's River	*General Hunter*	Apr. 15, '64	Sunk
Red River, La.	U.S.S. *Eastport*	Apr. 15, '64	Sunk
James River, Va.	U.S.S. *Com. Jones*	May 6, '64	Sunk
St. John's River	*H. A. Weed*	May 9, '64	Sunk
St. John's River	*Alice Price*	Jun. 19, '64	Sunk

---

227 "The Confederate General," Volume V, page 71
228 "History of the Confederate States Navy," page 753
229 This is just another example of the use of the "profit motive" by the Confederate Government to encourage activity in the commercial sector which would supplement or support government war making capabilities.
230 "History of the Confederate States Navy," page 753

Mobile Bay, Al.	U.S.S. *Tecumseh*	Aug. 5, '64	Sunk
James River, Va.	*Greyhound*	Nov. 27, '64	Sunk
Mobile Bay, Al.	U.S.S. *Narcissus*	Dec. 7, '64	Sunk
Roanoke River	U.S.S. *Otsego*	Dec. 9, '64	Sunk
Roanoke River	U.S.S. *Bazely*	Dec. 10, '64	Sunk
Roanoke River	*Launch No.5*	Dec. 10, '64	Sunk
Charleston, SC	U.S.S. *Patapsco*	Jan. 15, '65	Sunk
Cape Fear River	U.S.S. *Osceola*	Feb. 20, '65	Slight damage
Cape Fear River	Launch, *Shawmut*	Feb. 20, '65	Sunk
Georgetown, SC	*Harvest-Moon*	Mar. 1, '65	Sunk
Cape Fear River	*Thorn*	Mar. 4, '65	Sunk
Blakely River	U.S.S. *Althea*	Mar. 12, '65	Sunk
Charleston, SC	*Bibb*	Mar. 17, '65	Slight damage
Charleston, SC	U.S.S. *Massachusetts*	Mar. 20, '65	Slight damage
Blakely River	U.S.S. *Milwaukee*	Mar. 28, '65	Sunk
Blakely River	U.S.S. *Osage*	Mar. 29, '65	Sunk
Blakely River	U.S.S. *Randolph*	Apr. 1, '65	Sunk
Blakely River	*Ida*	Apr. 13, '65	Sunk
Mobile Bay, Al.	U.S.S. *Scioto*	Apr. 14, '65	Sunk
Blakely River	*Cincinnati*	Apr. 14, '65	Sunk
Mobile Bay, Al.	U.S.S. *Itasca*	Apr. 14, '65	Sunk
Mobile Bay, Al.	U.S.S. *Rose*	Apr. 14, '65	Sunk
Alabama River	*St. Mary's*	Apr. 14, '65	Sunk
Mobile Bay, Al.	RB *Hamilton*	Apr. 14, '65	Sunk
Ashley River, SC	U.S.S. *Jonquil*	Jun. 6, '65	Serious damage

On December 12th, 1862, a Federal squadron of five ships, including the U.S.S. *Cairo, Pittsburgh, Marmora, Signal*, and *Queen of the West* were operating on the Yazoo River. The Confederates had positioned a series of command-detonated torpedoes in the river and began detonating them as the Federal ships approached. The first two explosions were harmless, but the third torpedo went off directly under the *Cairo's* bow, below the waterline. Within 12 minutes, the *Cairo* was sunk.[231] The U.S.S. *Cairo* was the first Federal ship of the war to be sunk by a torpedo.

The *Cairo* was a 560-ton ironclad warship.[232] Its sinking by a single

---
231 *History of the Confederate States Navy*, page 753
232 US Department of the Navy, Naval Historical Center, www.history.navy.mil/photos/sh-usn/usnsh-c/cairo.htm

torpedo proved the lethality of this new technology. For the South, this new weapon added a new relatively inexpensive dimension to the war for control of the rivers and ports of the Confederacy!

Torpedoes were deployed for at least two different purposes. First, as with the *Cairo*, the torpedoes were deployed with the intention of sinking or damaging an enemy vessel The torpedo was placed along a navigable route, with no obvious sign of its presence, in the hopes that an enemy vessel would come along and strike it. A second potential use was to create a known hazard that would channel enemy ships into a kill zone for other weapons systems. This tactic is clearly demonstrated at the Battle of Mobile Bay, where a combination of mines and underwater pikes were deployed to drive attacking ships into the fire of Fort Morgan. Ships that did not heed the hazard, like the U.S.S. *Tecumseh* at Mobile, demonstrated to their peers the foolishness of colliding with one of the Southern torpedoes.

An excellent example of the Confederacy's strategy to develop technologies to offset the tremendous Union advantage in material assets was the combination of submersible or partially submersible craft with the torpedo.

The first work done on submarines in the Confederacy was done in New Orleans by a combination of private investors and inventors who hoped to take advantage of the legislation passed by the Confederate Congress designed to provide economic incentive for privateers to attack Federal naval shipping. The *Pioneer* was the first submarine constructed in the South. It underwent several tests, sinking a target barge, to demonstrate its lethality against a floating craft. The *Pioneer* had a crew of three and was propelled through and under the water by arms strength. Two of the three-crew members provided motion by turning a crank that spun the propeller. The *Pioneer* was issued a Letter of Marque by the Confederate government but sank before it could be employed against the Federal fleet attacking New Orleans.

The developers of the *Pioneer* moved to Mobile when New Orleans fell. They began work on a new, larger submarine, the *Hunley*. This new craft was much larger, forty feet long, and carrying a crew of up to nine. Again, the means of propelling the vessel through or under the water was human arm strength. The craft could make three knots under this means of propulsion. The *Hunley's* initial mode of attack was to tow a torpedo towards the intended target. The *Hunley* would submerge, dive under the target, and literally drag the torpedo into the victim. The *Hunley* would be on the opposite side of the hull of the target when the torpedo would explode, shielding the submarine from any adverse effects of the blast.

Trial runs were made in Mobile Bay, and at least one crew was killed.

The *Hunley* was transported to Charleston, South Carolina via railroad, on flat cars, as a result of orders by General Beauregard.[233] Once in Charleston, tests continued, and several more crews were lost. As a result, Beauregard ordered that the *Hunley* cease its dives and instead be used as surface torpedo craft. This required a change in the mode of attack. A spar would have to be added, and the *Hunley* would now act as a ram, driving or placing its weapon against the target's hull. The torpedo itself would be filled with 90 pounds of gunpowder.

Confederate ingenuity continued to play a role in the eventual combat use of the *Hunley*. Because of the great distance in terms of miles, from the Charleston wharf to the Federal blockading fleet, and the need to preserve human strength for the final rush towards the target, the *Hunley* would work in concert with the C.S.S. *David*,[234] a partially submerged torpedo boat, which would tow the *Hunley* from the wharf to a location outside Charleston Harbor within sight of the blockaders. This trip was made several times, but each time weather or adverse tides prevented the *Hunley* from executing the attack.[235]

Finally, on the afternoon of February 17th, 1864, conditions were right for an attack. Lt. George Dixon, of the Confederate States Army, commanded the *Hunley* as she set off. James Tomb, an Assistant Engineer, commanding the C.S.S. *David* advised Lt. Dixon that the Confederate States Navy was not conducting the operation.[236] When the two craft separated, probably sometime after 7 p.m., the *Hunley* was about two miles from its intended target, the U.S.S. *Housatonic*.

---

233 *Divided Waters,* page 406
234 The C.S.S. *David* had made an attack against the U.S.S *New Ironsides*, severely damaging her.
235 *Divided Waters,* page 406
236 Ibid

Figure 5 – C.S.S. *Hunley*
Image was provided by the US Department of Navy, Naval Historical Center

The Union fleet had been on a higher alert since the attack by the C.S.S. *David*. Admiral Dahlgren, U.S.N., had ordered all monitor class ships to have picket boats set out to watch for more torpedo boat attacks. In addition, heavy iron netting was draped over the sides of vessels to catch any spar torpedoes. And as a final precaution, ships were encouraged to anchor in shallower water to facilitate recovery should the vessel be successfully attacked.[237]

The *Hunley* approached quietly, with only her two conning towers protruding above the water-line. During her approach, she was spotted by a deck officer, an alarm was rung, and some small arms fire was discharged on the approaching submarine, but nothing could be done to prevent the attack. At approximately 8:45 p.m., the *Hunley's* torpedo was detonated, creating a huge hole in the hull of the *Housatonic*. While the Yankee ship sank rapidly, only five of 158 crewmen were lost.

But the *Hunley* vanished without a trace. Whether the concussion from the explosion, so near her fragile hull, opened a leak or the ship was carried out to sea could not be known. She had lost her sixth crew.

---

237 Ibid.

Torpedo boats were yet another way to deploy torpedoes against Union ships. As we have seen in the *Hunley* story, the C.S.S. *David*, a partially submerged craft, had successfully attacked the U.S.S. *New Ironsides*. The *Ironsides*, the largest ship in the Federal fleet, though not sunk, was damaged so severely that she had to be taken out of the line for a year to effect structural repairs.

Torpedo boats were a light, relatively inexpensive means to counter the much heavier Federal ships. They were powered by steam engines, and thus even when partially submerged, were tied to the surface because of their need for oxygen to burn.

In Richmond, a squadron of four torpedo boats C.S.S. *Squib, Wasp, Hornet,* and *Scorpion*, built at the Rocketts Navy Yard, operated under the command of Lt. "Savez" Read. They participated in the Battle of Trent's Reach, as a kind of advanced party, responsible for opening the barrier in the river so that the ironclads could move down the James River to attack the Federal squadron.

On April 9, 1864, the C.S.S. *Squib*, commanded by Lt. Hunter Davidson, made its way down the James River, passed through the Federal fleet during the dark of night, and eventually attacked the U.S.S. *Minnesota*, flagship of the James River Squadron. The mine exploded too near the waterline to cause serious damage.[238]

Wars are fought on many dimensions. Three of the most important dimensions are national will, money, and manpower. The development of the torpedo and the means to deliver it addressed all three. Where the South had little money or resource to build large conventional warships, they had the ingenuity and the strategic insight to push a new technology to its limits. Each time a torpedo successfully sank a Union vessel, it cost the north tens of thousands of dollars. The deployment of torpedoes was not overly dependent on manpower, but the potential cost to the enemy was fairly high in terms of trained sailors. And finally, the creation of a new lethal hazard weakened the will of commanders and helped create a perception in the north of those "infernal Southern scoundrels" who will do anything to win.

---

238 *Sea Hawk of the Confederacy*, page 159

Chapter Eleven —

Conclusion

In conclusion, I would like to deal with many of the misconceptions about the Confederate leadership and the issues related to naval warfare. Some of these misconceptions were created or strongly supported by influential Southern historians themselves.[239] Others are a result of a bias by those who write history from the "winning side" perspective. And still, others have been perpetuated simply by the lack of available published material on the subject. The disparity between the number of Union and Confederate veterans who fought in the armies, as opposed to the navies, also helped to minimize the telling of the accurate roles of both the Confederate and Union navies until recently. In any event, I believe that, as inadequate and incomplete as this summary is, it clearly demonstrates that the national and naval leadership, and those who worked on Research and Development (R & D) of new naval technologies, were well aware of the strategic importance of the navy and worked diligently to meet the challenge presented them. Did the South suffer from a shortage of industrial where-with-all … absolutely! But like the renowned armies of the Confederacy, the men associated with the Southern naval effort adapted to their nation's position of inferiority with ingenuity, daring, cunning, and a resolute commitment to the Cause.

In 1888, E.A. Pollard, in his complete history of the war titled *The Lost Cause,* was harsh in his criticism of his government, claiming the Davis administration did not appreciate the importance of constructing a strong navy.[240] However, Admiral Porter, U.S.N., held a very different opinion of the Confederacy's efforts. In an essay describing Union operations against New Orleans in 1862, he writes, "The energy and

---

239 *The Lost Cause*, page 191, Pollard writing of the US Navy, "The Federals had one immense and peculiar advantage in the war; and they were prompt to use it." This is the first sentence in his section titled Naval Operations in 1861. In Chapter 2 we reviewed the true size and operational readiness of the US Navy, and found only 42 commissioned ships, and most of these were deployed far from America.

240 *The Lost Cause*, page 192, "In no respect was the improvidence of this Government more forcibly illustrated than in the administration of its naval affairs; or its unfortunate choice of ministers more signally displayed that in its selection as Secretary of the Navy of Mr. Mallory of Florida. …"

forethought displayed by the South seems marvelous when compared to the North during the same period of time. ..." The Admiral goes on to say that the Federals did not have one ironclad in the fleet that conducted the operations against New Orleans and says they were only motivated to act with conviction on the issue of building ironclads after the Battle at Hampton Roads.[241]

J. Thomas Scharf in *The History of the Confederate Navy* is also highly critical of the government's lack of energy and direction with respect to naval affairs. And given that this voluminous history was published almost simultaneous to Pollard's *The Lost Cause*, the Confederate government received critical evaluations on their Naval efforts in two very powerful works done by Southern authors and published within months of one another.

But as we have seen, the Confederate government, both Provisional and once moved to Richmond, were acutely aware of the importance of naval affairs. The Provisional Confederate Congress, as one of its early acts, created a Committee on Naval Affairs. And President Davis immediately sent Raphael Semmes to the northeast ports of New York and Boston as a purchasing agent to procure ships and any other materials that could assist in the creation of a Confederate Navy. And again, I would refer to Admiral Porter's own words, where he describes an appreciation for the work done by the Confederates in New Orleans to have two ironclads (C.S.S. *Manassas* and C.S.S. *Louisiana*) available for service.

While both Scharf and Pollard have done yeoman work in giving us wonderful, broad, heavily researched accounts representing some of the first comprehensive writings of the Southern views on the war, I would submit that as more and more is researched and written about the Confederate Navy, the appreciation for the efforts of all concerned will rise. One great hamstring to this process will be the loss of so many Confederate Naval Records. But, much has already been done, and it is merely a matter of presenting this information to the serious student body of the "late unpleasantness" which will eventually reverse the opinion of the state of the Confederacy's Naval Affairs.

---

241 "Our Cake is all dough," *Battles and Leaders of the Civil War*, Page 126

The views of Northern writers or writers from the perspective of the victorious Union (who were not present to fight the Confederate Navy) have also helped to limit an appreciation of the South's naval prowess. Some examples that are easy to demonstrate would include the persistent habit of many to refer to the ironclads' Battle at Hampton Roads as the "*Monitor* and *Merrimac*,"[242] when the Southern ship was commissioned the C.S.S. *Virginia*. And, many histories allude to these ships as the first ironclads (presenting the concept of parallel development of ironclads) when in fact the C.S.S. *Manassas* was the first American ironclad to become operational and the first to engage the enemy.

Again, I must cite Admiral Porter's work, where he states clearly that the North had to be pushed into developing ironclads, after the scare the C.S.S. *Virginia* gave the Lincoln administration. Whether President Davis, Secretary Mallory, and others were farsighted, or whether "necessity was the mother of invention" can be debated. What cannot be debated is the Confederate government's enthusiasm for the development of a new class of ships capable of offsetting the tremendous numerical advantage the Union built up once the war began in earnest.

The Confederacy's understanding of the importance of technology in naval affairs is even further demonstrated when one considers the pioneer work done in the fields of torpedoes, submarines, and partially submerged craft. Again, the circumstances of the South, specifically with regard to financial resources and industrial capacity, encouraged Southern policy-makers and inventors to work together to offset the stated Northern advantages. In both of these fields, the Confederacy led the way; the U.S.S. *Cairo* being the first ship sunk by a torpedo, and the U.S.S. *Housatonic* being the first ship sunk by a submarine, the C.S.S. *Hunley*.

In addition, when one considers that any inclusion of naval events would ultimately lead the interested student to the sympathies for the South exhibited in the Caribbean Islands, and in England and France and other European nations, one might start to wonder about the fidelity of international friendships long assumed to be unblemished. And then there would also have to be a consideration of the various unlawful acts of the Federal Navy, including the affair in Bahai, Brazil where

---

242 *This Hallowed Ground*, page 68, In his description Mr. Catton never address the Confederate ship as the C.S.S. *Virginia*.

the C.S.S. *Florida* was attacked and captured while at anchor with her guns unloaded as prescribed by the port's rules and regulations.

In Bruce Catton's *This Hallowed Ground*, the author completely fails to mention an important aspect of the mission of the *Star of the West* with respect to Fort Sumter in the spring of 1861. Instead, Mr. Catton tells of the plight of the Federal soldiers within the fort. He tells of their limited food supplies, and writes, "Mr. Lincoln sent a messenger to tell the governor of South Carolina that Washington meant no particular harm but that a cargo of food for Sumter's garrison would be coming down directly..." [243] He then indicates that the local Southern authorities decided to bombard Fort Sumter before the additional food supplies could arrive.

What Mr. Catton fails to mention is that the *Star of the West* carried not only food but also 200 reinforcements to help man Fort Sumter! And how important were these reinforcements? Mr. Catton writes that because of the weak force manning Ft. Sumter, the Confederates could have taken the fort anytime. He also says bluntly, "There was no war. As far as the government was concerned, the men in Sumter had not an enemy in the world. Yet they were in fact besieged. ..."[244] The official calendar of the war, published as a part of Battles and Commanders by the United States War Department in 1906 does not mention the firing on the Star of the West on April 11th by cadets of THE CITADEL, instead, beginning the War on April 12th with the bombardment of Fort Sumter. Is it the position of the U.S. government that firing on a Federal ship, loaded with reinforcements and supplies, is not an act of war?[245]

Catton's version of the story seems to portray the South as pitiless, and itching for a fight, when told that a mere 85 Yankee soldiers held Fort Sumter, and were running out of food. He too forgets to inform the reader of Lincoln's attempt to reinforce Sumter under the guise of re-supply. The Lincoln Administration's use of deception and guile to help create a situation where General Beauregard and the Southern policy-makers felt compelled to act before the Union could strengthen their position on Southern soil was important to building the perception that it was the South and not the North who wanted war.

Mr. Catton does not mention the Confederate Navy at Island No.

---

243 *This Hallowed Ground*, page 21
244 *This Hallowed Ground*, page 21
245 *Battles and Commanders*, page xv

10, and instead refers to "a makeshift Confederate fleet that protected Memphis," and mentions only a tug at the Battle of Forts St. Phillip and Jackson south of New Orleans. These minimal references to the Confederate naval forces that battled superior Union naval forces on the Mississippi River, leaves the reader completely unaware of the ironclads, C.S.S. *Manassas*, and C.S.S. *Louisiana*, and the two Confederate squadrons which fought at both ends of the river.[246]

To be fair, Mr. Catton's work, *This Hallowed Ground*, is a brief overview of the War, only 187 pages long. The absence of narration concerning the naval war is common to many authors. I merely highlight this one, by a highly regarded author, to demonstrate why the achievements of the Confederate Navy are not common knowledge, even among those who read often on the War Between the States.

I should like to take a moment to list the most obvious examples of success with respect to the Confederate Navy;

The expeditious and effective building of the Confederate States Navy as reported by the *Official Records of the Union and Confederate Navies*. This document indicates that the Confederate States Navy had more than 200 ships on the rolls during the War.

The successful tests of the submarine *Pioneer* at New Orleans in 1861.

The construction of the submarine *Hunley*, its shipment via rail to Charleston, and its successful sinking of the U.S.S. *Housatonic* off Charleston Harbor.

The use of Letters of Marque to stimulate private investors into the building of both the first submarines and the first ironclad, the C.S.S. *Manassas*.

The deployment and use of the first ironclads C.S.S. *Manassas* and C.S.S. *Louisiana* in the War Between the States at the Battle of Forts St. Phillip and Jackson, south of New Orleans.

The sinking of the first warship, the U.S.S. *Cairo*, in history by a torpedo (mine).

The successful naval defense of Charleston, South Carolina.

The successful conduct of Southern commerce that sank more than 200 Federal commerce ships and caused another 700 to change flags from the United States to foreign powers, virtually decimating the U.S. Merchant Marine.

---

246 *This Hallowed Ground*, page 64

As stated at the beginning of this work, it was not the intention of the author to cover all the major engagements or naval actions. For example, I did not consider the C.S.S. *Stonewall*, an armored ship built in France, with the intention of sailing the high seas and attacking the blockading forces. I also did not address the Red River Campaign, the Fort Fisher Campaign, or other major campaigns and battles that included naval aspects. Instead, I have attempted to provide an overview, from the Confederate perspective, on the naval war. I have attempted to introduce you to the significant men who played important roles in the Confederate Navy.

Before we discuss some of the weaknesses of the Confederacy's naval efforts, I would like to summarize what I believe signifies its successes.

Central to the Confederacy's successes were the three hundred plus officers who resigned their commissions from the United States Navy and entered the service of the Confederacy. This dedicated corps of leaders created from nothing a navy that would include almost 400 vessels during the four years of war. They would help create the infrastructure, including 18 separate shipbuilding facilities spread across the South, and develop and manufacture cannon and ordinance that would rival those of the industrial North. And, they would provide the leadership required to lead men on the high seas of the world and on the rivers, bays, lakes, and harbors of the North American continent. Semmes, Read, Wilkenson, Buchanan, Tatnall, Brooke, Beall, and hundreds of other officers created a naval history filled with courage, daring, ingenuity, and dedication.

And Secretary Mallory and his clerks and other administrators worked ceaselessly to find the resources necessary to continue the fight.

Probably the single most important Confederate naval success, with respect to strategic effect, was the impact of the South's cruisers on the Federal commercial fleet. In J. Thomas Scharf's work, logs of the captures of the Confederacy's cruiser fleet are provided. The 19 commerce raiders identified by Scharf captured 258 ships.[247] Most of these prizes were destroyed, the remainder of these ships were bonded and released to shuttle prisoners back to United States, or were converted to Confederate use as cruisers or blockade runners. The impact of this campaign on the northern economy was devastating. Insurance rates for U.S.

---

247 *History of the Confederate Navy*, pages 814 -818

commercial ships rose to such an extent that more than 700 U.S. ships were transferred to foreign flags to prevent them from being sunk by the likes of the C.S.S. *Alabama, Florida,* and *Shenandoah.* The damage to the Yankee commercial fleet inflicted by the Confederate cruisers was so severe that the United States of America's commercial tonnage capacity in 1910 was only a third of that in 1860.[248]

This element of the war directly attacked the financial, shipping, and trade industries of the United States. The war in this theatre struck directly at an element of the national will. It also helped to demonstrate to Europe and the rest of the world that the Confederacy could find a way to strike at the Union. Europeans benefited from the Confederate raids in that most of the 700 Yankee ships' whose flags were transferred, were transferred to European nations. And interestingly, many of the most effective commerce raiders were built in Europe and somehow landed in Southern hands despite the neutrality laws passed by those nations.

A second strategic success was the rapid organization of the Department of the Confederate States Navy and the building of more than 20 operational ironclads. Of course, the C.S.S. *Virginia's* fight with the U.S.S. *Monitor* in Hampton Roads is the most famous. But other ironclads, like the C.S.S. *Manassas, Louisiana, Arkansas, Tennessee,* and *Albemarle* all proved to be extraordinary ships severely, punishing the Union ships they fought. In Charleston, South Carolina, a squadron of ironclads successfully ventured out to challenge the blockaders and protect the port from sea-borne capture. On the James River in Virginia, the ironclad squadron protected Richmond and had to be destroyed by their sailors when the Army of Northern Virginia withdrew west from the capital.

In the cases of Charleston and Mobile, the presence of ironclads greatly assisted in helping to prevent the capture of vital Southern ports. These ports sustained the supply lifeline provided by the blockade-runners until late in the war. (Here again, the Confederate Navy is found in the ownership and operation of some the most active blockade-runners.) And in Virginia, the presence of the C.S.S. *Virginia*, for forty-five days,[249] slowed the advance of McClellan's army up the Peninsula. Later, the Southern ironclads of the James River Squadron would

---

248 *The Civil War Archive, The History of the Civil War in Documents*, page 618
249 *History of the Confederate Navy*, pages 221

prevent the Yankees from sending their own ironclads up the James River and into Richmond.

The ironclads also helped convince the Europeans that the South was a legitimate and serious foe for the Union. In Hampton Roads, both the French and English had warships present. These representatives of Europe were eyewitnesses to the devastation done by the C.S.S. *Virginia* to some of the most powerful of the Yankee wooden fleet, the U.S.S. *Cumberland* and *Congress*, on March 8th, 1862. And they would also witness the titanic battle between the two ironclads the next day. With the string of Confederate victories which would follow after General Robert E. Lee assumed command of the Army of Northern Virginia, late in the spring of 1862, and combined with the success of the Confederate cruisers on the high seas, the outcome of the war had to appear in question to impartial observers on the other side of the Atlantic Ocean.

The last great success of the Confederate Navy was its energetic incorporation of developing naval technologies into its defensive scheme. The development of the torpedo, submersible, and partially submersible craft added greatly to the Confederate defensive efforts on the rivers and within their harbors. As discussed, the torpedoes were an inexpensive means to add a new hazard to even the largest Union vessel. As we saw when we considered the defenses of Charleston, the combination of strong forts and batteries placed in depth, combined with ironclads, torpedoes, and submersibles, made a defensive position that even the greatly enlarged U.S. Navy would not attempt to overwhelm.

As successful as the Confederate Navy was, there are clear areas where disappointment characterized the effort.

In the largest sense, there does not seem to have been a national strategic planning group that attempted to identify and link the strategic needs and priorities of the Navy and the Army. There was a lack of coordination between the Confederate armies and navies concerning overall strategy and prioritizing of cities, ports, and other facilities that were necessary to the conduct of the war. Of strategic importance was the loss of both the Pensacola Naval Yard and the Norfolk Naval Yard. In the case of Pensacola, Confederate forces were removed from that point in order to allow General Bragg to ferry troops to General A.S.

Johnson for the Shiloh Offensive.[250] But the loss of Pensacola provided the Federals with an excellent station for operations along the Gulf coast. It also prevented the South from utilizing the port as a naval base and required the destruction of two partially completed Confederate gunboats.

The loss of Norfolk was even more important. The deep draft of the C.S.S. *Virginia* would not allow her to retreat up the James River to safety. Therefore, with the loss of the Gosport Navy Yard, the *Virginia* was without a home and had to be destroyed. The failure or inability to defend Norfolk from a Federal land assault created a situation that ended the career of the South's most valued warship, the C.S.S. *Virginia*. And the end of this ironclad opened a free and unthreatened supply line for Union forces operating on the Peninsula after its demise. Had the Confederacy been able to build the Norfolk area into a major bastion of Southern land and naval power, the threat to Richmond from the seaward could have been greatly reduced, and the possibility of assisting in the defense of coastal North Carolina would have been facilitated. Further, continued use of Norfolk, in combination with Richmond, as builders of ironclads, could have dramatically changed the North's priorities with respect to defense of their capital and the eastern seaboard. Once the *Virginia* was lost, the James River Ironclad Squadron operated on the upper James, near Richmond. These ironclads could have sowed much pain and aggravation in the Chesapeake but were unable to get past Trent's Reach, and thus were useless in attempting to change the course of the war in the East.

In strategic terms, the Federals demonstrated a much higher appreciation for the importance of Naval and Amphibious Warfare from the outset. The most oft cited reflection of this is Lincoln's Proclamation of a blockade. But the blockade took more than a year to put in place. However, Union assaults on the Atlantic coast started almost immediately. The South did not possess the manpower, industry, or financial assets to build fleets to launch amphibious assaults on the coasts of New Jersey. But, had they been able to hold on to Norfolk and the Gosport Naval Yard, and then combined the naval forces that could be built at Gosport and Richmond, they could have posed a real threat to Federal possession of the Chesapeake and forced the Yankees to dedicate resources to winning the battle.

---

250 *History of the Confederate States Navy,* Page 37

Of course, all this discussion of a successful land defense of Norfolk requires a complete survey of the Confederacy's position in December and January 1861-62 to determine where the forces were that could have been transferred to Norfolk in time to construct a stout defensive position.

In the west, the South was never able to get a naval force on the Mississippi – Ohio River complex behind the Federal flotillas, though Yankee correspondence demonstrates just how fearful they were of such an action. At Fort Pillow, for example, Commodore Davis, U.S.N., was warned not to allow the Confederate Squadron known as the River Defense Force, under Captain Davis to get past him, and up the Mississippi into the Yankee rear.[251]

As with Jackson's Foot Cavalry and the South's cavalry formations under Forrest and Stuart, much damage and mayhem could have been caused if well-led Confederate naval forces had been able to gain the Yankee rear. Had the Confederates been able to get a naval force of some strength behind the Yankee Mississippi River squadron, the chaos and confusion caused would have helped tie up Yankee resources and greatly increase political opposition to Lincoln's War in the western states. And, just as the loss of Fort Donelson, on the Cumberland River, had caused a massive Confederate withdrawal from Kentucky, so a successful counter on the Ohio River could have threatened Union supply lines.

Tactically, situations occurred which the local Confederate Naval leadership was not prepared for, one of those categories of events was success. An example would be Charleston in January 1863, when the C.S.S. *Palmetto State* caught the U.S.S. *Mercedita* by surprise and seriously damaged her. Captain Stellwagon, U.S.N., offered his surrender and requested help in evacuating his sailors. But the Confederates were not prepared for such a contingency, and the Federal ship was not so badly damaged that when the Confederates moved on, the Federals were able to salvage the ship. A prize missed. How many times did the same scenario play out? Surely, not enough to change the outcome of the war. Maybe. Who can tell? What is obvious is that important war materials which could have been under Confederate operational control, and prisoners who could have been taken, and papers which might

---

251 Ibid, page 257

have had some intelligence value were not taken.

In addition, and of great disappointment, is the fact that most Confederate ironclads were lost as a result of self-destruction to avoid capture. A quick survey of the most effective of the Confederate ironclads indicates:

C.S.S. *Manassas* lost as a result of battle damage at Forts St. Phillip and Jackson

C.S.S. *Louisiana* lost through self-destruction to avoid capture, after participating in the battles of Forts St. Phillip and Jackson, because her engines had not been installed.

C.S.S. *Mississippi* (incomplete) lost through self-destruction at New Orleans to prevent capture.

C.S.S. *Virginia* lost through self-destruction in Hampton Roads to prevent capture.

C.S.S. *Arkansas* lost through self-destruction on the Red River, after engine failure to prevent capture.

C.S.S. *Tennessee*, sister to the *Arkansas*, partially constructed at Memphis was lost through self-destruction to avoid capture.

C.S.S. *Albemarle* sunk as a result of catastrophic damage caused by a torpedo,

C.S.S. *Tennessee* (Mobile) surrendered to Union forces after incurring battle damage that prevented further combat.

C.S.S. *Baltic* decommissioned and used for parts for other ironclads.

C.S.S. *Neuse* lost through self-destruction to prevent capture.

C.S.S. *Huntsville* and *Tuscaloosa* surrendered to Yankees at the conclusion of the war.

C.S.S. *Columbia* sank in Charleston Harbor when it struck a wreck.

The five ironclads of the James River Squadron and three of the Charleston Squadron were lost through self-destruction to avoid capture as Confederates abandoned those cities.

C.S.S. *Raleigh* ran aground near the mouth of Cape Fear River and broke apart.

C.S.S. *North Carolina* foundered as a result of a storm.

C.S.S. *Atlanta* defeated in battle and captured.

C.S.S. *Savannah* lost through self-destruction to avoid capture

While this is not a complete list, it demonstrates the number of times Confederate ironclads were destroyed by Confederate forces to avoid capture. Only the *Manassas, Tennessee, Albemarle,* and *Atlanta* listed above, were actually destroyed or disabled sufficiently by Yankee fire to end their service.

In two cases, stationed at Richmond, and Charleston, there were ironclads operating in pairs or more. It is disappointing to realize that no plan could be devised to employ these vessels so that they might cause damage to the enemy. That is not to say that the captains and their crews did not serve with gallantry, only that these powerful vessels could not be deployed so as to allow their power to be exercised on enemy vessels as an element of a larger scheme to win the war.

Many of the South's ironclads were only partially completed before they had to be destroyed. This reflected a combination of the lack of prioritization of defending the shipbuilding sites by the army commanders and a lack of manufacturing assets, whether it be machinery, rail capabilities, or skilled technicians to complete the project sufficiently so as to be able to relocate the partially completed ship when the site was threatened with capture.

Waste was a clear associate of the Confederate Navy and naval affairs. In Europe, the offering of cotton bonds, expected to raise millions for the purchase of ships and ordinance in Europe, was ruined by wild fluctuations caused by financiers in Europe. And the Confederacy repeatedly spent funds to build ships that had to be destroyed before they neared completion. And then there were the expenditure of funds to purchase naval assets outside the routine chain of command by the Confederate Congress. Some of these wasteful actions could have been avoided.

From the Southern perspective, the armies of the South will always dominate the study of the War. In terms of pure size, the Southern armies were 100 times larger than the navies. In the post-war years, the combined strengths of Union and Confederate Army veterans dwarfed those of the combined navies. This affected the politics of the Post War years immediately following peace and the shaping of the story that was to become our accepted history.

However, the continued study of the Confederate Navy will help to ensure that future students of the war will have a better grasp of the efforts, successes, and frustrations of those charged with waging the naval war for the Confederacy.

Appendix 2

Roll of Confederate Naval Officers

Admirals

Buchanan, Franklin
Semmes, Raphael

Captains

Rousseau, Lawrence
Forrest, French
Tatnall, Josiah
Randolph, V.M.
Hollins, George N.
Ingraham, D.N.
Baron, Samuel
Lynch, William F.
Sterett, Isaac S.
Lee, S. S.
Whittle, William C.
Hunter, William H.
Farrand, E.
Tucker, John R.

Commanders

Thornburn, Robert D.
Robb, Robert G.
Mason, Murray
McBlair, C.H.
Fairfax, A. B.
Page, Richard R.
Chatard, Frederick
Sinclair, Arthur
Kennedy, C.H.
Brent, Thomas W.
Mitchell, John K.
Maury, Matthew F.
Tucker, John R.
Page, Thomas Jefferson
Minor, George
Pinckney, R.F.
Rootes, Thomas
Hartstene, H. J.
Henderson, James L.
Muse, William T.
Hunter, Thomas T.
Cook, James W.
Spotswood, C.F.M.
Brown, Isaac
Maury, William L.
Maffitt, John N.
Barney, Joseph N.
Wood, Taylor J. N.
Bullock, James D.
Harrison, G.W.
James H. North
Johnson, J. W.
Pegram, Robert B.
Davidson, Hunter
Brooke, John M.
Kell, J.
Webb, William A.
Sinclair, George T.
Glassell, William T.

First Lieutenants

Renshaw, F. B.
Poindexter, C. B.

Mark K. Vogl

Lewis, H. H.
Gwathmey, W.
Murphy, P. U.
Guthrie, John J.
Rutledge, John
Morgan, Van R.
Winder, Edward L.
Parker, John H.
Kennard, J. S.
Wilkinson, John
Morris, C.M.
Fauntleroy, C.M.
Maury, John S.
Hays, Charles W.
Simms, C.C.
Myers, Julian
Warley, A.F.
Bennett, John W.
Carter, J.H.
McLaughlin, A.
Parker, W.H.
Jones, J. Pembroke
Murdaugh, William H.
Rochelle, James H.
Sharp, William
Waddell, James I.
McGory, Charles P.
Carter, Robert R.
Hamilton, John R.
Johnson, O. F.
Eggelston, John R.
Chapman, R. T.
Loyall, B.B.
Word, W.H.
Shepperd, F.E.
Dozier, W.G.
Bradford, W.I.
Dalton, H.H.

Evens, W.E.
Shyrock, G.S.
Porter, T.K.
Graves, C.J.
Mills, T.B.
Whittle Jr., W.C.
Kerr, W.A.
Grimball, J.
Hall, W.B.
Averett, S.W.
Claiborne, H.B.
Borchert, G.A.
Cenas, Henry
Butt, W.R.
Pollack, W.W.
Wharton, A.S.
Domin, T.L.
Harrison, T.L.
Hoole, J.L.
Hoge, F.L.
Reed, E.G.
Borum, C.
Johnston, J.V.
De Bree, A.M.
Minor, R.D.
Van Zent, N.H.
Corkie, D.P.
Fry, J.
Campbell, W.P.A.
Blake, J.D.
Dennington, J.W.
Pebot, T.P.
Porcher, P.
Alexander, J.W.

Appendix 3

Roll of Confederate Naval vessels1

This list was compiled by beginning with the list provided in Battles and Commanders. Ships were then added to the list from other sources as they were found. Footnotes identify the additions or additional information. A level of confusion can be expected because, in many instances, several ships possessed the same name. Efforts have been made to identify sources, etc. This is not a complete roll of Confederate ships.

A second roll follows, which reflects the ships listed in the official records of the war.

Ship's Name	Commander	Type Ship
Alabama	Raphael Semmes	Commerce Raider
Albemarle	James Cook	Ironclad
Alert[252]		Tender
Anglia[253]		Steamer
Arctic		
Arkansas	Isaac N. Brown	Ironclad
Arrow[254]		Steamer, gunboat
Atlanta[255]		Blockade-Runner
Atlanta[256]		Ironclad
Baltic	C. C. Simms	Ironclad
Bayou City[257]		Cotton-clad Steamer
Bragg		
Beaufort	W. H. Parker	Wooden gunboat[258]

---

252 *The History of the Confederate Navy*, page 21, seized by Alabama upon secession.
253 *Battles and Commanders*, page 153
254 *The Confederate Privateer*, page 47
255 Ibid, The *Atlanta* would be transformed into a Commerce Raider, *Tallahassee*, which was later renamed the *Olustee*.
256 Ibid, originally a blockade runner named the *Fingal*
257 *The Confederate Navy, A Pictorial History*, page 124
258 *The Confederate Navy, A Pictorial History*, page 240

Beauregard		Gunboat[259]
Bombshell[260]	Lt. Albert Hudgins	Gunboat
Boston[261]		Commerce Raider
Calhoun[262]		Commerce Raider
Calhoun[263]		Tow boat
Chattahoochie		
Charleston	Isaac N. Brown	Ironclad
Chesapeake[264]	John C. Braine	Steamer
Chickamaugua[265]		Commerce Raider
Chicora	Thomas T. Hunter	Ironclad
City of Richmond		tender[266]
Clarence	C. W. Read	Commerce Raider
Columbia[267]		Ironclad
Confederate States[268]		Receiving ship
Cornubia		Blockade runner[269]
Cotton	Fulton	Cotton-clad Gunboat[270]
Cotton Plant[271]		
David		Torpedo boat
Drewry	C. H. Fauntleroy	Wooden gunboat[272]
Defiance	McCoy	
Diana	Semmes (son of)	Gunboat[273]
Eastport	Lt. Brown	Ironclad[274]

---

259 *The Confederate Navy, A Pictorial History*, page 102
260 *Rebel Reefers*, page 70 & 71
261 Ibid
262 *The History of the Confederate Navy*
263 *Blue and Gray at Sea, Naval Memoirs of the Civil War*, "Excerpts of a Rebel Reefer" page 65
264 *The Confederate Navy, A Pictorial History*, page 165, a captured vessel, she was retaken in British waters.
265 Ibid
266 *The Confederate Navy, A Pictorial History*, page 223
267 Ibid
268 *Rebel Reefers*, page 7
269 *The Confederate Navy, A Pictorial History*, page225
270 *Destruction and Reconstruction*, chapter VIII
271 *Rebel Reefers*, page 71
272 *The Confederate Navy, A Pictorial History*, page 240
273 *Destruction and Reconstruction*, Chapter IX
274 *Naval Strategies of the Civil War*, page 109

El Tousson[275]		Ocean going ram
Ellis[276]	Muse	
Era No. 5[277]		Transport
Echo[278]		Commerce Raider
Edwards[279]	Cooke	
Fredericksburg	W. H. Parker	Ironclad
Florida	John N. Maffitt	Commerce Raider
	Charles M. Morris	
Gaines	John W. Bennett	
Georgia	William Maury	Commerce Raider[280]
General Rusk[281]		Steamer
*Governor Moore**	Bevery Kennon	
General Quitman	Grant	
Georgia	William Gwathmay	Ironclad
J. P. Jones		Oscar L. Johnson
Gray[282]		Steam cutter
Gunnison[283]		Torpedo boat
Hampton	John S. Maury	Wooden gunboat[284]
Huntsville	Julian Meyers	Ironclad
Huntress	W. B. Hall	
	William G. Dozier	
	Charles M. Morris	
Harriet Lane	Nicholas Barney	
Hunley[285]		Submersible
Isaac P. Smith[286]		Gunboat
Ivy		Gunboat[287]

---

275 *Battles and Commanders*, page 269
276 *The Confederate Privateer*, page 109
277 *The Confederate Navy, A Pictorial History*, page 133
278 Ibid
279 *The Confederate Privateer*, page 108 & 109
280 Ibid
281 *The Confederate Privateer*, page 208
282 *The History of the Confederate Navy*, page 21, purchased by South Carolina upon secession.
283 *The Confederate Privateer*, page 204
284 *The Confederate Navy, A Pictorial History*, 240
285 *The History of the Confederate Navy*
286 *The Confederate Navy, A Pictorial History*, page 130, captured Union vessel.
287 *The Confederate Privateer*, page 153

Jeff Davis[288]		Commerce Raider
Isandiga	Joel S. Kennard	
Indian Chief	J. H. Ingraham	
Jackson[289]		Ironclad
Jackson[290]		Paddle-wheel gunboat
John Bell		
John F. Carr[291]		Sidewheel steamer
Josiah H. Bell[292]		Sidewheel steamer
Judah		
Juno	Phillip Porcher	
Junaluska[293]		
Jeff Thompson		
Jamestown	Thomas Jefferson Page	
Lewis Cass[294]		Revenue Cutter
Little Rebel		
Livingston[295]		
Louisiana		Ironclad
General Lovell		Gunboat
Lucy Gwinn[296]		Merchant steamer
Manassas	A. F. Warley	Ironclad
Maven[297]		Steamer
McRea	Lt. Gwathmay[298]	Gunboat
Merrimac		Blockade Runner[299]
Mississippi[300]		Ironclad

---

288 Ibid
289 Ibid Also known as the *Muscogee*, presently on display at the Civil War Naval Museum at Columbus, Ga.
290 page 65
291 *Cottonclads! The Battle of Galveston and the Defense of the Texas Coast*, page 123
292 Ibid
293 *The Confederate Privateer*, page 109
294 *The History of the Confederate Navy*, page 21, seized upon secession by Alabama
295 *The Confederate Navy, A Pictorial History*, page 104
296 *Cottonclads! The Battle of Galveston and the Defense of the Texas Coast*, page 123
297 *Rebel Reefers, The Organization and Midshipman of the Confederate States Naval Academy*, page 13
298 *The Confederate Privateer*, page 154
299 *The Confederate Navy, A Pictorial History*, page 225
300 Ibid, never completed in New Orleans, was destroyed.

Missouri[301]		Ironclad[302]
Morgan[303]		
Mosher[304]	Sherman	Tug
Nashville	Robert B. Pegram	Commerce Raider[305]
Nashville		Ironclad
Neuse	William Sharp	Ironclad
Neptune[306]		Cotton-clad steamer
Nansemond		Wooden gunboat[307]
North Carolina	William S. Muse	Ironclad
Pioneer[308]	John K. Scott	Submersible
Price		
Palmetto State	John Rutledge	Ironclad
Patrick Henry	John R. Tucker	C.S.N. Academy
Pickens[309]	Lt. Kennon	Cutter
Polk[310]		
Queen of the West[311]		Ram
Raleigh[312]		Gunboat, 1 gun
Raleigh	John Wilkinson Armstrong	Ironclad
Richmond		Ironclad
Rappahannock	Charles M. Fauntleroy	Ironclad
R. E. Lee[313]		Blockade-Runner
Roanoke	M. F. Clarke	Gunboat[314]
Roebuck[315]		
Resolute	J. Pembroke Jones	

---

301 *The History of the Confederacy*
302 *The Confederate Navy, A Pictorial History*, page 132
303 Ibid
304 *Blue and Gray at Sea*, "Autobiography of George Dewey, Admiral of the Navy," page 27
305 Ibid
306 *The Confederate Navy, A Pictorial History*, page 124
307 *The Confederate Navy, A Pictorial History*, page 240
308 *The Confederate Navy, A Pictorial History*, page 174
309 *The Confederate Privateers*, page 42 & 154
310 *The Confederate Navy, A Pictorial History*, page 104
311 *The Confederate Navy, A Pictorial History*, page 133, captured Yankee ship
312 *The Confederate Privateers*, page 102
313 *The Confederate Navy, A Pictorial History*, page 225
314 *Rebel Reefers*, page 75
315 *Cottonclads! The Battle of Galveston and the Defense of the Texas Coast*, page 124

Ship	Commander	Type
	William B. Hall	
Retribution[316]		Commerce Raider
Royal Yacht[317]		
Savannah[318]		Receiving ship
Savannah	John Kell	Ironclad
	Wilburn Hall	
Selma	Peter U. Murphy	
Shrapnel[319]		
Shenandoah	James I. Waddell	Commerce Raider
Slidell[320]		
Sumter	Raphael Semmes	Commerce Raider
Sumter[321]		Gunboat
Stonewall	Thomas Jefferson Page[322]	Ironclad cruiser
Sampson	Joel S. Kennard	Steamer[323]
Tacony[324]	C. W. Read	Commerce Raider
Tallahassee[325]	John Taylor Wood	Commerce Raider
Tuscarora[326]	Lt. Huger	Gunboat
Tuscarora[327]		Ironclad
Tuzkaluza (Tuscaloosa)	Charles H. McBlair	Commerce Raider
Tennessee	James D. Johnson	
Tennessee	Franklin Buchanan	Ironclad
Texas[328]		Ironclad
Thomas Jefferson[329]		Paddlewheel steamship

---

316 *Rebel Reefers*, page 75
317 *The Confederate Privateers*, page 233
318 *Rebel Reefers, The Organization and Midshipman of the Confederate States Naval Academy*, page 13
319 *Rebel Reefers*, page 104
320 *Rebel Reefers, The Organization and Midshipman of the Confederate States Naval Academy*, page 13
321 *The Confederate Navy, A Pictorial History*, page 102
322 *The Confederate Navy, A Pictorial History*, page 249
323 *Rebel Reefers, The Organization and Midshipmen of the Confederate States Naval Academy*, page 13
324 Ibid
325 *The Confederate Navy, A Pictorial History*, page 249
326 *The Confederate Privateers*, page 154
327 *The Confederate Navy, A Pictorial History*, page 249
328 Ibid
329 *Rebel Reefers*, page 7

Torpedo	Hunter Davidson	Converted tug[330]
Torch	Frank Shepper	
Teaser	J. W. Alexander	Converted tug/ Gunboat[331]
Uncle Ben		Sidewheel steamer[332]
General Earl Van Dorn	J. S. Hollins	
Virginia (*Merrimac*)	Franklin Buchanan	Ironclad
Virginia II	Robert B. Pegram	Ironclad
Watson[333]		Towboat
Wm. Aiken[334]		
Winslow[335]		Commerce Raider
Water Witch	P. T. Pelot	
Webb	W. B. Hall	Gunboat
	C. W. Read	
Warrior	Stephenson	
Yadkin	W. A. Kerr	
Yorktown	Nicholas Barney	
York[336]		Commerce Raider

---

330 *The Confederate Navy, A Pictorial History*, page 240
331 *The Confederate Navy, A Pictorial History*, page 109
332 *Cottonclads! The Battle of Galveston and the Defense of the Texas Coast*, page
333 *The Confederate Privateers*, page 154
334 "*The History of the Confederate Navy*, page 21, seized from Federal government upon secession.
335 Ibid
336 Ibid

Appendix 4

Confederate Commerce Raiders

SHIPS	DATES OF ACTION
C.S.S. *JEFF DAVIS*[337]	June '61 to Aug. '61
C.S.S. *SUMTER*	July '61 to Jan. '62
C.S.S. *WINSLOW*	July '61 to Aug.'61
C.S.S. *YORK*	August 1861
C.S.S. *NASHVILLE*	Nov. '61 to Feb. '62
C.S.S. *ECHO*	July 1862
C.S.S. *ALABAMA*	Sep. '62 to Jan. '64
C.S.S. *RETRIBUTION*	Jan. '63 to Feb. '63
C.S.S. *FLORIDA*	Jan. '63 to June '64
C.S.S. *GEORGIA*	Apr. '63 to Oct. '63
C.S.S. *BOSTON*	June 1863
C.S.S. *CLARENCE*[338]	June 1863
C.S.S. *TACONY*[339]	June 1863
C.S.S. *TUSCALOOSA*	July '63 to Sep. '63

---

337 Operated as a Privateer, *History of the Confederates States Navy*, page 78
338 Captured by the C.S.S. *Florida* on May 6th, 1863, commissioned into the Confederate Navy and placed under Lt. Read. Read imaginatively added quaker cannons making the *Clarence* an effective commerce raider.
339 Captured by the C.S.S. *Clarence*, Lt. Read transferred his flag to the *Tacony*. Quaker guns were added to the C.S.S. *Tacony*.

C.S.S. *TALAHASSEE*   August 1864

C.S.S. *CHICKAMAUGUA*   October 1864

C.S.S. *OULSTEE*[340]   November 1864

C.S.S. *SHENNANDOAH*   Nov. '64 to June '65

---

[340] The C.S.S. *Tallahassee* was converted to a blockade, and then reconverted to a cruiser and renamed the C.S.S. *Oulstee*.

Appendix 5

The Confederate Ironclads

New Orleans Ironclads

C.S.S. *Manassas*
C.S.S. *Louisiana*
C.S.S. *Mississippi*

Figure 6 – C.S.S. Manassas
Image was provided by the US Department of Navy, Naval Historical Center

C.S.S. *Manassas* …New Orleans … 12, Oct. 1861 purchased by the Confederate States government, converted from a commercial tug boat. First American ironclad engaged in battle, at the Head of the Passes, Oct. 12, 1861, where it drives off the Federal blockade squadron. The *Manassas* will take in the Battle for New Orleans at Forts Jackson and St. Phillip.

Figure 7 – C.S.S. *Louisiana*
Image was provided by the US Department of Navy, Naval Historical Center

C.S.S. *Louisiana* ... duel paddlewheel, and duel propeller screw. The Louisiana was larger than any of the federal ships and had it been fully operational during the battle for New Orleans it is very possible the Federals would have been turned back. During the battle the *Louisiana* was anchored along the river bank and used as a floating battery.

C.S.S. *Mississippi* ... sister to the *Louisiana*, she was not completed when the Federal fleet moved up the Mississippi River to seize New Orleans. When Captain Sinclair, the ship's captain failed to find a means to pull her up-river, she was set afire, and adrift and allowed to float down the river. The *Mississippi* was 260 feet long, 58 feet extreme breadth, 15 feet depth of hold.[341]

---

[341] *History of the Confederate States Navy*, page 269

Photo # NH 57830 CSS Virginia, wash drawing by Clary Ray

Figure 8 – C.S.S. *Virginia*
Image was provided by the US Department of Navy, Naval Historical Center

C.S.S. *Virginia* ... Norfolk, Va. ... February, 1862 constructed from the hull of the U.S.S. *Merrimac*. The emergence of this ship on the Chesapeake Bay had members of the Lincoln Cabinet warning Lincoln to abandon to White House.

The *Virginia* was 263 feet long, 51 feet at the beam. She was 3,200 tons and consumed 3,400 pounds of anthracite coal per hour.[342] She required between 22 and 24 foot draft depending on her weight. Her battery consisted of two 7-inch Dahlgren pivot guns, and eight 9-inch rifled Dahlgren shell guns in her broadside. She had a crew of 300 men.

Lt. John Wood, C.S.N. wrote about the *Virginia*: " From the start we saw that she was slow, not over 5 knots, she steered so badly that, with her great length, it took 30 to 40 minutes to turn. She drew 22 feet, which confined us to a comparatively narrow channel in the Roads, and the engines were our weak point. She was as unmanageable as a waterlogged vessel."[343]

The *Virginia* was destroyed on May 10, 1862, by her Captain, Commander Tattnall, after Norfolk, Virginia and the Gosport Naval Yard were re-captured by the Federals. A Court of Inquiry found Tattnall wrongly destroyed the vessel, but a subsequent Courts Martial found

---
342 *The Confederate Navy, A Pictorial History*, page 81
343 *The Civil War*, page 149

his actions justified. The deep keel of the vessel left nowhere for her to go after the loss of Norfolk.[344]

Ironclads of Charleston, South Carolina

C.S.S. *Palmetto State*
C.S.S. *Chicora*
C.S.S. *Charleston*
C.S.S. *Columbia*

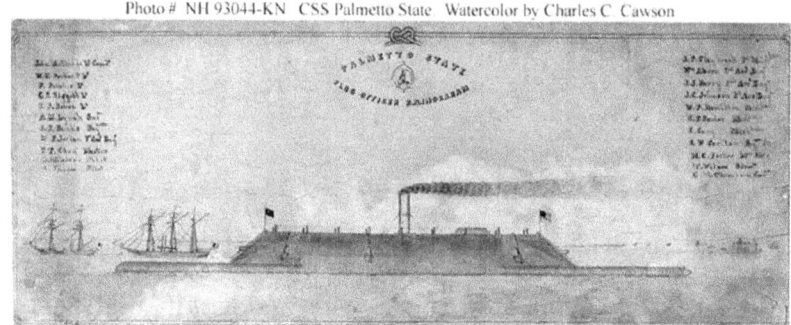

Figure 9 – C.S.S. *Palmetto State*
Image was provided by the US Department of Navy, Naval Historical Center

C.S.S. *Palmetto State* ... Charleston, South Carolina ... Her armament included an 80-pound rifled gun forward, a 60-pound rifled gun aft, and two 8-inch shell guns, one on each broadside. An image of the *Palmetto State* depicts three gun ports broadside indicating the bow and aft guns could pivot to either port or starboard.

C.S.S. *Chicora* ... Charleston, South Carolina ... Launched 1862, accompanied *Palmetto State* in action of 31 January 1863 driving off Federal blockaders.

C.S.S. *Charleston*

C.S.S. *Columbia* ... Charleston, South Carolina ... Launched 10 March, 1864, sunk January 12th, 1865, when it struck a wreck near Fort Moultrie.

---

344 *History of the Confederate States Navy*, page 221

The Tarheel Squadron

C.S.S. *Albemarle*
C.S.S. *Neuse*
C.S.S. *North Carolina*
C.S.S. *Raleigh*

Figure 10 – C.S.S. *Albemarle*
Image was provided by the US Department of Navy, Naval Historical Center

C.S.S. *Albemarle* ... Edwards Ferry, North Carolina ... April 1864

C.S.S. *Neuse* ... Kinston, North Carolina ... March, 1865. The *Neuse* was one of three ironclads built on the inland waterways of North Carolina. The ship was completed and launched but prevented access to the Carolina coast because of low water levels in the Neuse River. She was destroyed when Yankee cavalry threatened capture.

C.S.S. *North Carolina* ... Wilmington, North Carolina ... Launched in October 1863, she was used as a guard ship. She foundered in September 1864, as a result of worm damage.

C.S.S. *Raleigh* ... Wilmington, North Carolina ... Launched fall of 1863. She ventured out to attack seven blockaders in the vicinity of New Inlet, 6 May 1864, in order to assist blockade runners attempting to leave Wilmington. She ran aground on May 7th near the entrance of the Cape Fear River and broke apart.

Ironclads of Mobile Bay, Alabama

C.S.S. *Baltic*
C.S.S. *Tennessee*
C.S.S. *Nashville*
C.S.S. *Huntsville*
C.S.S. *Tuscaloosa*

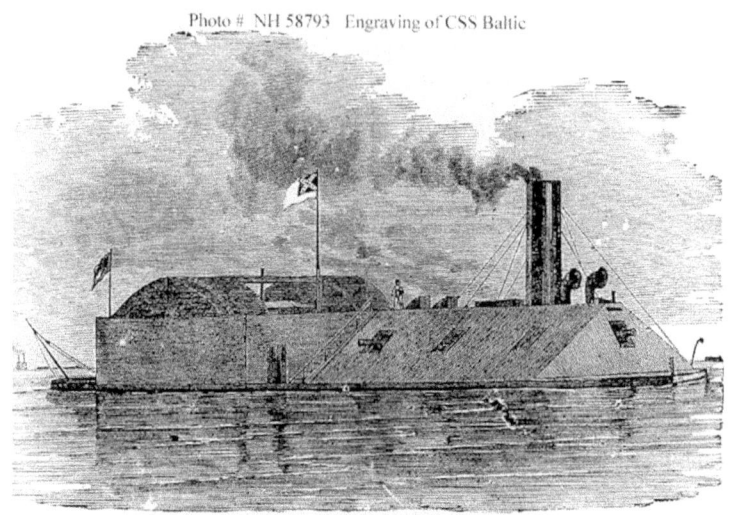

Figure 11 – C.S.S. *Baltic*
Image was provided by the US Department of Navy, Naval Historical Center

C.S.S. *Baltic* ... Philadelphia, Pennsylvania, and Mobile Alabama... 1860 purchased by the State of Alabama, converted to a warship and transferred to the Confederate States Navy, 1862. She was in poor condition, dismantled as an ironclad in 1864, and converted to the first mine-layer.

C.S.S. *Nashville* ... Montgomery, Alabama ... 1863, launched incomplete from Montgomery, moved to Mobile, but was never completed. Did not participate in the defense of Mobile.

Figure 12 – C.S.S. *Tennessee*
Line engraving from *Harper's Weekly* published on 3 February 1866.
Image was provided by the U.S. Department of Navy, Naval Historical Center

C.S.S. *Tennessee* ... Selma, Alabama ... Launched March 1864, stationed at Mobile by June 1864. Flagship for Admiral Buchanan, C.S.N. Escorts included C.S.S. *Gaines, Morgan,* and *Selma.*

C.S.S. *Huntsville*
C.S.S. *Tuscaloosa*

Ironclads of Savannah

C.S.S. *Atlanta*
C.S.S. *Savannah*
C.S.S. *Georgia*

Figure 13 – C.S.S. *Atlanta*
Image was provided by the US Department of Navy, Naval Historical Center

C.S.S. *Atlanta* ... Scotland and Savannah ... 1861, operated first as the *Fingal*, a blockade runner, carried a large shipment of weapons into Savannah. When Savannah was effectively blockaded, the *Fingal* was converted into an ironclad and renamed the C.S.S. *Atlanta*. She first appeared in mid-1862. Was defeated and captured in Wassau Sound in June 1863.

Figure 14 – *Rebel Turtle Ram*
Image was provided by the US Department of Navy, Naval Historical Center

C.S.S. *Savannah* ... Savannah, Georgia ... Launched 30 June 1863, was destroyed to prevent capture 21 December 1864.
C.S.S. *Georgia* ... Savannah, Georgia ... 1862, The *Georgia* leaked so bad she was called "swamp in a box."

James River Squadron

C.S.S. *Richmond*
C.S.S. *Texas*
C.S.S. *Fredericksburg*
C.S.S. *Virginia II*

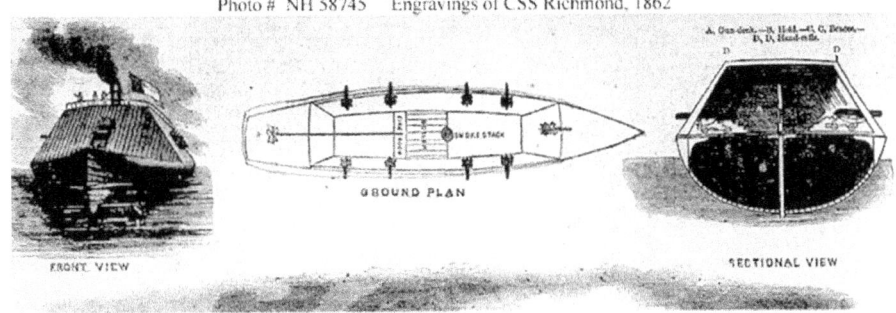

Figure 15 – C.S.S. *Richmond*
Image was provided by the US Department of Navy, Naval Historical Center

C.S.S. *Richmond* ... Norfolk, Virginia ... Construction began in Norfolk, launched incomplete and towed to Richmond when Norfolk was abandoned to the Yankees.

C.S.S. *Texas* ... Richmond, Virginia ... January 1865 launched incomplete. The *Texas* was captured at the fall of Richmond.

Figure 16 – C.S.S. *Fredericksburg*
Image was provided by the US Department of Navy, Naval Historical Center

C.S.S. *Fredericksburg*... Richmond, Va. ... Launched mid-1864, part of the James River Squadron. Sole Confederate ironclad to reach the Federal ships at Trent's Reach.

C.S.S. *Virginia II* ... Richmond, Va. ... 1864 ... Part of the James River Squadron, participated in three engagements on the James before being sunk on April 3, 1865.

Figure 17 – C.S.S. *Stonewall*
Image was provided by the US Department of Navy, Naval Historical Center

C.S.S. *Stonewall* ... Bordeaux, France ... Commissioned at sea in 1865, after France delayed her delivery, she was the Confederacy's only ocean-going ironclad. She was intended to break the blockade. She left Ferrol, Spain in March 1865, but was surrendered to Spanish authorities in Cuba with news of the Confederacy's surrender.

Ironclads of the Mississippi River

Figure 18 – Building of the C.S.S. *Arkansas*
Image was provided by the US Department of Navy, Naval Historical Center. They site *Battles and Leaders of the Civil War* Volume III, page 573, as their source.

C.S.S. *Arkansas* … Memphis, Tennessee, Yazoo City & Greenwood, Mississippi … Removed from Memphis when Yankees captured the city, her sister the *Tennessee*, was destroyed. She ventured out against the Federal in July 1862, running two Federal fleets before arriving at Vicksburg. Was destroyed by the Confederates, after an engagement with the U.S.S. *Essex* when her engines failed.

Appendix 6

Blockade Runners

Confederate Blockade Runners
Strategic Summary - 2018

References
History of the Confederate States Navy, Thomas Scharf
The Blockade Runners, Dave Horner
The Confederate Navy, A Pictorial History, Phillip Van Doren Stern

Maritime geography of the South
3,549 miles of coastline[345]
189 inlets, bays and rivers[346]
Destination ports[347]
Initially Runners went from Europe to Southern cities, but that changed as the blockade tightened.
Nassau 560 miles to Charleston
Bermuda 674 miles to Wilmington (3 days)
Cuba for Mobile and Gulf ports[348]
Matamoros, Mexico to Brownsville, (Union attempted to blockade Matamoros, but U.S. Courts said they could not do that.)[349]

Diplomatic and legal aspects
 Because Lincoln declared a blockade, he accidentally recognized the Confederacy as a foreign nation. If he had proclaimed our southern ports were closed, he would have avoided foreign recognition of the South![350]
 A port remained open for 30 days after the announcement of its blockade.
 The Confederate government regulated how much of the ship's

---

345 The Confederate Navy, Pg. 62
346 Ibid
347 *The Blockade Runner*, Pg. 15
348 Hampton Roads Naval Museum
349 *The Confederate Navy*, Pg. 62
350 Talked about extensively in Scharf's history of the Confederate Navy and in Van Doren Stern's book, Pg. 62

freight could be for non-war related items. Inspections were conducted by Confederate authorities of every ship that entered a Southern port.

Union Navy strength
Eventually 700 ships and 105,000 men. Initially used whatever is available, that they can get their hands on.
Jan. 1862 there were 160 ships in the blockade.[351]
Oct. 1862 there were 256 ships on blockade duty.[352]
Jan. 1865 there were 471 ships in the blockade.[353]
Captured blockade runners could be used as blockade chasers.
Federals built 1,000-ton sloops of war to chase runners, and were armed with 32-pounders.
500-ton, shallow draft gun boats armed with pivot guns were used in rivers and bays.

C.S.N. Blockade Runners
The first government owned blockade runners.

1. C.S.S. *R. E. Lee*
   a. Dec. '62 to Nov. '63 21 successful runs in 10 months, exporting 6,000 bales of cotton, worth 2,000,000 in gold.[354]
2. C.S.S. *Phantom*
3. C.S.S. *Merrimac*
4. C.S.S. *Cornubia*

Missions of the blockade runners
Export cotton to Europe to create revenue for purchases of military and naval needs.
Import military, medical and food necessities.
Carried mail to Europe, and agents and communications for both the Confederacy and for European nations and companies.
A small percentage, about 5 percent, of the hull could carry luxuries and commercially valuable freight.

---

351 *The Confederate Navy*, Pg. 62
352 *The Confederate Navy*, Pg. 112
353 Ibid
354 *The Blockade Runners*, Pg. 6

Financing of Blockade Runners

British private citizens made investments.

1864, U.S. Counsel in London writes that 90 percent of Blockade Runners are owned by the British.

Cotton sold 5 cents/pound in Charleston, re-sold in Europe at 50 cents a pound.

British and other Europeans composed most of the crews for Confederate runners.

New York Sun reports 10 dollars in quinine in Nassau grows to 400 to 600 dollars in Charleston.[355]

Phillip Van Doren Stern, wrote average runners carrying 1,600 bales of cotton, monthly expenses and profits: 80,465 dollars expenses, and 172,000 earnings, profit averages 91,535 per month.[356]

Confederate Cotton Bond[357]

Ehrlangers Bank in France offer to make a $25,000,000 loan to the Confederacy to be financed through cotton. Secretary of State Judah Benjamin negotiates loan for $15,000,000 which equaled 3,000,000 British pounds.

Terms

$15,000,000 in bonds offered for sale in France at 90 percent par. (Example one-thousand-dollar bond sold at 900 dollars) Bonds pay 7 per cent interest. Bonds could be used to purchase cotton at 7 cents a pound, or redeemed at one hundred percent par in twenty years. This loan is signed 28 January, 1863

Bonds are issued March 19 and actually do very well. But by April, counter pressure (undetermined) began to drive the price of the bonds down. The CSA acts to stabilize the bond price, spending more than $12 million, reducing their net cash available from the loan to $2.6 million, from a 15-million-dollar loan!

Blockade Shipping Companies[358]

John Fraser of South Carolina

Importing and Exporting Companies of South Carolina (Bee Company)

Paid dividends of 5,000 dollars, 2,000 dollars and 2,000 dollars plus

---

355 *The Blockade Runners,* Pg. 8
356 *The Confederate Navy,* Pg. 63
357 *The Confederate Navy,* Pg. 157
358 *The Blockade Runners*

50 per share.
    Anglo – Confederate Trading Company
    Paid two dividends in 1864, 1,500 and 1,000 dollars
    Palmetto Importing and Exporting Company
    Paid a dividend of 2,000 dollar per share

Technology[359]
    Steam replacing sail, or supplementing it.
    Anthracite coal – almost no smoke
    Steam exhaust is released into the ocean directly to eliminate sound.
    Low, sleek silhouettes, lower funnels
    Iron hulls replacing wood
    "Sidewheelers outclassed screw propellers"[360]
    Gray or sky-blue paint used to camouflage the ships.
    Later runners could top 20 mph, the C.S.S. *Little* did 22 mph.
    Clyde Class Runners, manufacturers on the Clyde River, Scotland
    250 to 280 feet long

Blockade Runner Tactics
    Arrive in the vicinity of the port at high tide
    Arrival night should be without moon
    Storms, bad weather was an ally of the runner
    Rockets carried and used to misdirect federal pursuers – different colors meant different things to the federals.
    Use the coastline as a means to hide an approaching or exiting runner.
    At sea, runners would fly the colors different from the Confederacy, and could have several sets of owner and shipping papers.

Effectiveness of the Blockade
    400 ships entered the South from April to August 1861
    84 percent of attempts made it to port in Carolina in 1863
    83 percent of attempts made it to port in Carolina in 1864
    As late as 1864, the Confederate States government reported blockade runners carried out 5.3 million dollars' worth of cotton, while

---

[359] *The Confederate Navy*
[360] *The Blockade Runner*, Pg. 8

importing 8.6 million pounds of meat, 1.9 million pounds of saltpeter, 5 million pounds of coffee, 69,000 rifles, 97 packages of revolvers, 43 cannon, and 2,639 packages of medicine.[361]

35 blockade runners were waiting in Nassau as the war ended.[362]

In 1864 the Confederacy still possessed four important ports, Wilmington, Charleston, Mobile, and Galveston. Most historians, analysts indicate Southern retention of these ports was strategic as the lifeline for the South.[363]

Casualties of Blockade Runners[364]
    1,149 runners captured (210 were steamers)
    355 runners destroyed (85 were steamers)
    Total value estimated at $35,000,000

---

361 *Civil War Times Illustrated*, December 1991, Mr. Lincoln's Blockade by V.C. Jones
362 *Civil War Times Illustrated*, December 1991, Mr. Lincoln's Blockade by V.C. Jones
363 *The Civil War and Reconstruction*, Pg. 451
364 *The Blockade Runner*, Pg. 13

Appendix 7

C.S.A. SUBMARINE SERVICE

TIME LINE

Sept. 25, 1861 — Robert Minor draws sketches of a propeller for a submarine boat

Nov. 1861 — Tredegar Iron Works charges Cheeney[365] 3,000 dollars for labor, and 2,000 for materials.

Nov. 8, 1861 — John Brooke writes; "Cheeney will be ready to start on the submarine expedition soon. Com. Maury will alarm the enemy by his attempts – which have already proved unsuccessful."

Nov. 1861 — Mrs. Baker, an agent of Alan Pinkerton attends the test of a submarine on the James River below Rocketts.

Feb. 1862 — Initial tests of the *Pioneer* in New Orleans Specifications: 30 feet long, 10-foot diameter at mid-section, one clockwork torpedo, crew of two to three. The sub weighed four tons.

Jan. 1863 — Harbor Trial of *Pioneer II/American Diver*, a second predecessor of the *Hunley*

Feb. 1863 — Trials of the new *Pioneer II* results in a sinking of the ship near Ft. Morgan in Mobile Bay. This version of the ship had a crew of five and a spar torpedo. (The Louisiana State Museum is in possession of a submarine they thought was the *Pioneer*, but now believe it is a second submarine, unnamed.)

April 1863 — Work begins on the construction of the *Hunley* at Parks and Lyons Machine Shop in Mobile, Al.

July 1863 — Trials in Mobile Bay

August 1863 — Beauregard orders the boat to Charleston. Transported via rail to Charleston, South Carolina

August 29, 1863 — *Hunley* sinks during dry run test

October 15, 1863 — *Hunley* sinks for the second time.

January 1864 — *Hunley* is towed by a David to the mouth of the Harbor several times in the hopes of finding blockers within range.

February 17, 1864 — *Hunley* attacks and sinks *Housatonic* in 28 foot.

---

365 Cheeney was an engineer from New York

The Confederate List of Submarines

The Pioneer	New Orleans, La.
Unnamed craft	Richmond, Virginia
Unnamed craft, possibly *American Diver*,	St. John's Bayou, La.
Pioneer II	Mobile, Al.
Hunley	Mobile, Al. and Charleston, S.C.
Five unnamed craft (one shipped to Houston, Tx)	Shreveport, La.

C.S.A. SUBMARINE SERVICE

The Submarine Service of the Confederacy is an enigma composed of a quilt of mysteries, from the Mississippi and Gulf of Mexico to the Atlantic and the James River. It is an area of Confederate Naval history still actively explored. In February 2020, the Smithsonian magazine featured an article titled "Explosive" was published to explain the loss of the *H.L. Hunley*. We will talk about this later, but it is an excellent example of the continued research being done on the Confederate States Navy and the Confederate Submarine Service.

The maritime effort of the Confederate States of America, 1861 – 1865, is one of the most misunderstand and under-reported aspects of the War for Southern Independence. It is almost inconceivable, a nation born in war could accomplish as many magnificent feats as the Confederate States of America Navy.

However, from the first, I must suggest that one must assume a less conventional understanding of "the navy." Because of the Confederacy's birth in the face of war, mission and not convention must define the entire Confederate maritime effort as the navy.

The first step in fully appreciating the Confederate States Navy is to recognize the conglomerative and cumulative effort President Davis, Secretary Stephan Mallory, the Confederate Congress, Southern financiers and international investors, and ingenious inventors and machinists. This group demonstrated the human characteristics of leadership, ingenuity, innovation, strategic vision, and political acumen. All of this resulted in the creation of cutting-edge modern navy paid for on a shoe-string.

Their joint effort resulted in the building of a naval/maritime organization of:

Operation of 26 Ironclads,

17 Privateers[366] (privately owned, not counting submarines),

11 Commerce Cruisers[367] (naval ships),

And at least 1,650 Blockade Runners (great majority owned by investors foreign and domestic), and an unknown number of tenders and also, possibly a dozen or so DAVIDS operating in Charleston, Houston, Mobile, and Shreveport. But maybe the most startling aspect of this vast armada are the ten or more vessels of the Confederate Submarine Service which operated outside of the Confederate Navy.

Imagination, ingenuity, boldness, courage, seamanship, and the application of cutting-edge technologies were the hallmarks of the Southern naval-maritime war effort. Because so many records of the Confederacy were destroyed, the story of the Confederate Navy is incomplete and cloaked in mystery.

The Confederate Submarine service is possibly the most enigmatic mystery of all. Because of the secret nature of the submarine service, the small number of men involved in the building and operating the submarines, and the exceptionally high death rate of crews, we are left with few records and few firsthand accounts.

Here, we will try to tell the mysteries in chronological order.

Richmond, Virginia
Submarine, 1861-1862[368]

Mystery Number One: The Richmond submarine, 1861 - 1862

John Coski, of the Museum of the Confederacy, in his book, *Capital Navy*, tells that there was an effort in Richmond in 1861 and 1862 to manufacture and operate a submarine(s) on the James River. The work was done at the Rocketts shipyard on the James River.

The man behind the effort was a New Yorker, who joined the Confederacy, William G. Cheeney, after the efforts on behalf of the federals to build such a craft were rebuffed. The evidence of the unnamed vessel is slight but solid:

There are bills from the Tredegar Iron works for two thousand dol-

---

366 Brig Jeff Davis was the most successful with 40 prizes. *The Confederate Navy*, P.48
367 *The Confederate Navy*, Pgs. 47 - 50
368 *Capital Navy*, P. 116 – 120

lars for component parts (listed) and three thousand dollars for a labor force of five men.

There is a drawing in a notebook of a propeller for the craft.

In addition, there is the written report of Mrs. Baker, a federal agent, to Alan Pinkerton describing events on the James River.

According to Mrs. Baker, sometime in November 1861, she attended a test of a submerged vessel downstream from Rocketts. Alan Pinkerton in his book, *The Spy of the Rebellion*, recalls her report:

… a large scow had been towed into the middle of the river, and the submarine vessel was to approach it and attach a magazine, containing nearly half a bushel of powder to which was attached several deadly projectiles, and this was to be fired by a peculiarly constructed fuse, coiled on board the submarine vessel.[369]

Mrs. Baker tells us the submarine submerged about one-half mile from the scow and made its way towards the target. Baker describes a float could be seen moving on the water, painted green, attached to the submarine to provide air to the men below, which was the only visible sign of the craft as it moved. The float approached the scow, remained for some time before withdrawing several hundred yards, then after a time, the scow exploded!

In his footnotes, John Coski even reports there is some speculation that the submarine in Richmond was powered by steam!

Mystery Number Two: A submarine or a David?

But, the most startling thing Baker reported was that this craft was only a small model of a larger one being built. In fact, *Harper's Weekly* reports an "infernal machine" caught by the U.S.S. *Minnesota* in the Chesapeake Bay, on October 9th, 1862.

Operations in New Orleans, Louisiana,
1861 - 1862

Most students of the Cause are aware of the *H.L. Hunley* operating from Charleston Harbor and know of its earlier predecessor the Pioneer.

The effort to construct, test, and launch submarines in New Orleans and Mobile was organized as a commercial venture outside the Confederate States Navy.

---

369 P.117 – 188, *Capital Navy*

The Confederate Congress adopted a modified form of the Letter of Marquis that authorized payment for the value of a ship and its cargo if sunk by a vessel in possession of a Letter. This differed from earlier applications of the Letter, in that ships had to be captured and brought to port for inventory and sale by the maritime Court. But with her ports under blockade, and neutral ports not willing to accept Confederate captures, the Confederates had to alter the Letter so as to induce investors to create privateer ships.

Robert Barron, James McClintock, and Baxter Watson applied to Richmond for a Confederate States of America Letter of Marque[370] in March of 1862. Their purpose for construction of the C.S.S. *Pioneer* was financial.

The vessel was built of ¼-inch riveted iron plate from old boilers. A crankshaft its power source. It would hold two men.[371] She was scuttled in Lake Pontchartrain in May 1862 to prevent her from being taken by the Yankees as they approached New Orleans. Submariner development work on the Gulf of Mexico was moved to Mobile.

Mystery Number Three:

A complete story of the South's efforts in submarine warfare would discover the *Pioneer II* in Mobile, a possible immediate predecessor to the *Hunley*. And there is another name which surfaces, the *American Diver*. The *American Diver* could be another name for the *Pioneer II*, or it may be a completely different ship.

Mystery Number Four: Is a found submarine in St. John's Bayou the *Pioneer II*, or another boat?

There is a submarine constructed near New Orleans that was found just outside Lake Pontchartrain in the St. John Bayou. It was initially believed to be the *Pioneer*, but as of February 2020,[372] after sketches of the *Pioneer* were found and compared to the found submarine, it was determined this was more likely another craft; possibly the *American Diver*. It is presently held and displayed at the Louisiana State Museum in Baton Rouge.

---

370 A side note concerning Letters of Marque is important here. The Confederate Congress changed the traditional parameters of the concept of a Letter of Marque to include payment for destruction of enemy ships.
371 P. 212, *Ships of the Civil War, 1861 – 1865*, Kevin Doughterty.
372 Ibid

Events in Mobile, Alabama

"Horace L. Hunley, McClintock and Baxter moved on to Mobile to begin work on a second submarine, Pioneer II. This craft was larger, with a crew of five. Shelby Foote reports on tests done, including successful test attacks against two flatboats in Mobile Harbor. *Pioneer II* was probably the submarine described by a Confederate deserter on 26 February 1863 to the Senior Officer of the Federal Blockade off Mobile:

On or about the 14th, an infernal machine, consisting of a submarine boat, propelled by a screw which is turned by hand, capable of holding five persons, and having a torpedo which was to be attached to the bottom of a vessel and exploded by means of clockwork, left Fort Morgan at 8 p.m. in charge of a Frenchman who invented it. The intention was to come up at Sand Island, get the bearing and distance of the nearest vessel, dive under again and operate upon her; but on emerging they found themselves so far outside the island and in so strong a current (setting out) that they were forced to cut the torpedo adrift and make the best of their way back.

She was second in a line of three submarines that included *Pioneer* and *H.L. Hunley*.[373]

Additionally, *Pioneer II* proved it could remain submerged for two hours.[374] However, it sank near Ft. Morgan during a test, the crew surviving.[375]

Features of the *H.L. Hunley*

The craft was constructed from a steam boiler that was narrowed fore and aft. The vessel was forty feet long, three and half feet in breadth at mid height, and four feet keel to the base of the two coning towers.[376] Coning towers were fore and aft, each with water tight portals.

The *Hunley* had two ballast tanks to alter the specific gravity of the submarine, and thus help submerge the ship. A pump was used to pump water out of the tanks, or out of the inside of the submarine. Three five-hundred-pound keel plates could be shed to lighten the vessel and help it rise.

---

373 Part of the text is incorporated from the United States Navy's Dictionary of American Naval Fighting Ships, a work in the public domain.
374 P. 896. *The Civil War, A Narrative, Fredericksburg to Meridian*, Shelby Foote
375 P. 108, *A Short History of the Civil War at Sea*
376 P. 108, *A Short History of the Civil War at Sea*

Near the forward coning tower were two fins, one on each side of the ship. These fins were the principal means to submerge and raise the ship. A rudder, placed behind the propeller provided steerage.

Tests were run in Mobile, where the first crew was lost. She was called to Charleston by General Beauregard, and she arrived there on two flat cars sometime in the first half of August 1863.[377]

Weapon technologies of a submarine

Placing and detonating the torpedo had several approaches. Detonation of the torpedo (mine) could be accomplished four ways;

electric through rubber covered wire,

percussion, i.e., contact against a hull

igniting a detonator via lanyard,

and lastly, the use of a clock to set off the detonator.

Shelby Foote explains the initial method for attacking union ships: "Her method of attack was quite as novel as her design. Towing at the end of a 200 foot line a copper cylinder packed with 90 pounds of powder and equipped with a percussion fuse , she would dive as she approached her target, completely under it, then elevate a bit, drag [the] towline across the keel until the torpedo made contact and exploded, well astern of the submarine , whose crew would be cranking hard for a getaway, still under water. …"[378] Rising on the opposite side of target from where the torpedo would explode would shield the submarine from the explosion.

This methodology was tested in Mobile Bay twice, using flatboats as the targets. Both tests were successful.

Events in Charleston

An alternate method of attack was devised after General Beauregard directed that *Hunley* remain above the sea level, and not submerge after the loss of the second crew and Horace Hunley, during tests in Charleston. The *Hunley* was to be operated like a DAVID, the Confederacy's prototype version of a World War II torpedo boat. A DAVID was similar in size to the *Hunley* and looked much like a submarine, most the vessel was submerged under water, propelled by a steam engine, with a torpedo mounted on a protruding spar. The torpedo would be attached to the target with a spike. The submarine could then back

---

377 P. 216, *Ships of the Civil War, 1861 – 1865*, Kevin Dougherty
378 P. 896, *The Civil War, A Narrative Fredericksburg to Meridian*

away, and detonate through the lanyard.

In Charleston Harbor, the *Hunley* sank the first time when a ship it was moored to moved, thus flipping the small craft so that its open hatches allowed water to rush in. Five of the crew were lost.

On October 22, 1863, the *Hunley* went down again. This time the craft was moving under its own power in the harbor, submerged, and returned to the surface. When recovered, the ghastly bodies of the crew were too much for General Beauregard to accept. He ordered the ship not be used any further.

However, a third crew was gathered, commanded by an Army Lt. George E. Dixon of Alabama. Dixon is believed to have helped in the construction of the *Hunley*. Beauregard changed his orders but directed that the *Hunley* stay above the surface and act as DAVID.

On at least two other sorties, a DAVID was used to tow the *Hunley* out of Charleston harbor. But there is no mention of a DAVID during its final voyage.

Around 1800 hours, or 6 pm, on February 17th, the *Hunley* set off to attack the U.S.S. *Housatonic*. At about 2045 hours, a look-out on the U.S.S. *Housatonic* sighted something 75 to 100 hundred yards off the ship and rang the alarm. But, before the ship could move an explosion mid ship, near the magazine, blew a large hole in the ship. It sank in 28-foot water, five of its crew dying. Most of the crew ended up in the yardarms, above the waves, and were saved by small craft from neighboring ships.

Mystery Number Five: The loss of The *Hunley*

One of the true mysteries of the War for Southern Independence is the last moments of the *Hunley*.

Both Confederates and Yankees in the vicinity of the attack report that they saw a blue light after the explosion. The blue light was to be the signal from the *Hunley* to shore that the attack had been successful.

So what happened to the *Hunley*? When and how did it sink?

The *Hunley* Museum has the remains and has painstakingly worked to remove a hundred and fifty years of barnacles and sediments from both the interior and exterior of the craft. Damage to the vessel has been examined to determine the cause of its sinking. But they are undecided on what happened. On their web page, they describe the elements of the mystery:

The Mystery of the *H.L. Hunley* sinking
As completely provided by the *Hunley* Museum.
As of June 2019:

Here is what we know as of now....

Crew Remains: Archaeologists excavating the *Hunley* after its recovery in 2000 found the crew members' remains were largely found at their stations, with no sign of panic or desperate attempts to escape the submarine.

The remains also show no new injuries, suggesting whatever happened to the *Hunley* was not violent enough to break the crew's bones. Since the bodies decomposed more than a century ago, any flesh or tissue wounds the crew may have experienced that night will never be known.

Possible Answer: Now researchers at Duke University believe they have the answer. Three years of experiments on a mini-test sub have shown that the torpedo blast would have created a shockwave great enough to instantly rupture the blood vessels in the lungs and brains of the submariners.

'This is the characteristic trauma of blast victims, they call it 'blast lung,' Dr Rachel Lance.

You have an instant fatality that leaves no marks on the skeletal remains. Unfortunately, the soft tissues that would show us what happened have decomposed in the past hundred years.[379]

The March 2020 Smithsonian magazine published the article "Explosion," by Rachel Lance, describing her scientific efforts to discover what happened to the *Hunley* crew.

Hunley Location on the Seabed: One of the many reasons it took so long to find the *Hunley* was because her location was not where most expected. Searchers usually looked between the shore and the wreck of the *Housatonic*, assuming she must have been lost between those two points as the submarine attempted to return home. In fact, she was found on the sea-side of the *Housatonic*, about 1,000 feet (less than half a mile) from the Union ship's wreck site.

Damage to Submarine: When the *Hunley* was recovered, signs of obvious damage were noticed immediately, including a large hole in

---

[379] *The Telegraph*, August 23, 2017, Sarah Knapton, "Mystery deaths of H.L. Hunley submarine crew solved — they accidentally killed themselves."

the aft ballast tank. It is tempting to look at the holes and appendages that broke away and assume they are scars remaining from the night of the historic attack. However, most of the damage happened slowly over time while the *Hunley* rested on the ocean floor for over a century. In fact, much of the damage to the sub is the result of unforgiving underwater currents and scouring sand.

The Rudder was found detached and underneath the vessel. Based on where it was found, lying beneath the keel, it seems the rudder broke off the submarine not long after it sank.

The Forward Conning Tower held five viewports. Captain Dixon used these to navigate and as his windows to the outside world. One of the viewports is completely missing. There is now a grapefruit-sized hole in its place. Since a broken off iron fragment from the missing view port was found in the sediment at the very bottom of the submarine, this damage could have happened very early, potentially even the night of the attack.

Hatches: The hatches that sat on top of the forward and aft conning towers served as the only access points into and out of the submarine. Scientists found one hatch was locked, and the other was not. The forward conning tower was found unlatched. This could be significant, but the hatch was heavy enough that it would stay sealed while the submarine was underwater and upright. The aft hatch was found locked. If the crew had been desperately trying to escape, it is reasonable to assume both hatches would have been unlatched.

Ballast Pump Settings: When the *Hunley* mysteriously vanished, most students of history assumed the eight-man crew drowned. That may not be true.

The pumps are still in the same position they were on the night the submarine was lost. Those settings could reveal what steps — if any — the crew may have taken to try and save their lives.

A preliminary study of the pump system shows that it was not set to pump water out of the crew compartment. This discovery suggests the crew may not have drowned, but died of some other cause.

Blackout Mode: The *Hunley* was in Blackout Mode when she was lost. The submarine had a series of 10 topside ports that provided the crew a small measure of ambient light when the *Hunley* cruised on the surface. These small glass ports were equipped with iron covers that could make the ports watertight and also block any light from escaping the sub, and possibly alerting ships to their presence. These ports were all found closed.

Historical Records: Some historical evidence suggests the *Hunley* did not sink immediately after the attack, and light, perhaps in the forms of signals, was seen by both Union and Confederate sources. Records indicate the *Hunley* crew was to signal to shore if they were successful in sinking the Union warship.

Robert Flemming, a sailor on the U.S.S. *Housatonic*, was standing bow lookout watch the night the *Hunley* attacked. About 45 minutes after the attack, Flemming — who survived and retreated to the *Housatonic's* rigging to await rescue — said he spotted a blue light on the water, just ahead of the U.S.S. *Canandaigua*, the first Navy ship to arrive on the scene.

When the *Canandaigua* got astern, and laying athwart of the *Housatonic*, about four ships lengths off, while I was in the fore-rigging, I saw a blue light on the water just ahead of the *Canandaigua*, and on the starboard quarters of the *Housatonic*.

Robert Flemming

Flemming's report of a blue light could be consistent with the testimony of a Confederates at Battery Marshall, who said Dixon said he would show "two blue lights" when he wanted a signal fire lit on the beach of Sullivan's Island.

In addition to Flemming's testimony, we have two others:

Lieutenant Col. Dantzler at Battery Marshall reported on February 19th, 1864, "The signals agreed upon to be given in case the boat wished a light to be exposed at this post as a guide for its return were observed and answered."

In 1866, Jacob Cardoza recounted, "The officer (Dixon) in command told Lieutenant-Colonel Dantzler ... if he came off safe, he would show two blue lights. The lights never appeared."

Was Flemming the last man to see the *Hunley* for more than a century? If he was, his account could suggest a tragic end for the *Hunley*. If the submarine was "just ahead" of the *Canandaigua*, which was sailing to rescue Union sailors, it could have created a wake that toppled the submarine or hit it directly. Also, because the *Hunley* had no ports facing aft, the crew might not have even known a ship was bearing down on the submarine.

Sediment In-filling: After the *Hunley* filled with water, sediment suspended in the water column settled along the bottom of the submarine. Analysis of the deposition of sediment indicates some additional material filling the submarine over time may have entered near the forward conning tower. The breach in the forward conning tower is the most likely source and would explain some of the courser sediment discovered in early deposits at Dixon's station.

Mystery Number Six: The Shreveport submarines.

Events in Shreveport, Louisiana

There's evidence the Shreveport subs existed. Reports of Union spies in Shreveport, as well as Confederate reports, detail the appearance and dimensions of the submarines as well as operations to put mines in Red River for a Union invasion that never came. Five submarines were built, with one sent to the Houston/Galveston area in Texas and lost in transit. The late historians and authors Eric Brock and Katherine Brash Jeter did considerable research on the subs and the Confederate Navy Yard and found documentation that a number of machinists and engineers who had built the *Hunley* and other submarines for the South were in Shreveport the last year of the conflict.[380]

Dr. Gary Joiner, a professor at L.S.U. said, "(The local subs) had the same everything except they had one hatch instead of two on the *Hunley*." Joiner said, "They didn't have ribs. They were done in the fashion of a boiler." Joiner thinks the lost subs are still under land or mud, probably in good condition, much like a Union ironclad that was in the Yazoo River for eight decades only to be salvaged in pretty good condition."[381]

Mystery Number Seven: Which submarine is this?
Who made this drawing?

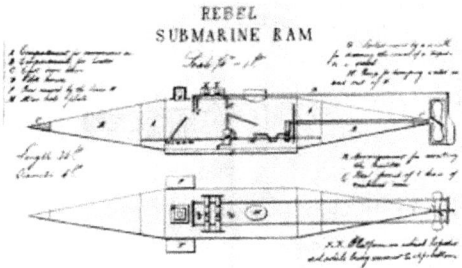

Figure 19 Rebel Submarine Ram

---

380 Article from Shreveport, La *Times*, Jan. 2015 by Prime.
381 Ibid

Some final notes

Here three possible means of detonating the mine, and they do NOT have a decided position on what was used.

The submarine may always be displayed in a water solution because of the fragility of the craft.

Mystery is a central element of the Confederate Submarine Service!

Magnolia Cemetery is where the three Charleston *Hunley* crews are buried. Among the dead at Magnolia is Brigadier General Micah Jenkins, C.S.A., Class of 1854, THE CITADEL.

SOURCES

Coski. John M., *Capital Navy*, Savas Beattie, LLC, N.Y., N.Y., 2005

Dougherty, Kevin J, *Ships of the Civil War, 1861 – 1865*, Amber Books Ltd, 2013

Foote, Shelby, *The Civil War A Narrative, Fredericksburg to Meridian*, Vintage Books, New York, 1963

Knapton, Sarah, "Mystery deaths of *H.L. Hunley* submarine crew solved — they accidentally killed themselves." *The Telegraph*, August 23, 2017

Musicant, Ivan *Divided Waters, the Naval History of the Civil War,* Castle Books, New York, 1995

Prine, John Andrew, "Mystery of missing Civil War Submarines resurfaces," *The Shreveport, La. Times*, Jan. 24, 2015

Rachel Lance, "Explosive," *Smithsonian*, March 2020

Still, Jr., William N., (Editor), *The Confederate Navy*, Conway Maritime Press, 1997

Thomsen, Brian M., *Blue and Gray at Sea*, Tom Doherty Associates Book, New York, 2003

Tucker, Spencer, *A Short History of the Civil War at Sea*, Scholarly Resource, Inc, Wilmington, Del. 2002

Bibliography

Anderson, Bern, Admiral USN, (Ret.), *By Sea and by River, The Naval History of the Civil War*, Da Capo Press, Inc. 233 Spring Street, New York, New York 10013 1962

Bergeron, Arthur, Jr., *Confederate Mobile*, University Press of Mississippi, Jackson & Loudon, 1991

Blay, John S., *The Civil War, A Pictorial Profile*, Bonanza Books, Crown Publishers, New York, 1958

Bond, O.J., Col., *The Story of THE CITADEL*, Garrett and Massie Inc., Richmond, Va., 1936, Reprinted Southern Historical Press, 275 West Broad Street, Greenville, S.C. 29602 1989

Bradford, Ned (Editor), *Battles and Leaders of the Civil War*, Hawthorne Books Inc., NY Copyright 1956

Brooke, George M. Jr., (Editor), *Ironclads and Big Guns of the Confederacy, The Journal and Letters of John M. Brooke*, University of South Carolina Press, Columbia, South Carolina, 2002

Campbell, R. Thomas, *Sea Hawk of the Confederacy*, Burd Street Press, Shippensburg, Pa.17257-0152, 2000

Campbell, R. Thomas, *Southern Fire, Exploits of the Confederate Navy*, Burd Street Press, printed by Beidel Printing House, Inc. 63 West Burd Street, Shippensberg, Pa 17257 Copyright 1997

Catton, Bruce, *This Hallowed Ground*, Doubleday & Company, Inc., Garden City, New York, 1956

Commager, Henry Steele, (Editor), *The Civil War Archives, the History of the Civil War in Documents*, 1950, 1973, Bobbs Merrill Company, Black Dog Leventhal Publishers, Inc., New York 2000

Conrad, James Lee, *Rebel Reefers, The Organization and Midshipmen of the Confederate States Naval Academy*, Da Capo Press, Perseus Book Group, Cambridge, Ma. 2003

Davis, Burke, *Gray Fox, Robert E. Lee and the Civil War*

Davis, Burke, *The Long Surrender*, Random House, New York 1985

Davis, Jefferson, *The Rise and Fall of the Confederate Government*, Volume I & II, Da Capo Press Inc., New York 1990

Davis, William C., (Editor), *The Confederate General*, Volumes 1 – 6, National Historical Society, 1991

Esposito, Vincent J., Col,. *The West Point Atlas of the Civil War*, by Frederick A. Praeger Publisher, New York, 1962

Foote, Shelby, The Civil War, A Narrative – Volume I Fort Sumter to

Perryville, Vantage Books, Copyright 1974, September 1986

Foote, Shelby, *The Civil War, A Narrative – Volume III Red River to Appomattox*, Vantage Books, Copyright 1974, September 1986

Frazier, Donald S., *Cottonclads! The Battle of Galveston and the Defense of the Texas Coast*, Ryan Place Publishers, 2730 Fifth Avenue, Fort Worth, Texas 1996

Freeman, Frederick and Kismaric, Carole, *Duel of the Ironclads*, Time-Life Books, New York, 1969

Government Printing Office, *Official Records of the Union and Confederate Navies in the War of the Rebellion.*

Greene, Francis Vinton, *The Mississippi*, Charles Scribner Sons, New York, 1881, reprinted by The Archive Society, 130 Locust Street, Harrisburg, Pa. 1992

Hansen, Harry, *The Civil War*, Bonanza Book, New York, 1962

Horner, Dave, *The Blockade Runner*, Illustrations by Jack Woodson, Dodd, Mead & Company, New York, 1968

Pollard, E.A., *The Lost Cause*, by written in 1866, Gramercy Books, Random House Company, 40 Engelhard Avenue, Avenel, New Jersey 07001, 1994

Porter, David, Admiral, *The Naval History of the Civil War*, General Publishing Company, Toronto, Canada, Dover Publishing, Mineola, NY 1998, Sherman Publishing Company, New York, 1886

Randall, J. G. and Donald, David, *The Civil War and Reconstruction*, Second Edition, DC Heath and Company, Lexington, Massachusetts, 1969

Robinson, William Morrison, Jr., *The Confederate Privateers*, University of South Carolina Press, Columbia, South Carolina, 1990 originally published Yale University Press, 1928

Scharf, J. Thomas *History of the Confederate State Navy*, 1888, published recently by Gramercy Books, Random House Value Publishing, 40 Engelhard Avenue, Avenel, New Jersey 07001, 1996

Semmes, Raphael, *The Confederate Raider ALABAMA*, Selections from "Memoirs of Service Afloat during the War Between the States," edited with an introduction by Phillip Van Doren Stern, Fawcett Publications Inc., Greenwich, Conn., 1962

Stern, Philip Van Doren, *Secret Missions of the Civil War*, Wings Books, Random House Value Publishing Inc., 201 East 50th Street, New York, New York 10022, 1990

Stern, Philip Van Doren, *The Confederate Navy, A Pictorial History*,

Bonanza Books, New York, 1962

Summers, Harry G. Jr., Col., *On Strategy: the Vietnam War in Context*, Strategic Studies Institute, US Army War College, Carlisle Barracks, Pa.1982

Symonds, Craig, *Confederate Admiral, The Life and Wars of Franklin Buchanan*, Naval Institute Press, Annapolis, Maryland 1999

Texas A & M University Press, *The Civil War Adventures of a Blockade Runner*, William Watson, College Station, Texas 2001, first published by Unwin Brothers London, 1892

Thomsen, Brian M., (Editor), *Blue and Gray at Sea, Naval Memoir of the Civil War*, A Tom Dougherty Associates Book, 175 Fifth Avenue, NY, NY 10010, 2003

Williams, T. Harry, *PGT Beauregard, Napoleon in Gray*, Louisiana State University Press, Baton Rouge and London, 1955 (1991)

Woodworth, Steven E., *A Short History of the Civil War at Sea*, Scholarly Resources Inc., 104 Greenhill Avenue, Wilmington, De. 19805-1897

Wright, Marcus J. General (Editor). *Battles and Commanders*, U.S. War Department, Washington, D.C. 1906

Magazine Articles

AMERICAS, July/August 1994, "Naval Technology from Dixie," by Darryl E. Brock

America's Civil War, January 1993, Book Review by Jon Guttman of *Gray Raiders of the Sea; How Eight Confederate Warships destroyed the Union's High Seas Fleet*, by Chester G. Hearn

America's Civil War, September 2004, "Laying Claim to the Carolina Coast," by Gary W. Dolzall

Civil War Times, August 1996, "Reluctant Raider," by John M. Taylor

Civil War Times Illustrated, December 1971 "Mr. Lincoln's Blockade," by V.C. Jones

Confederate Veteran magazine, Volume II, 1999, "David and Goliath," by R. Thomas Campbell

Confederate Veteran magazine, Volume VI, 1996, "Unraveling the Mystery of the C.S.S. *Hunley*," by James L. McClinton, Ph.D. Special note, the C.S.S. *Hunley* was built in Mobile, Alabama and shipped via rail to Charleston.

Table of Figures

Front Cover The clash of the C.S.S. *Virginia* and the U.S.S. *Monitor*

Figure 1 The blockade-runner, C.S.S. *Robert E. Lee*   32

Figure 2 Commander Raphael Semmes   40

Figure 3 Charleston during the great war.   58

Figure 4 Piece of North Carolina currency   121

Figure 5 C.S.S. *Hunley*   144

Figure 6 C.S.S. *Manassas*   171

Figure 7 C.S.S. *Louisiana*   172

Figure 8 C.S.S. *Virginia*   173

Figure 9 C.S.S. *Palmetto State*   174

Figure 10 C.S.S. *Albemarle*   175

Figure 11 C.S.S. *Baltic*   176

Figure 12 C.S.S. *Tennessee*   177

Figure 13 C.S.S. *Atlanta*   177

Figure 14 *Rebel Turtle Ram*   178

Figure 15 C.S.S. *Richmond*   179

Figure 16 C.S.S. *Fredricksburg*   179

Figure 17 C.S.S. *Stonewall*   180

Figure 18 Building of the C.S.S. *Arkansas*   181

Figure 19 Rebel Submarine Ram   200

Ship Pics from the Naval History Heritage Command

Front Cover: The clash of the C.S.S. *Virginia* and the U.S.S. *Monitor* at Hampton Roads was provided by the U. S. Department of the Navy, Naval Historical Center

Figure 1 Title: USS Fort Donelson
Description: (1864-1865) At anchor, circa 1864-1865. This steamer was previously the Confederate blockade runner *Robert E. Lee*. U.S. Naval History and Heritage Command Photograph.
Catalog #: NH 53934

Figure 2 Title: Commander Raphael Semmes, CSN
Description: Photograph taken circa 1861-62, at the time he served as Commanding Officer of CSS *Sumter*. U.S. Naval History and Heritage Command Photograph.
Catalog #: NH 45799

Figure 3 Charleston during the great war. Photo is from the Library of Congress

Figure 4 Piece of North Carolina currency, Image was provided by the US Department of Navy, Naval Historical Center

Figure 5 Title: CSS *H.L. Hunley* Description: Drawing, Pen and Ink on Paper; R.G. Skerrett; 1902; Framed Dimensions 20H X 25W
Accession #: 45-125-P

Related Content
H.L. Hunley, a small hand-powered submarine, was built privately at Mobile, Alabama, in 1863, based on plans furnished by Horace Lawson Hunley, James R. McClintock and Baxter Watson. Her construction was sponsored by Mr. Hunley and superintended by Confederate officers W. A. Alexander and G. E. Dixon. Following trails in Mobile Bay, she was transported to Charleston, South Carolina, in August 1863 to serve in the defense of that port. On February 17, 1864, she was part of blockade duty off Charleston, approached the steam sloop of war USS *Housatonic* and detonated a spar torpedo against her side. The Federal

ship sank rapidly, becoming the first warship to be lost to a submarine attack.

However, *H.L. Hunley* did not return from this mission, and was presumed lost with all hands. Her fate remained a mystery for over 131 years, until May 1995, when a search led by author Clive Cussler located her wreck. In August 2000, following extensive preliminary work, *H.L. Hunley* was raised and taken to a conservation facility at the former Charleston Naval Base.

Figure 6 Title: "The *Manassas* struck us a Diagonal Blow"
Caption:
Description: Photo #: NH 79908 The *Manassas* struck us a Diagonal Blow Artwork by Bacon published in *Deeds of Valor*, Volume II, page 20, by the Perrien-Keydel Company, Detroit, 1907. It depicts CSS *Manassas* ramming USS *Brooklyn*, during the battle off Forts Jackson and St. Philip, on the Mississippi River below New Orleans, 24 April 1862. U.S. Naval History and Heritage Command Photograph.
Catalog #: NH 79908

Figure 7 Title: CSS *Louisiana*
Description: (1862-62) 19th Century photograph of a lithograph by Bowen & Company, depicting the ship as she appeared previous to the explosion that destroyed her in the Mississippi River near Fort St. Philip, 28 April 1862. U.S. Naval History and Heritage Command Photograph.
Catalog #: NH 1734

Figure 8 Title: CSS *Virginia* (1862-1862)
Description: Wash drawing by Clary Ray, 1898. Courtesy of the U.S. Navy Art Collection, Washington, D.C. U.S. Naval History and Heritage Command Photograph.
Catalog #: NH 57830

Figure 9 Title: CSS *Palmetto State* BandW
Description: (1862-1865) Wash drawing by Clary Ray, signed and dated 23 April 1897. Courtesy of the U.S. Navy Art Collection, Washington, D.C. U.S. Naval History and Heritage Command Photograph.
Catalog #: NH 57837

Figure 9 Title: CSS *Palmetto State* (1862-1865)
Caption:
Description: CSS *Palmetto State* (1862-1865) Watercolor by Charles C. Cawson, circa 1862, featuring the names of the ship's officers. Their names are given in Photo # NH 93044-KN ... (complete caption). Courtesy of the Navy Art Collection, Washington, DC. U.S. Naval History and Heritage Command Photograph.
Catalog #: NH 93044-KN

Figure 10 Title: CSS *Albemarle* (1864-1864)
Caption:
Description: At the Norfolk Navy Yard, Virginia, after salvage, circa 1865. Two ladies are standing on her deck, near a section of displaced casemate armor. Courtesy of Mr. J.C. Hanscom. U.S. Naval History and Heritage Command Photograph.
Catalog #: NH 63375

Figure 11 Title: CSS *Baltic* (1862-1864
Caption:
Description: Engraving published in *The Soldier in Our Civil War*, Volume II, depicting the ironclad ram Baltic at Mobile, Alabama. U.S. Naval History and Heritage Command Photograph.
Catalog #: NH 58793

Figure 12 Title: USS *Tennessee* (1864-1867, formerly CSS *Tennessee*)
Caption:
Description: Line engraving published in *Harper's Weekly*, 3 February 1866 as part of a group of engravings entitled The Iron-Clad Navy of the United States. See Photo # NH 73986 for the entire group of engravings. U.S. Naval History and Heritage Command Photograph.
Catalog #: NH 61434

Figure 13 Title: CSS *Atlanta* (1862-1863)
Description: Sepia wash drawing by R.G. Skerrett, 1901. Courtesy of the Navy Art Collection, Washington, DC. U.S. Naval History and Heritage Command Photograph.
Catalog #: NH 57819

Figure 14 Title: "The Rebel Turtle Ram Just Launched at Savannah."
Caption:
Description: Photo #: NH 51961 *The Rebel Turtle Ram Just Launched at Savannah*. Line engraving published in *Harper's Weekly*, January-June 1863, page 164. This view may have been intended to depict (however inaccurately) CSS *Savannah*, which was launched at Savannah, Georgia, in February 1863. U.S. Naval History and Heritage Command Photograph.
Catalog #: NH 51961

Figure 15 Title: CSS *Richmond*
Description: (1862-1865) Wash drawing by R.G. Skerrett, 1900, depicting the ship underway on the James River, Virginia, during the Civil War. Courtesy of the U.S. Navy Art Collection, Washington, D.C. U.S. Naval History and Heritage Command Photograph.
Catalog #: NH 75620

Figure 15 Title: CSS *Richmond*
Caption:
Description: (1862-1865) Line engraving, published in *Harper's Weekly*, 1862, depicting the ship as seen from off the bow, in plan view on the gun deck and in section through the hull. See Photo # NH 58746 for another image of *Richmond* that was published on the same page as these. All of these depictions, which are based on sketches captured in July 1862, are rather inaccurate. U.S. Naval History and Heritage Command Photograph.
Catalog #: NH 58745

Figure 16 Title: "The Rebel Iron-Clad Fleet Forcing the Obstructions in James River", 23 January 1865
Caption:
Description: hoto #: NH 59187 T*he Rebel Iron-Clad Fleet Forcing the Obstructions in James River, 23 January 1865* Line engraving, based on a sketch by A.R. Waud, published in *Harper's Weekly*, 11 February 1865, page 81. It depicts the Confederate ironclads *Virginia II*, *Richmond* and *Fredericksburg* attempting to run past the obstructions at Trent's Reach to attack Federal positions along the James River. U.S. Naval History and Heritage Command Photograph.
Catalog #: NH 59187

Figure 17 Title: CSS *Stonewall*
Caption:
Description: (1865) At Ferrol, Spain, in March 1865. This is a heavily retouched version of Photo # NH 42861. Courtesy of Mr. J. S. Barron, 1937. The original photograph was given to him by his father, Commodore Samuel Barron, who served in *Stonewall* as a Lieutenant. U.S. Naval History and Heritage Command Photograph.
Catalog #: NH 42862

Figure 18 Title: CSS *Arkansas* (1862-1862)
Caption:
Description: Line engraving after a drawing by J.O. Davidson, published in *Battles and Leaders of the Civil War*, Volume III, page 573, depicting the ship fitting out off Yazoo City, Mississippi, in June-July 1862. Assisting in the work is the CSS *Capitol*. U.S. Naval History and Heritage Command Photograph.
Catalog #: NH 73376

nhhcpublicaffairs@navy.mil

Figure 19 Rebel Submarine Ram
http://upload.wikimedia.org/wikipedia/commons/thumb/b/b6/PioneerSubDrawingShock.jpg/800px-PioneerSubDrawingShock.jpg

Other works by Mark K. Vogl

The Military Lessons of the Civil War, 1861-1865

The Rebel Mountain Reader

The Confederate Night Before Christmas

Southern Fried Ramblings with Grits and all the Fixin's

Because of Him

The White House Reclaimed, A Deplorable's View of the 2016 Election

The Adventure - Stolen Days

Mark's eighth book, *The Adventure Stolen Days* is available through The Scruppernong Press. www.scuppernongpress.com

The Adventure – Stolen Days tells the story of Dr. Nash Laurent, who spends a life time creating a Southern organization, PROJECT ALABAMA to finance and build a space-time ship with the intention of going back and saving the life of Stonewall Jackson at Chancellorsville. But by the time all is ready, Nash is just too old for the mission, and so he recruits Parks Walter, a NASA astronaut to go with his daughter Jeanne Marie and his son Michael back in time. But can this team do it? Can they save Stonewall Jackson's life? They have three ways to try, will any of those ways work? And what is Providence? If you try to change history are you fighting God's Will? This is *The Adventure – Stolen Days.*

www.ingramcontent.com/pod-product-compliance
Lightning Source LLC
Chambersburg PA
CBHW071959290426
44109CB00018B/2073